AF598878

Miss Swiss

DOESN'T HAVE A TITLE. IT'S A REGULAR STORY. IT DOESN'T NEED A TITLE.

I WANT TO TELL YOU A STORY. ONE DAY MIKO CAME AGAIN. DO YOU REMEMB

Lisa Lapinski
Miss Swiss

***

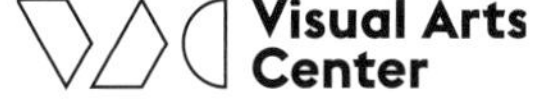

INVENTORY PRESS

.KO? HE WAS IN THAT PICNIC STORY. SO CHIP AND DALE WENT FOR A WALK

IN THE WARM, WARM SUN ALL THE WAY TO THE CAFÉ. SO NOW WENDY CAME F

CONTENTS

LITTLE PICNIC SNACK. ONE DAY, TINKER BELL WAS SICK ALL MORNING. I

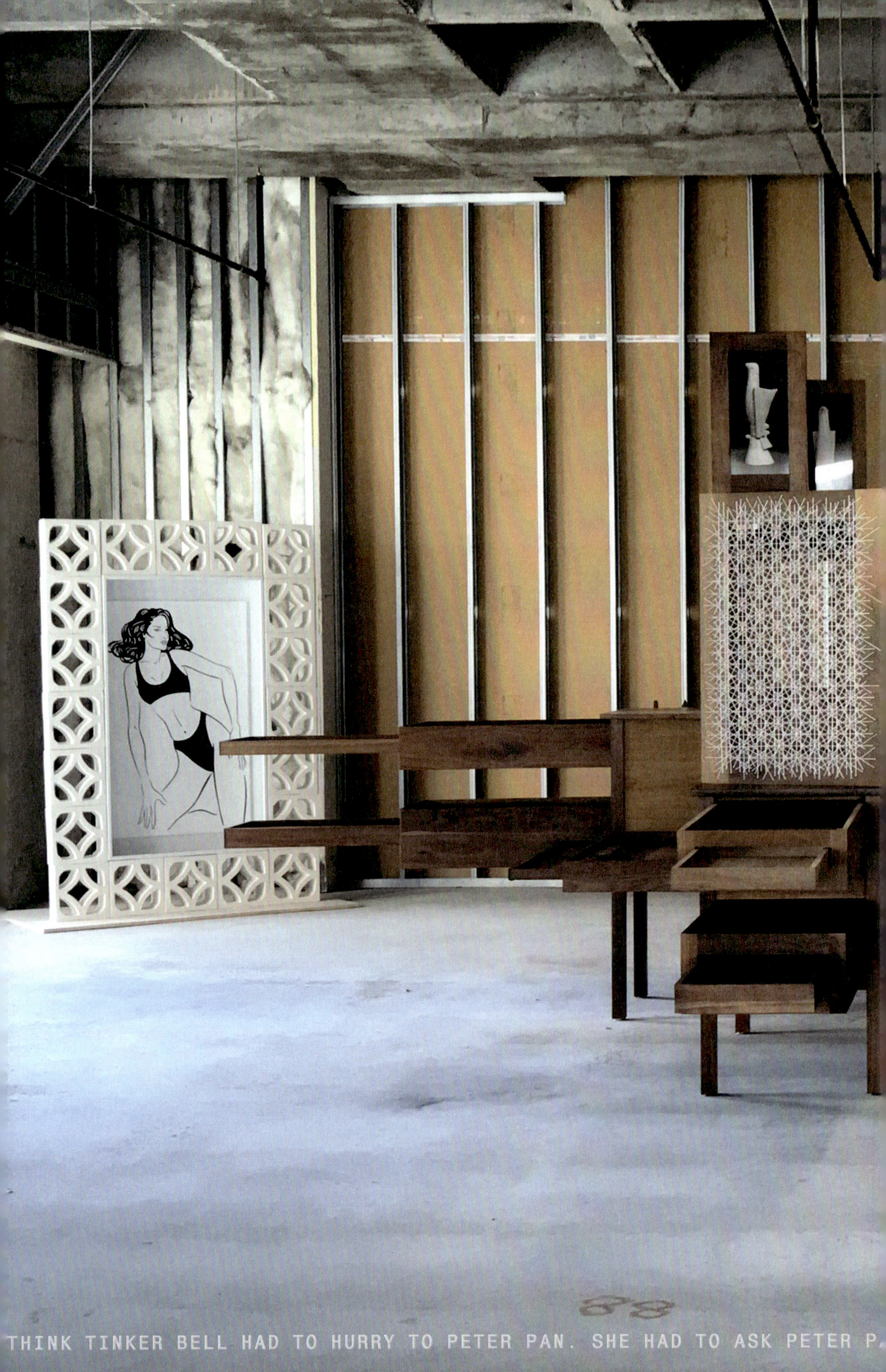

THINK TINKER BELL HAD TO HURRY TO PETER PAN. SHE HAD TO ASK PETER P

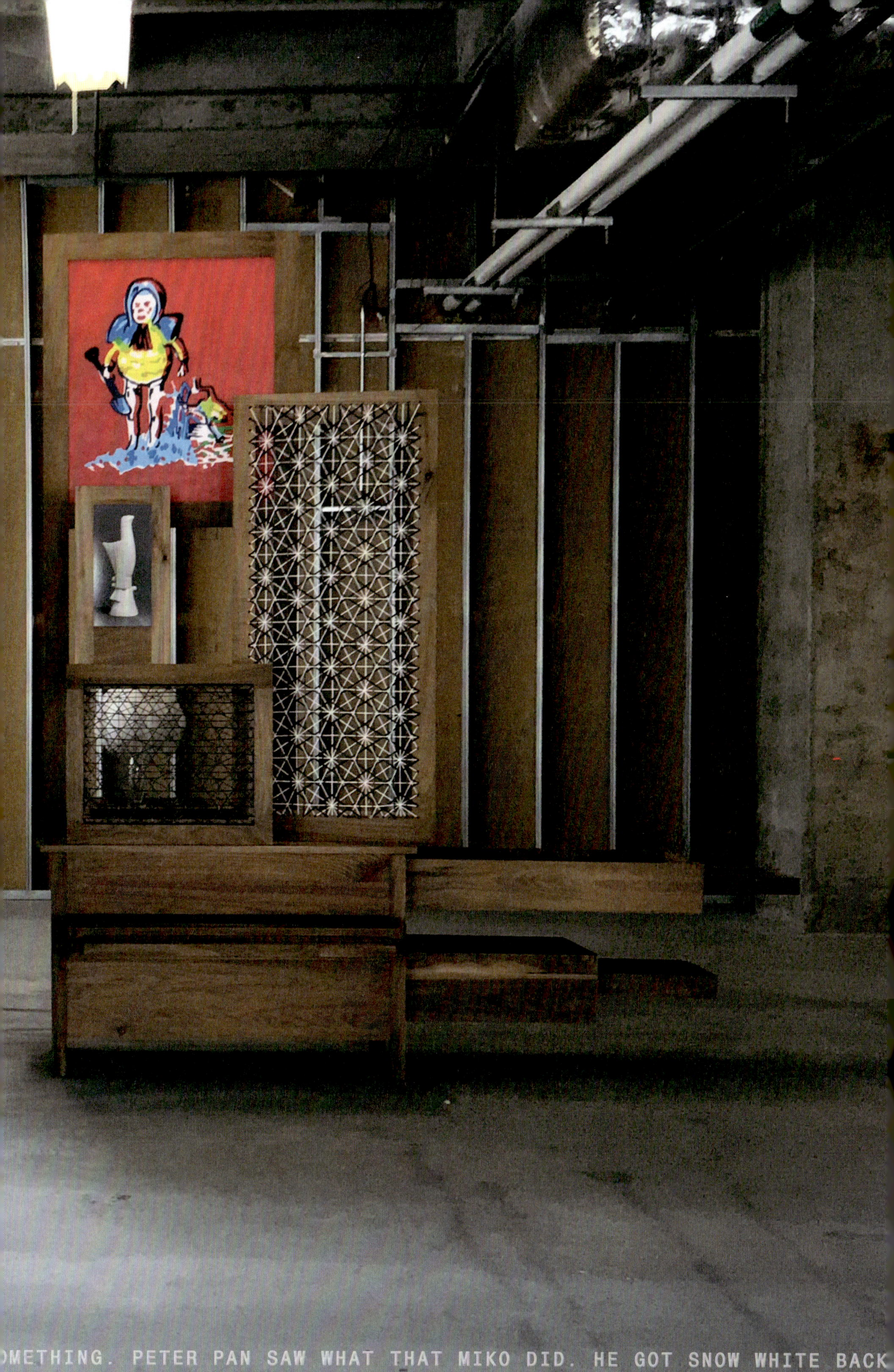

OMETHING. PETER PAN SAW WHAT THAT MIKO DID. HE GOT SNOW WHITE BACK

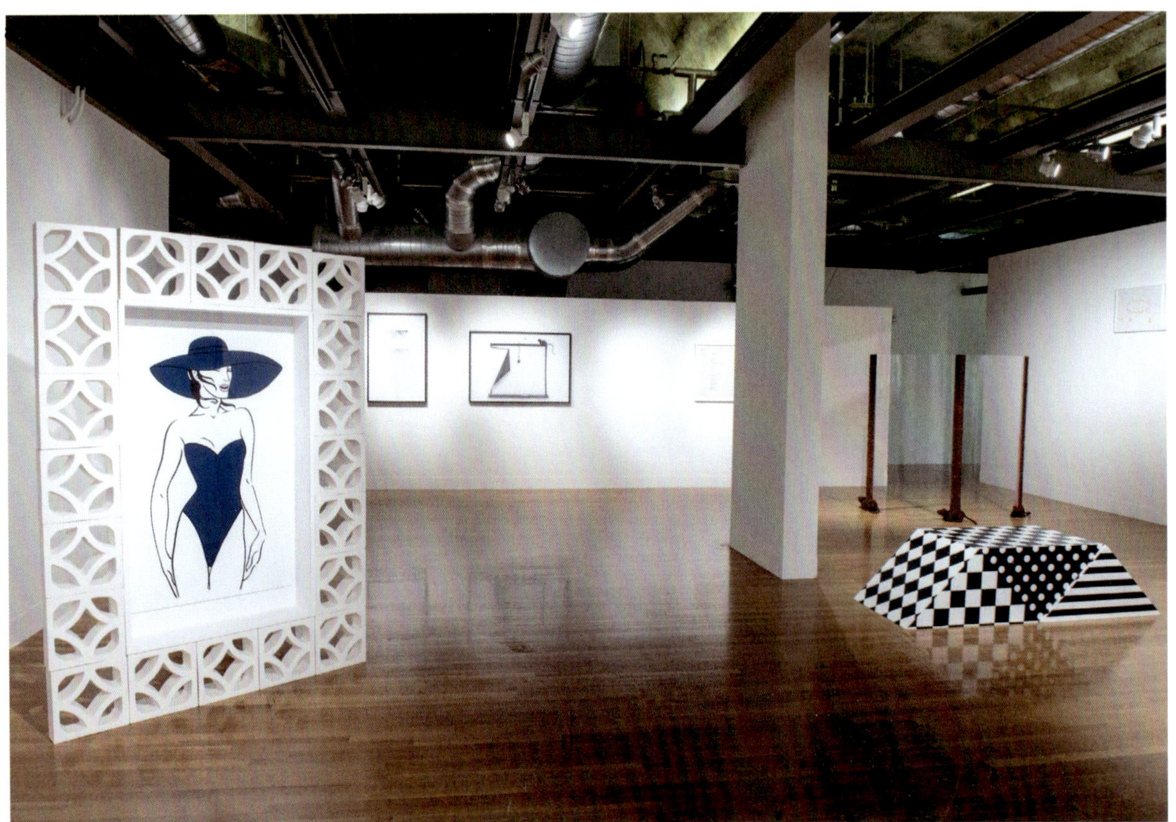

Lisa Lapinski: Drunk Hawking, installation view, Visual Arts Center, University of Texas at Austin, January 24–March 6, 2020.

previous spread

Lisa Lapinski, raw space, Biomedical Research Collaborative, Rice University.

THERE. SOFTLY: "CAN YOU SAY "THTHTHTHTHTH SNOW WHITE?" NOW KIKI A

MacKenzie Stevens

A Gathering of Friends

* * *

The first time I encountered Lisa's work was in 2017 at Kristina Kite Gallery in Los Angeles. I reached out to her in the summer of 2019 at the suggestion of Amy Hauft, an artist and former colleague at UT Austin, who had visited Lisa a few months earlier. I was pleasantly surprised when I emailed to ask if I could visit and she immediately said yes. We finally met that summer at a raw space on the campus of Rice University in Houston, where she has taught for over eight years, to view roughly thirty of her artworks.

There, in the hollows of a construction site with exposed brick and I-beams—think Soho-style loft in downtown Houston—and on an otherwise empty floor in a bustling bioscience research building stood the result of three decades of Lisa's practice. The occasion for this monumental gathering of work was serendipitous but also practical, as many of these objects had been recently returned to her after years spent on display in cities around the world, in exhibitions in both galleries, artist-run spaces, and museums. It was sort of an odd but beautiful homecoming, a reunion of old friends and acquaintances huddled together in this cavernous space. Little My and Snufkin—characters from Finnish author and artist Tove Jansson's beloved Moomins series of books and cartoons—stood opposite Holly Hobby's bow. Tobacco covered rats and camels were nearby. Waxed mini blinds and Lisa's slinky bikini girls were adjacent to the sprawling outfitted dressers comprising *Nightstand* (2006). This unbelievable conglomeration of "things" was the most fantastic way to be introduced, *really* introduced, to Lisa's work, to Lisa's world. We walked the space together and over the course of several hours we talked, and I learned. Little did I know that *this* encounter at *that* space would be a preliminary staging of the exhibition entitled *Drunk Hawking* that we would create together for the Visual Arts Center in spring 2020.

For *Drunk Hawking*, selections from the Houston space were relocated to the campus of the University of Texas at Austin, and there, for three months before COVID-19 would disrupt every aspect of our lives, the bikini girls brushed shoulders with wallpapered screen prints and altered readymade chairs/sculptures, and so on. Arranged in a relational configuration, with no real regard for dates or a standard chronological ordering, the tobacco laden and the heavily patterned were in very close proximity. To my delight, the crusty tobacco-dusted wallpaper stacks I had experienced in her storage in Houston in the summer of 2019 also found a place in *Drunk Hawking* ... not on the wall, but on the ground. Their crusty surfaces, made from shredded Bali Shag tobacco, was crunchy to the touch. They emitted the pungent and familiar smell of really good tobacco, the kind that makes you want to smoke even if you're not a smoker. The fragrant smell was present throughout the exhibition, in the form of rats, camels, and of course, these inconspicuous stacks.

The exhibition was accompanied by a text written by Kyle Dancewicz, reproduced here in its entirety. Bruce Hainley's contribution was originally delivered as an introduction to a talk Lisa gave at ArtCenter College of Design in Pasadena. In *Guess You Better Unwind It*, Sabrina Tarasoff disentangles Lisa's fascination with Disney characters whose malleability and ambiguity are a trope Lisa continues to explore. A conversation between Lisa and German linguist Viola Schmitt expands upon Lisa's process with an eye to her early experiences as an artist living abroad in the 1990s and her time as a graduate student at ArtCenter under the mentorship of Mike Kelley, as well as the role of philosophical concepts to her practice. The final text is a piece written by Lisa about her friend and colleague, artist Morgan Fisher.

BO CAME ALONG AND DONALD WAS RIDING ON THEIR BACK AND DONALD WAS

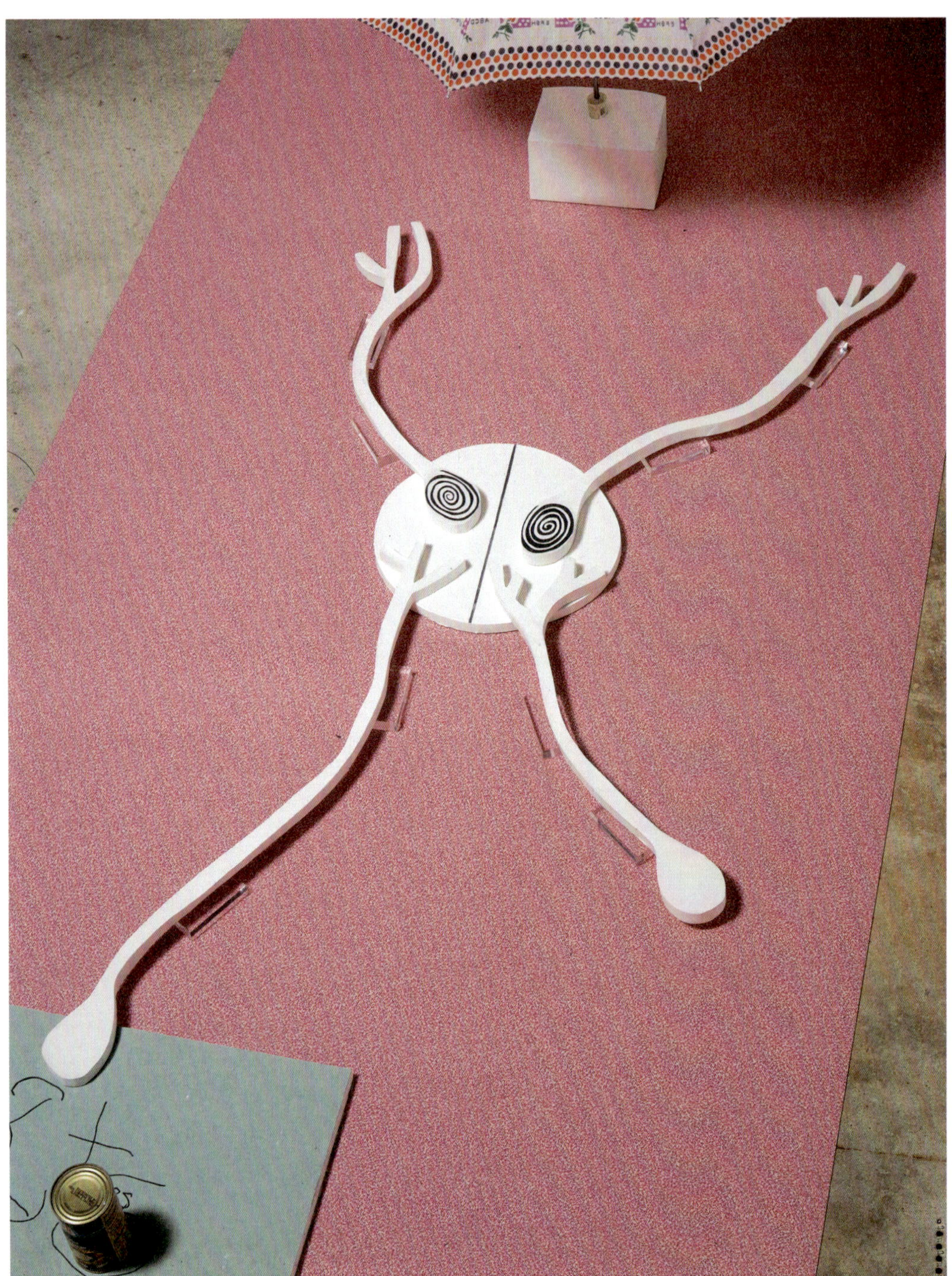

Sculpture for Horizontal Rain,
2000 (detail)
Hydrocal, screenprint on
wallpaper liner, drywall, Lucite,
linoleum flooring, can, umbrella
48 x 132 x 26 in.
(122 x 335.3 x 66 cm)

Sculpture for Horizontal Rain,
2000
Hydrocal, screenprint on
wallpaper liner, drywall, Lucite,
linoleum flooring, can, umbrella
48 x 132 x 26 in.
(122 x 335.3 x 66 cm)

following spread

[Clown Type] Face, 1999
Wallpaper, Xerox copy, staples,
canned hearts of palm
Dimensions variable

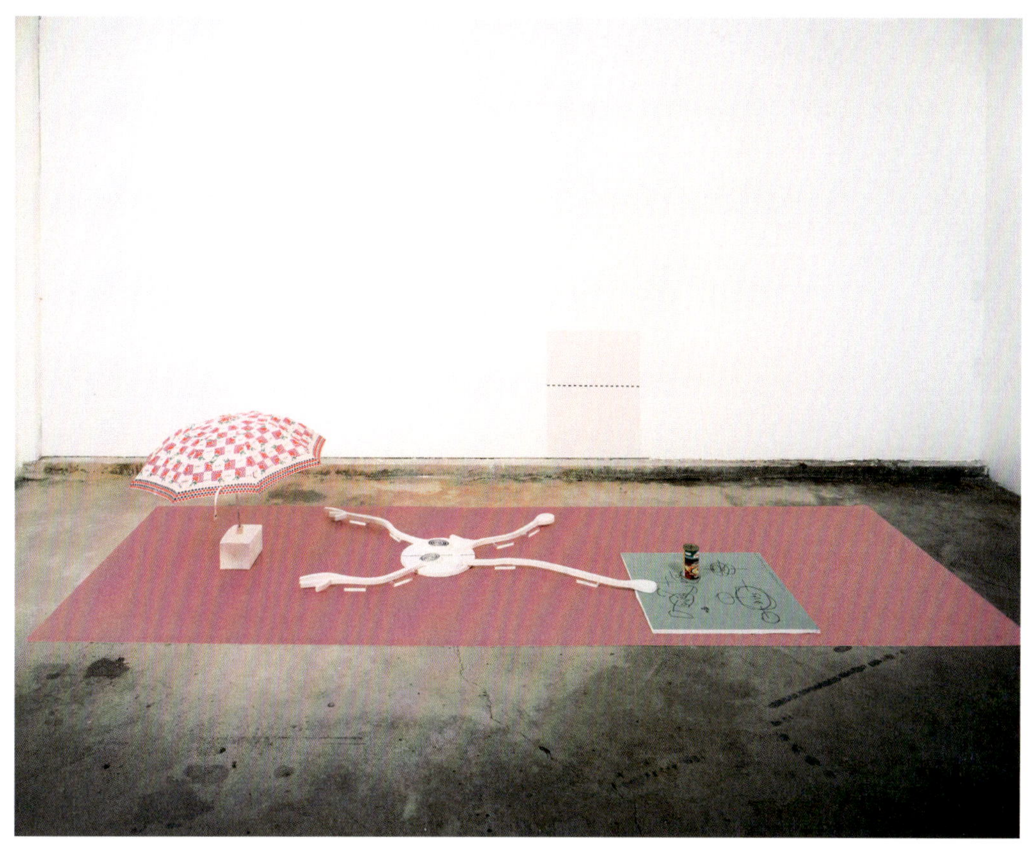

ENT TO SEE SNOW WHITE. SO SLEEPING BEAUTY CAME RIDING ON HER BIKE

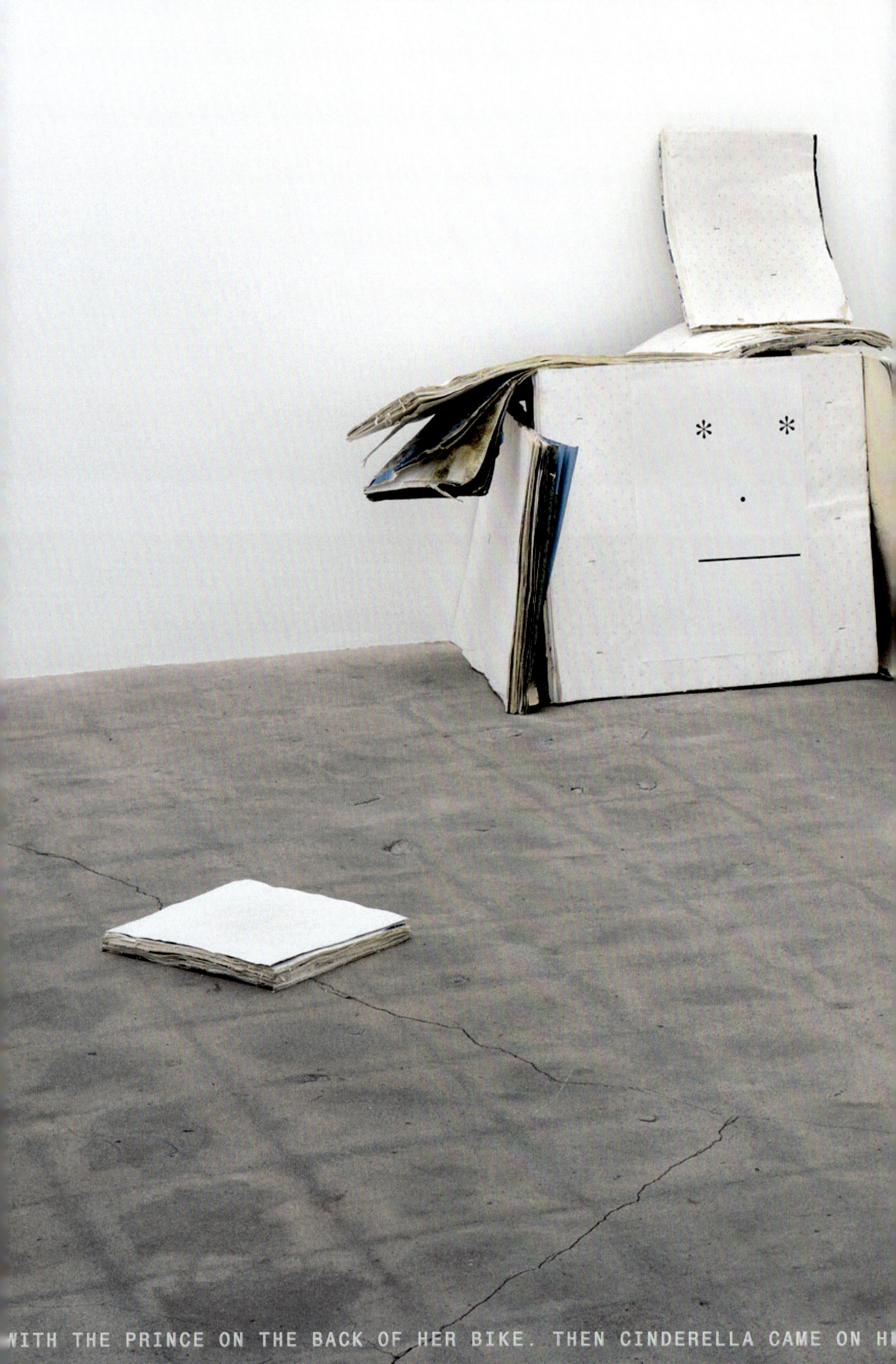

WITH THE PRINCE ON THE BACK OF HER BIKE. THEN CINDERELLA CAME ON H

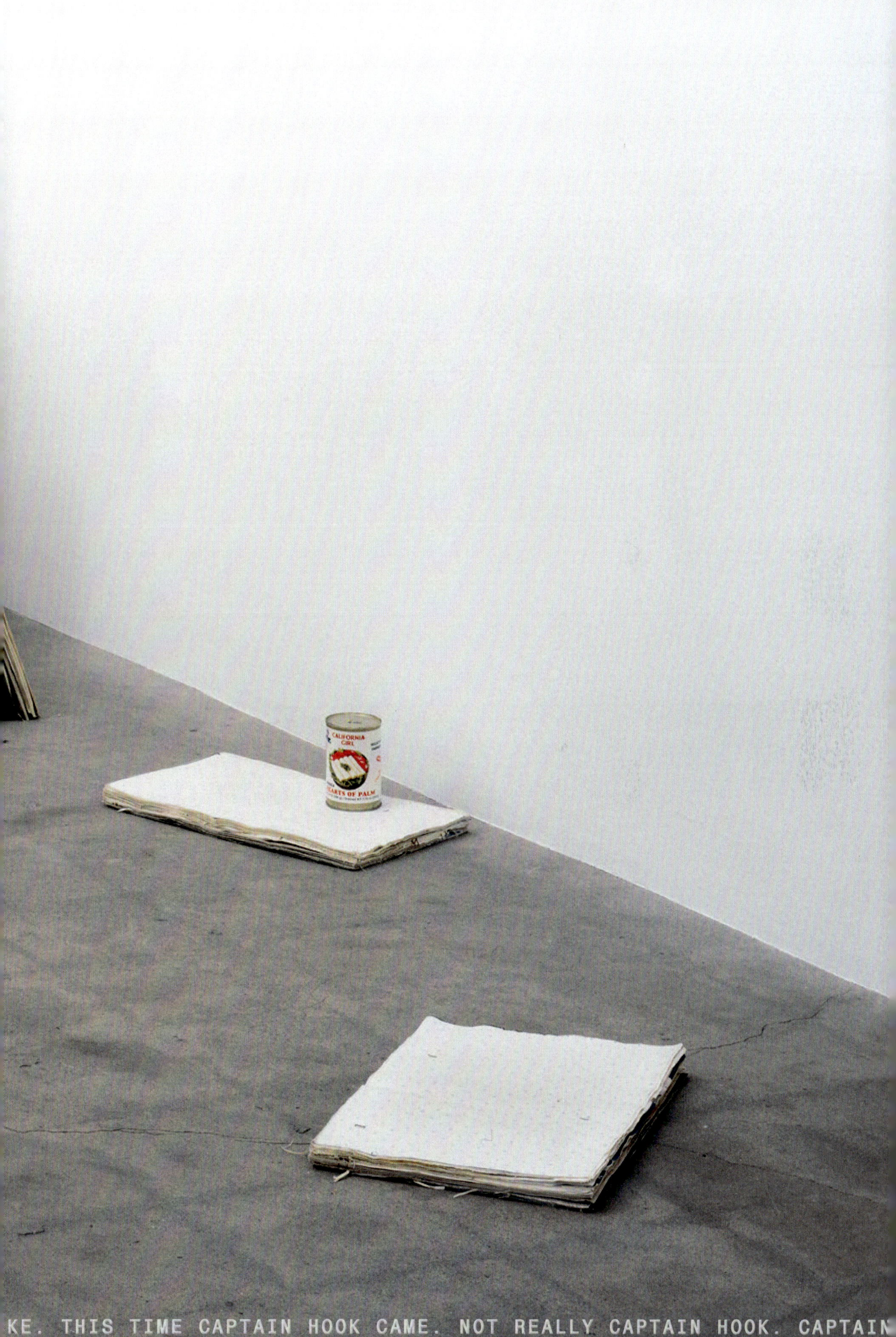

KE. THIS TIME CAPTAIN HOOK CAME. NOT REALLY CAPTAIN HOOK. CAPTAIN

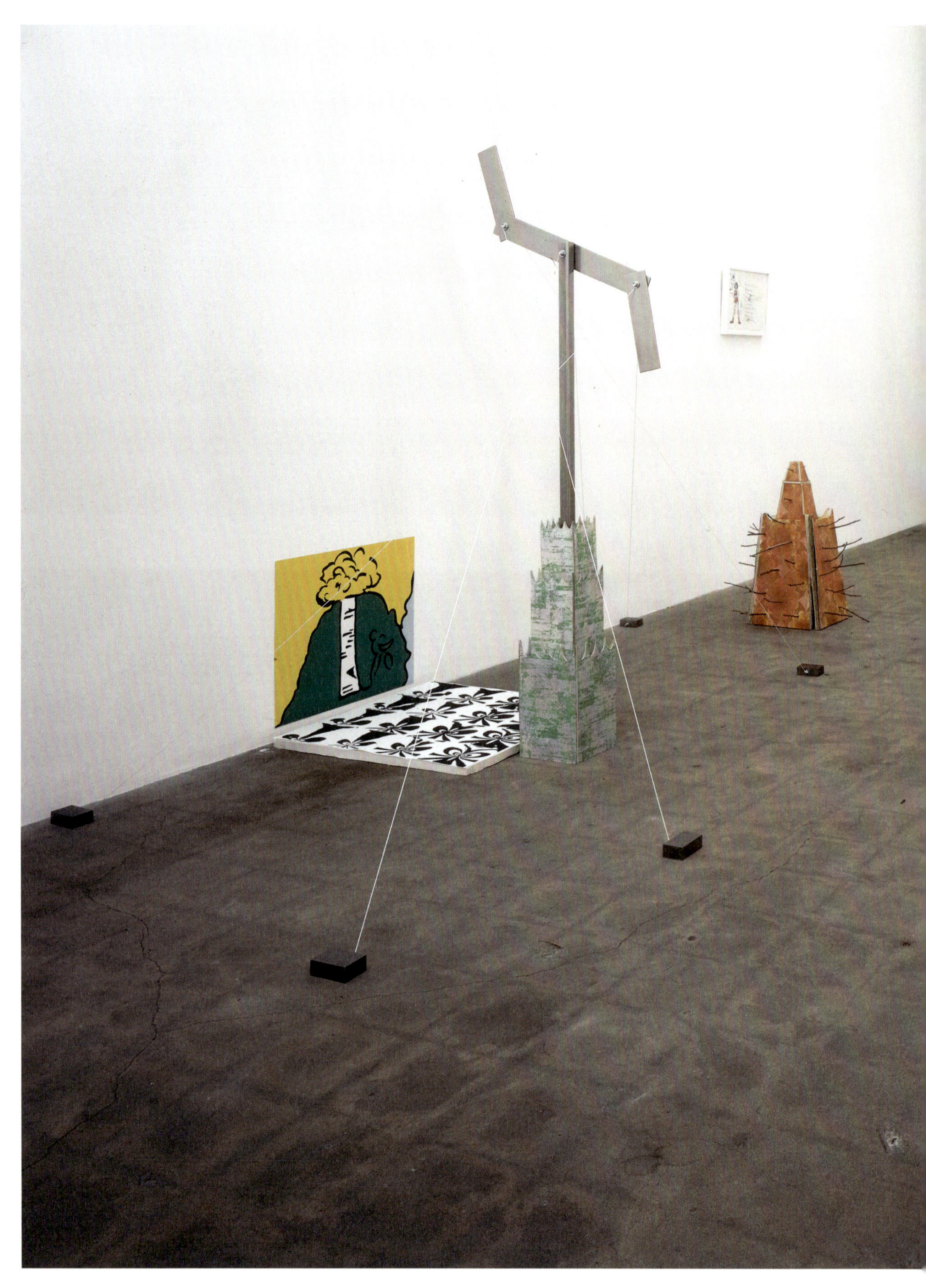

HOOK STAYED IN THE CAVE. HE STAYED IN THE LOST BOYS CAVE. ALSO, T

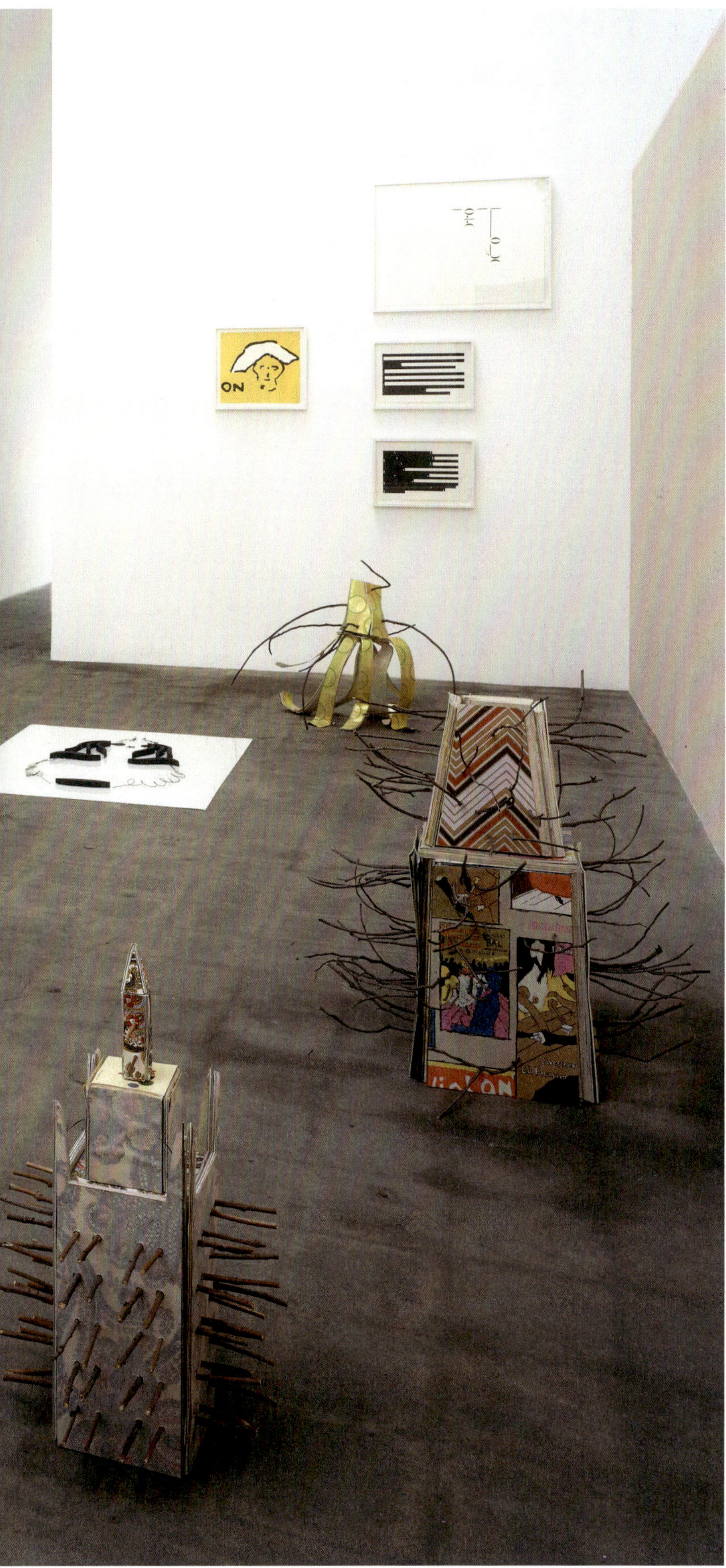

Untitled (Rimbaud Show)
Installation view,
Richard Telles Fine Art,
Los Angeles, November 17–
December 21, 2001

following spread

Untitled (Rimbaud Show)
Installation view,
Richard Telles Fine Art,
Los Angeles, November 17–
December 21, 2001

ST BOYS CAME TOO AND ALSO THIS TIME THE CROCODILE CAME ON A BIKE.

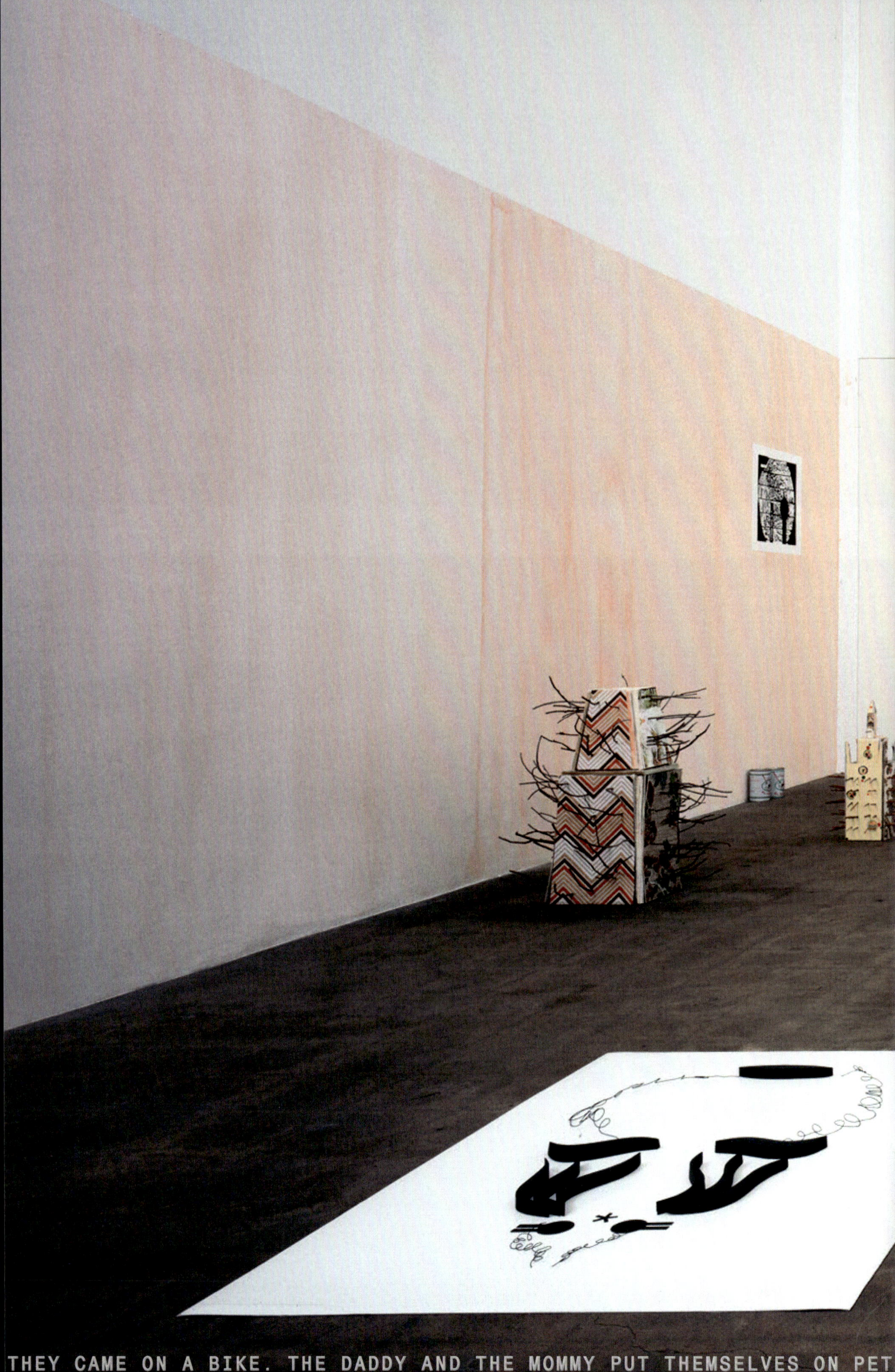

THEY CAME ON A BIKE. THE DADDY AND THE MOMMY PUT THEMSELVES ON PET

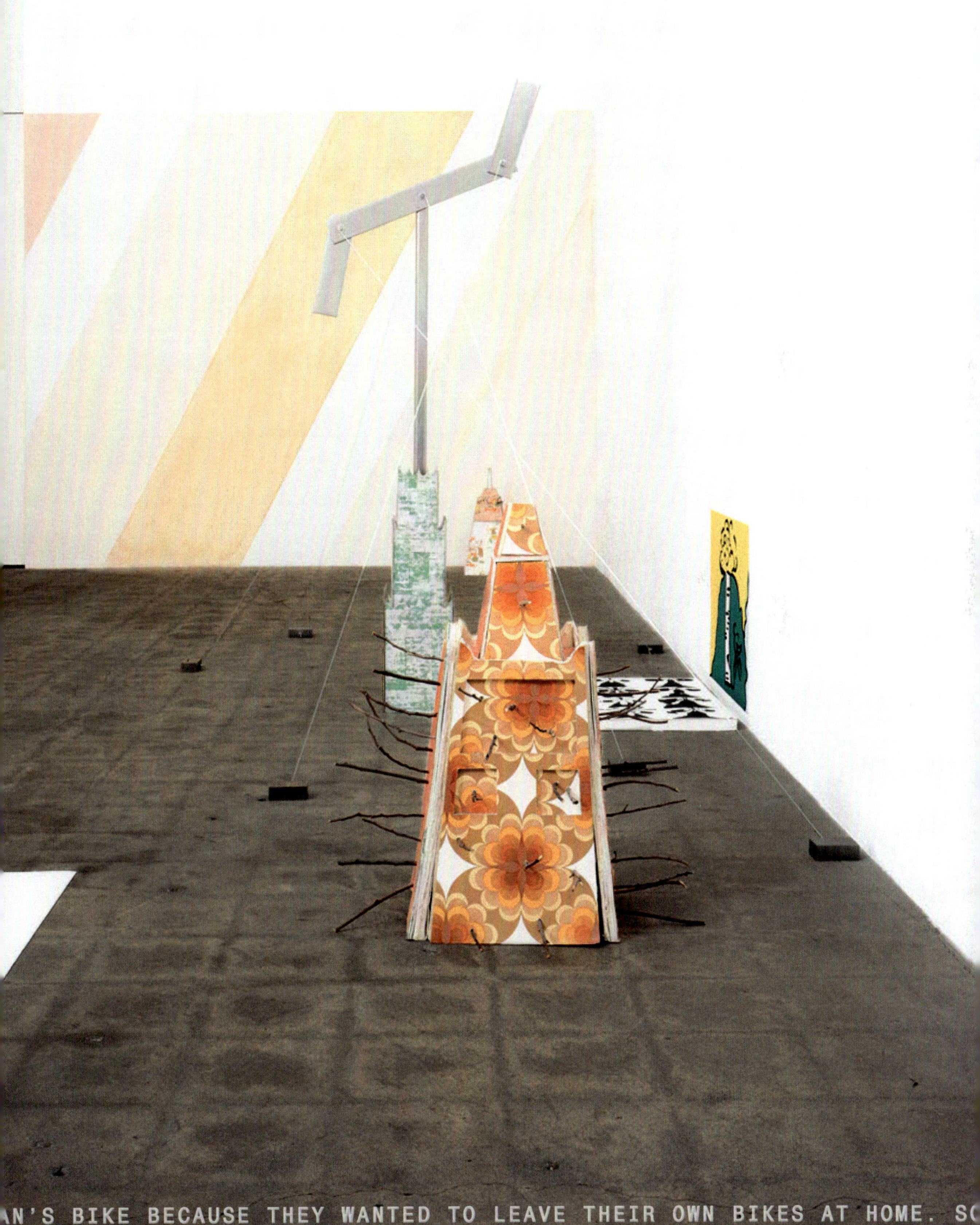

AN'S BIKE BECAUSE THEY WANTED TO LEAVE THEIR OWN BIKES AT HOME. SO

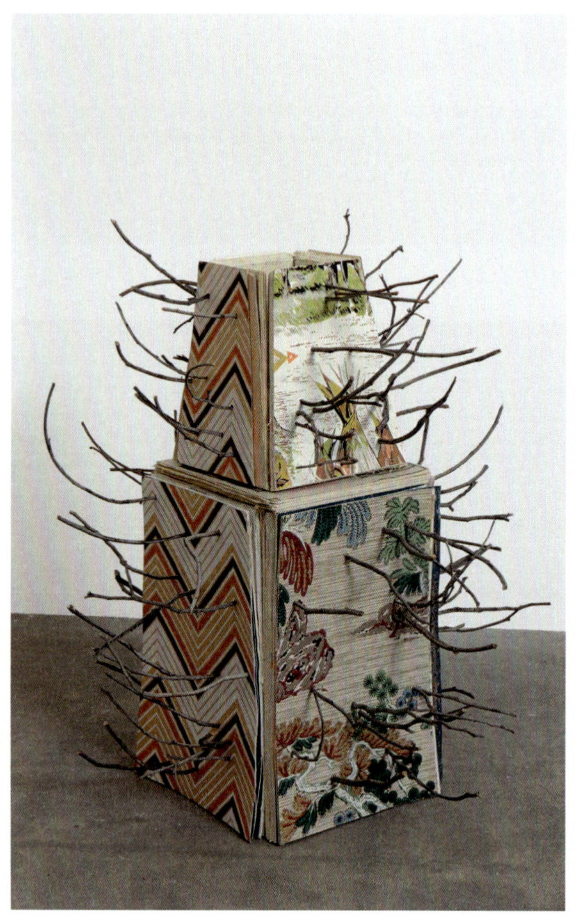

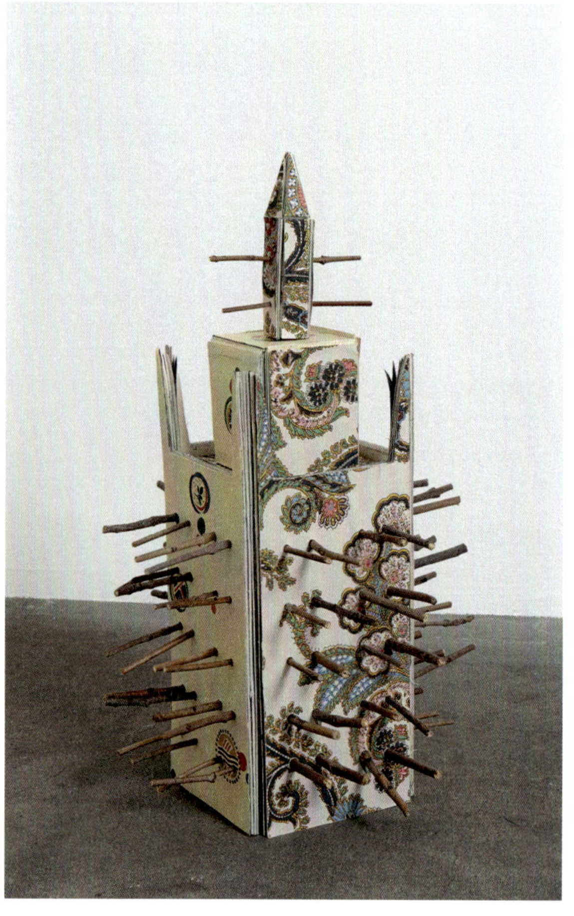

FOR THE LITTLE SISTER. NANNY WAS HOLDING THE SISTER ALL NIGHT. SH

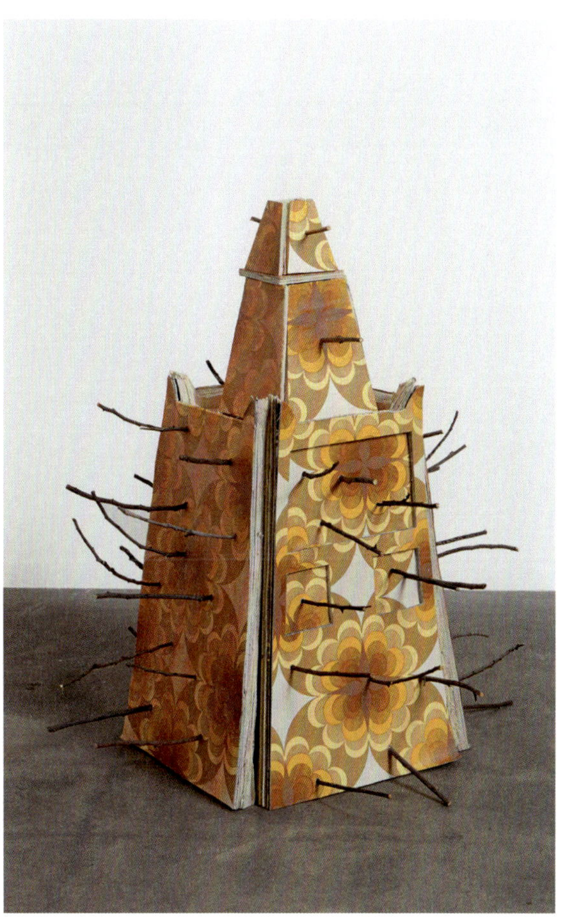

from left to right

Mosque of Boré, 2001
Wallpaper, adhesive, sticks, clay
28 x 29 x 29 in. (71.1 x 73.7 x 73.7 cm)

Mosque of Mopti, 2001
Wallpaper, adhesive, sticks
23 x 13 x 13 in. (58.4 x 33 x 33 cm)

Mosque of Sankoré, 2001
Wallpaper, adhesive, sticks
23 x 13 x 13 in. (58.4 x 33 x 33 cm)

AS TAKING CARE OF THAT SISTER WHO BELONGS TO WENDY. BUT NANNY DROPPED

Bruce Hainley

The “Is” in Lisa

* * *

I am going to begin by telling a little tale about Poiesis and Techne.

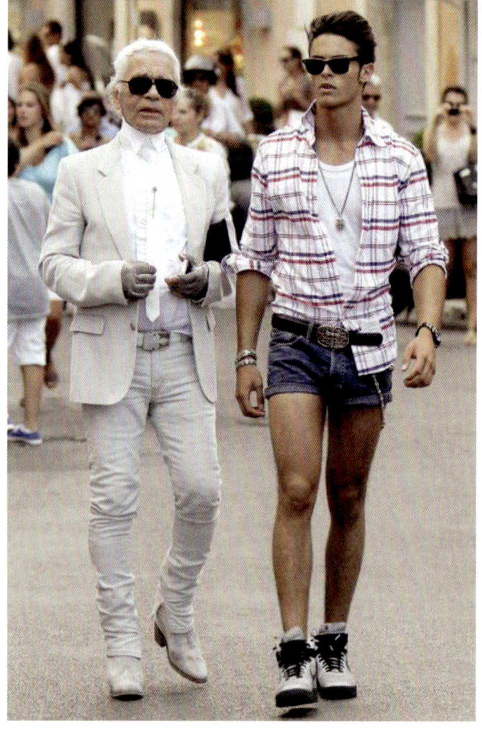

Karl Lagerfeld and Baptiste Giabiconi, 2016.

Here’s Poiesis, out for a stroll on the streets of St. Tropez, lost in thought (is it thought? What does thought look like, how do “smarts” appear?), troubled about whether he’s a product or something that produces … something. Perhaps a certain kind of frisson or affect? Pleasure? Envy? He has trouble putting any of these “thoughts” into words, but not into the world. When he walks down a St. Tropez street his gait is like watching someone dance for joy, and heads turn.

He spots Techne, and thinks, Phew! That’s the guy I need. Techne will help me make my thoughts and dreams come true.

Techne’s all too happy to oblige. He likes working with his hands, which is why he wears gloves, dove gray, protecting his instruments. He sizes up a situation and seizes the day.

They’re happier when they stroll together, and life’s a dream. People like what they do in tandem.

But then I thought, nahhhhhh …

Maybe instead I could say something about Lisa going to see, circa 1989, a rather infamous Los Angeles exhibition, *A Forest of Signs: Art in the Crisis of Representation*, organized by Ann Goldstein and Mary Jane Jacob at the Museum of Contemporary Art.[1] Although she didn’t know this in the moment (how could she? It would be almost a decade before she decided to apply to an MFA program, before, perhaps, she allowed herself to think of herself as an artist), she was seeing many works by those who would eventually become her teachers at ArtCenter College of Design: Mike Kelley, Stephen Prina, Larry Johnson. Two other artists at work in the critical forest would be teachers in other ways: Mitchell Syrop, whose vivid use of picture and text, a patois of buzzwords and branded jingoisms (“Lift and Separate”; “Academic Freedom”; “Live Nude”), is unparalleled and whose effect can be seen to brighten many of Lisa’s titles for specific works and entire shows; and Haim Steinbach, with whom Lisa would study in Como, Italy, during the summer prior to her receiving her MFA degree. If Syrop provided lessons in pictures and text, Steinbach gave seminars in objects and their syntax. Any crisis in representation was differently directed.

Which is to say that while completing a degree in continental philosophy, she sees, in Los Angeles, *A Forest of Signs*, encountering things, art (techniques, poetics), a representational crossroads, that would eventually—after a decade during which she spent time teaching English in Poland, South Korea, Hungary, and Portugal—help her determine how to become an artist.

At some point in the editing process for this catalogue, Lisa noted to me the weirdness of the progression, all the life in between seeing *A Forest of Signs* and applying to art school, that that exhibit stayed with her all those years, through most of the 1990s, while she was teaching in former communist turbine factories and traveling.

One work in particular, long lingering,Steinbach's *Untitled (Wakamba Gourds)* (1989), cauterized some wound or lack, and propelled and compelled some response or life trajectory. The sculpture (is it helpful, fleetingly, to consider Steinbach's shelves in relation to friezes?), its little bronze statuette, maternal, with bosomy, bottomy curves, balanced on laminated glass and the Kenyan storage gourds balanced on the faux wood grain of the rich brown plastic laminate shelf, condenses a history of Western modernism through material juxtaposition and placement, the exchange of forms alluding (surely?) to colonial traffic of bodies and artifacts as well as to figurative motifs that come to be called Culture. Circa 2000, no one, no other artist I knew apart from Lisa, spoke of and thought through as convincingly Steinbach's dynamic and brainy project, one that had been stupidly relegated, shoved—shelved—in a dark corner of the art basement marked "Shopper's Art" or with some other lazy, hackneyed phraseology. A famous (?) art critic once snorted and reprimanded me when, trying to respond to his question about which older artists were important to the younger LA artists I was most interested in, thinking of Lisa I said Steinbach's name.

Lisa Lapinski: The Fret and Its Variants, exhibition catalogue, Museum of Contemporary Art (MOCA) Los Angeles, 2008.

The ready-made is an occasion for so much discourse because it is so still. The tautological form is the stillest thing in the world. The ready-made is a motionless catastrophe; it occurs only once, and we are still trying to manage the after-effects. It is immovable not because it is heavy; it is neither light nor heavy. Conversely, Haim Steinbach is an artist almost singularly concerned with gravity. Appearance is not a realm where difference is constant, but one where equals become unequal and unequals become equal (necessarily); and this structure of appearance is the structure of the object that appears.[2]

This opening paragraph of Lisa's daunting essay on Steinbach, "Raider's Blanket," is a corrective not only to much of the blah-blah about his venture, but also about the lifelikeness of the readymade; exemplary of one artist thinking and writing about another, a thinking which Lisa, through her sculptural pursuits, carries out in other ways.

I'm not going to pursue this line of thinking either.

I find it difficult to express how art that means something to me means something; what, exactly, I should say about it, how much to expect to be paid for saying it, since no amount, nothing or actual artwork in exchange or something in between, ever seems quite right.

You'll have noticed that everything I've said so far depends upon a mix-up or miscegenation of the discreet, the indiscreet (as in indiscretion), and the discrete (as in individually separate and distinct).

People love when an artist, or anyone really, talks about art anecdotally, when professionals veer into an indiscreet mode.

When does the discreet shade and fade into the indiscreet? Can you always tell? When does the anecdote become history or historical?

1. The catalogue for Lisa's 2008 exhibit at MOCA, *The Fret and its Variants*, was designed by Mathias Poledna.[3] I don't know if this is still the case, but for some years after he designed that trig tome, Poledna abjured designing books for anyone else, any artist other than himself.

2. Together in Minneapolis for Lisa's solo show at Midway Contemporary Art, prior to the show at MOCA, I told Lisa I thought her debut Los Angeles institutional exhibit should be called *Monty Python Precedes Dungeons and Dragons*; Bennett Simpson, the curator, wasn't as convinced by the urgency or accuracy of that title. Lisa ended up giving it instead to a piece within—*The Fret and its Variants*—anyway.

3. I once witnessed Lisa throw a drink in a dealer's face, a man who long deserved it. The dealer was at that point still her dealer, and he can be lucky it wasn't lye. I want to say this happened as we were leaving Larry Johnson's Hammer survey, and it makes me recall that at the opening of *The Fret and its Variants*, a few years prior, Larry saying, mock-peevishly, a mode few pull off as well as he can, that such a tony, intellectual

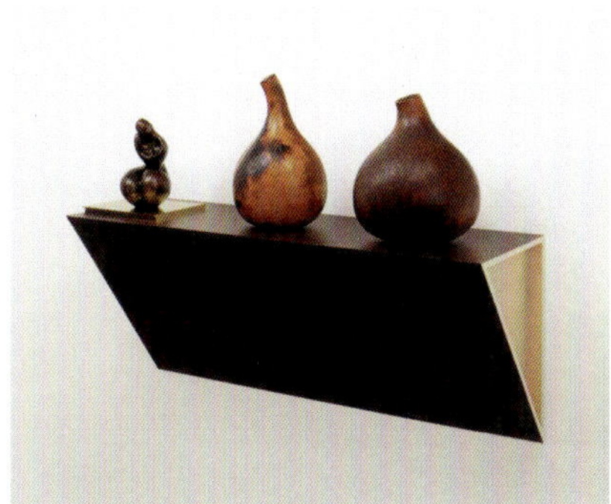

Haim Steinbach, *Untitled (bronze statuette, Wakamba Gourds)*, 1989. Plastic laminated wood shelf, bronze statuette, Wakamba gourds. 42 3/4 x 59 1/2 x 20 1/2 in. (108.6 x 151.1 x 52.1 cm).

ONSTER AND COOKIE MONSTER WAS BEHIND HIM AND HE GOT SOME COOKIES. HE crowd had never shown up for one of his openings. After checking with Lisa, she corrected my memory: she threw the drink into the dealer's face not at Larry's survey opening, but at group exhibit of LA sculptors that included her work.

4. Lisa was one of the first artists I made cry during a studio visit.

5. A few years ago, I went with Lisa and Kristina Kite to see Zach Woods perform improv at Largo, and afterwards we talked for a long time about how out of two random suggestions shouted from the audience—"airports" and "dinosaurs"—he and his stage partner wove together an hour and a half of play-acting, seemingly from almost nothing at all. Airports and dinosaurs, it might as well have been Monty Python and Dungeons and Dragons. Or Poiesis and Techne.

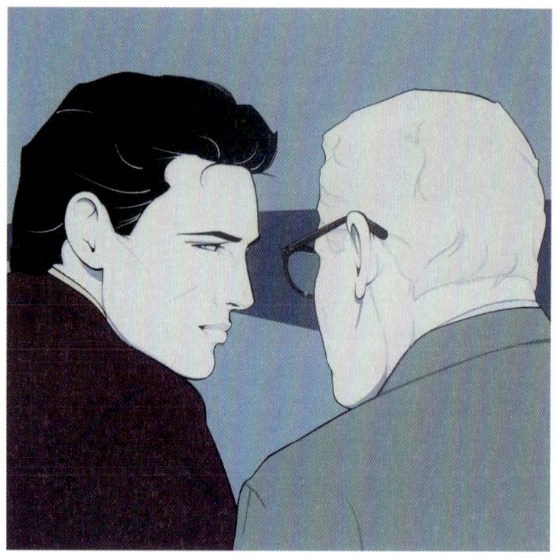

Patrick Nagel, Untitled, ca. 1980s.
Watercolor, gouache, pencil, ink on board.
20 1/2 x 20 in. (52.1 x 50.8 cm).

At what point did I slide into the relatively indiscreet with these five examples? Was it from the get-go? It's always possible to be more indiscreet or much less so, but when does any anecdote become the beginning of a theory?

And what about that other *discrete*, as in distinct?

When does an arrangement of discrete works or observations become an exhibit or an essay?

In looking back over Lisa's enterprise, strange objects I've been lucky enough to see since her first weepy weeks of graduate school and to think about and observe in many more illustrious circumstances, I would say that she calls attention to that moment when one thing becomes and/or meets or abrades another, things that one might often consider as discrete as Poiesis and Techne. Consider how art becomes an argument or a gourd becomes art, at some point after it's harvested. Or when mealy-mouthed identity politics becomes hardcore feminism. Or when one thing after another turns into a pattern, whether syntactical, representational, aesthetic, or facial, and the difficulty, almost an impossibility, of unseeing that pattern. I'm thinking of trying to unsee the swastikas made by the design pattern of the Chippendale fencing in *Christmas Tea = Meeting, presented by Dialogue and Humanism, formerly Dialectics and Humanism* (2007) as well as how the barest-bone reduction of faciality by Alexei Jawlensky could be even further reduced (or intensified?) to punctuation marks in *[Clown Type] Face* (1999).

All of which is a much less felicitous gloss on a statement of purpose composed when Lisa was in the early stages of the projects that have resulted in her solo exhibition *Holly Hobby Lobby* as well as the two shows she curated, at Midway Contemporary and at Rice University, that form and formulate some kind of dialogue with it: "I am interested in the paradoxical or even imaginary processes by which a sculpture might be advanced as a form of argument, as if it were a political pamphlet realized in three dimensions."[4]

In other words, her materializations of that blazing instant and process—imaginary, by which I mean no less than actual—when Poiesis cruises Techne, a form of argument or relationality sometimes known as Praxis.

PULLED THEM OUT OF PETER PAN'S OVEN. THEN WENDY WENT TO THE GROCE

1. *A Forest of Signs*: *Art in the Crisis of Representation*, Museum of Contemporary Art, Los Angeles, May 7–August 13, 1989.

2. Lisa Lapinski, “Raider’s Blanket,” in *Special Project*: *Mr. Peanut*, Haim Steinbach on Mike Kelley (Los Angeles: Overduin and Kite, 2008).

3. *The Fret and its Variants*, The Museum of Contemporary Art, Los Angeles, June 26–August 25, 2008.

4. *Holly Hobby Lobby*, Kristina Kite Gallery, Los Angeles, September 9–November 4, 2017; *Group Show (Anna Helm, Lisa Lapinski, Hirsch Perlman)*, Midway Contemporary Art, Minneapolis, September 16–November 4, 2017; *Pile the Wood High!*, Moody Center for the Arts, Rice University, February 2–May 19, 2018.

TORE TO BUY SOME PICKLES. WHEN SHE GOT BACK SHE HAD A LITTLE PICKLE

Analysandom
Installation view,
Richard Telles Fine Art,
Los Angeles, November 17–
December 21, 2001

THEM ON THE PAVEMENT. (DID THE SISTER GET HURT?) NO, SHE WAS STANDIN

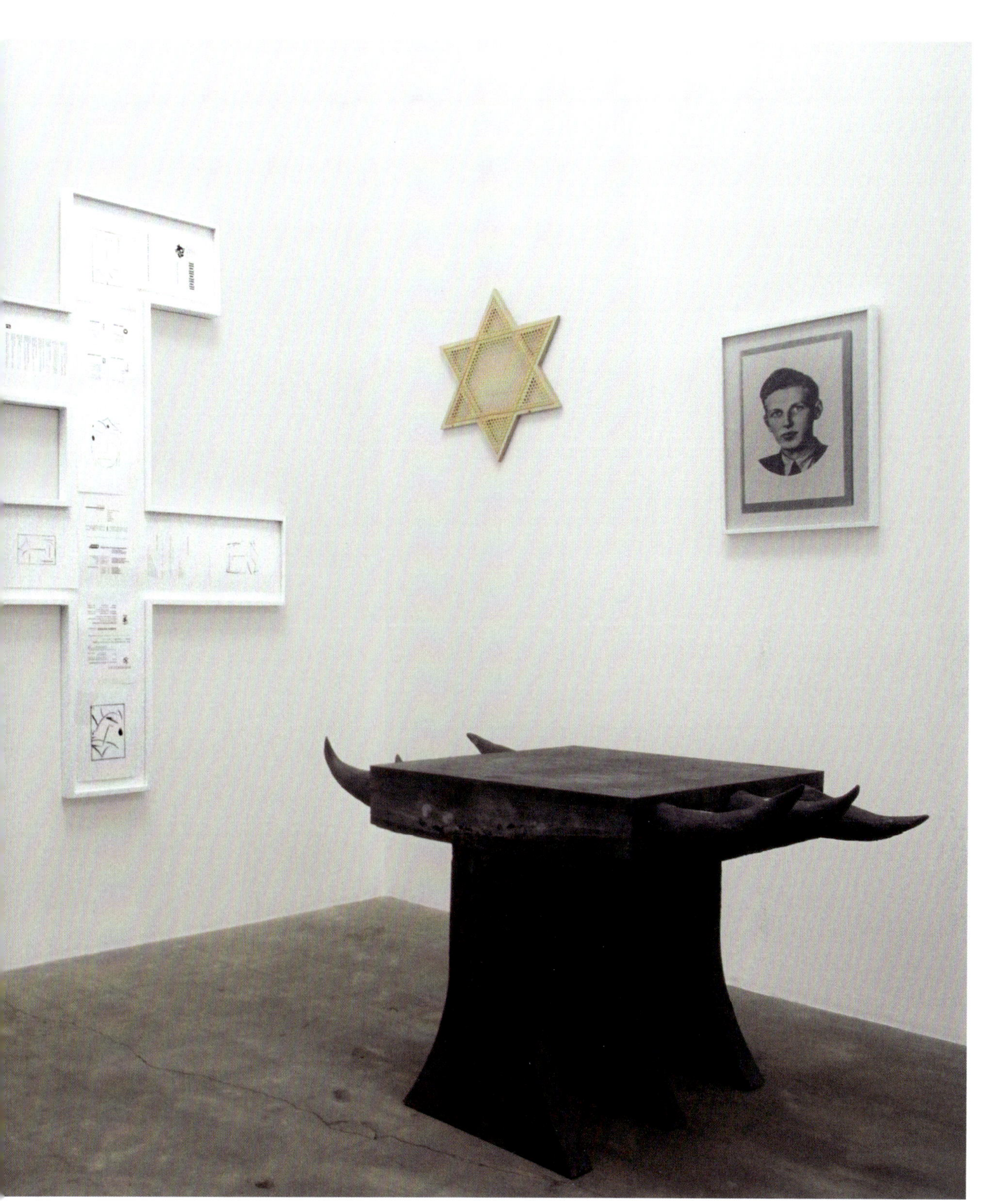

" ON THE PAVEMENT. GRAMPY WAS HOLDING BRONS. HE PUT A LITTLE CHAIR

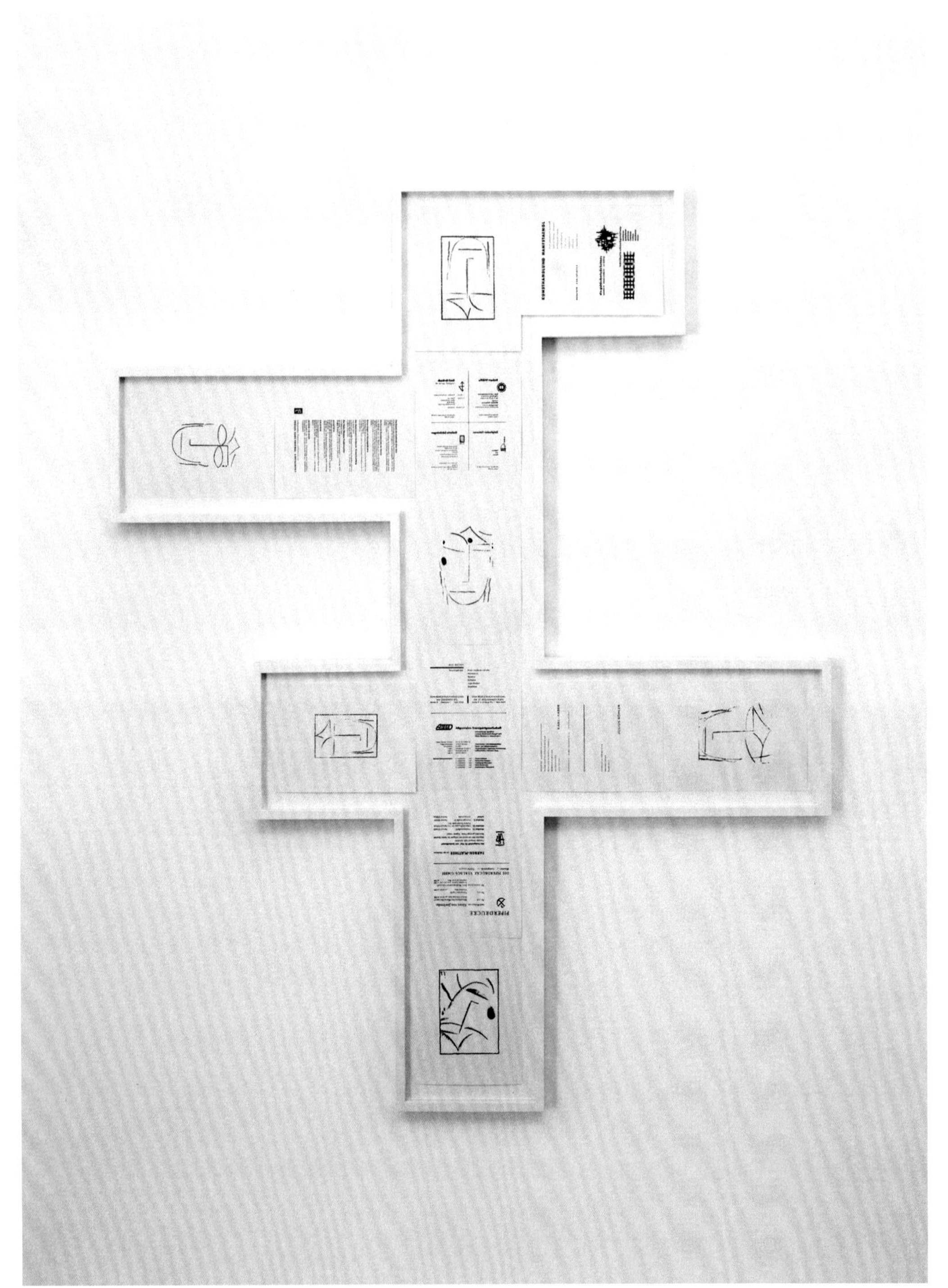

ON THE PAVEMENT JUST RIGHT FOR BRONS. AND HE PUT BRONS RIGHT ON IT

Rod Cross, 2002–03
Screen print on paper
72 x 57 in. (182.9 x 144.8 cm)

Untitled (Caned Star of David), 2003
Wood and caning
24 x 21 in. (61 x 53.3 cm)

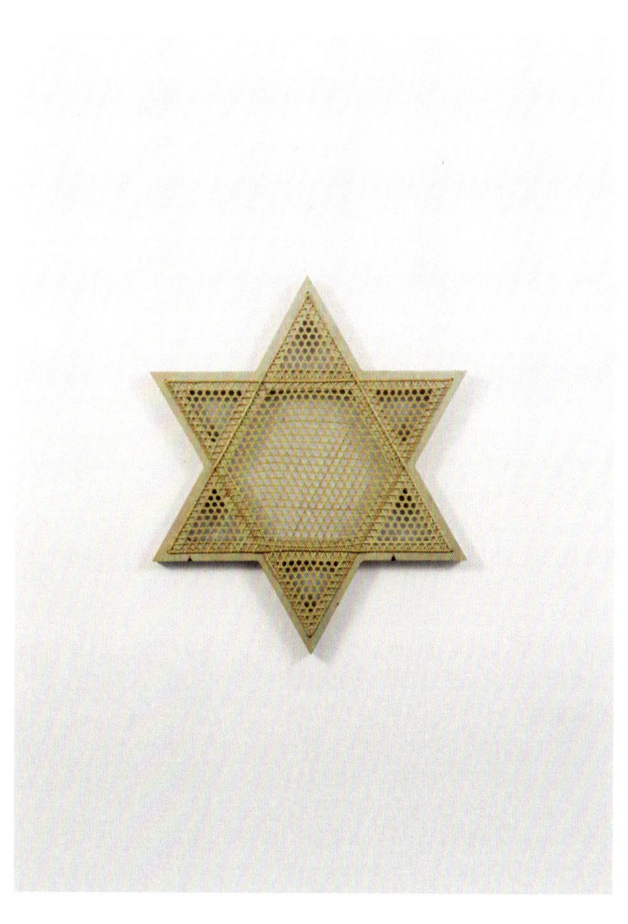

EN BELLE CAME WITH HER YELLOW DRESS AND BELLE GOT SOME CANDY. SHE

Graham Bader

Strolling Forms, Wandering Signs

* * *

What does a product logo smell like? How about for a Shaker, or for a fan of the austere glass cubes of post-minimalist sculptor Larry Bell? And what precise hold, beyond that of visual familiarity, do logos—or any visual form—even have on us? How do they occupy our thoughts, fill our senses, make space in our lives?

I've no idea if these exact questions occurred to Lisa Lapinski as she began her series of 2010 *Tobacco Camels*, a set of works that materialized Camel cigarettes' iconic logo as a real, live (though not living) tobacco camel—standing simply on a white plinth, ensconced in a Plexiglas cube atop a woven-cane base, perched high over a transparent columnar support or encased in a truncated pyramid. I *do* know that Lapinski, in making these works, was thinking about the material life of such familiar forms as Camel's camel—about how we know them, and how they become part of us, beyond simple visual recognition.

Lapinski's thoughts about the series began at Camel's home in Winston-Salem, North Carolina. Where—while touring the R. J. Reynolds headquarters during a visit to relatives—she noticed an oversized sculpture wrapped in translucent plastic that she quickly understood to be just such a "tobacco camel" as that she would soon come to make.[1] She couldn't see it, though; apparently due to a mold problem, the company's embodied insignia was literally under wraps. So Lapinski set out to make her own: she took a Camel cigarette pack to a Los Angeles taxidermist to have the basic form rendered in foam, found (through trial and error) just the right kind of tobacco—Bali Shag—to cover it, and then let the creature mutate in scale, housing, and perch across the series' distinct pieces. A new, old creature was born.

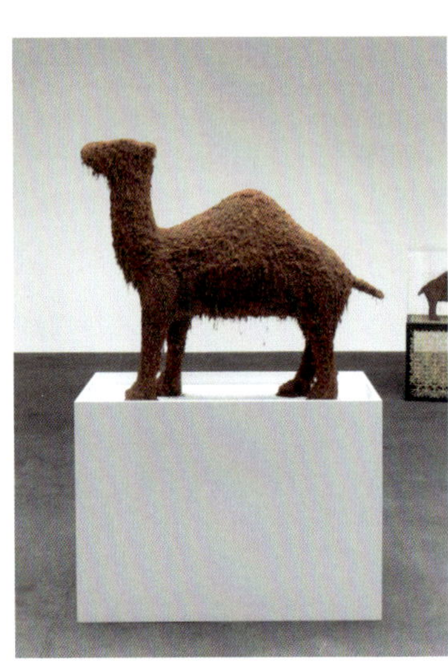

Lisa Lapinski, *Tobacco Camel #3*, 2011 (detail). Plastic foam, adhesive, tobacco, wood. 78 x 28 x 22 in. (198.1 x 71.1 x 55.9 cm).

And smell it did. As Zurich-based perfumer Andy Tauer has commented on the olfactory charms of raw tobacco:

> I love it for its multitude of facets. There is a wood line. There are dried fruits giving it a gourmand character … There is an animalic, furry, dirty line. And there is a quality that says "bathroom, used, not cleaned for a while," and so much more.[2]

I doubt any of this was on Lapinski's mind as she made her camels. And yet there they are, animalistic fur and dirt and even the suggestion of uncleaned bathrooms, in the shaggy underbellies and shedding scraps of her intricately rendered horde. Even if our noses aren't as finely attuned as Tauer's, his olfactory associations have strangely worked their way into the visual form of Lapinski's materialized icons. Their creaturely characteristics are there to be both smelled and seen.

In effecting this transmogrification of product insignia into multisensory experience, Lapinski inverts what logos are and how they function: no longer a mark whose

PUT OUT THE CANDY ON THE TABLE. BELLE CHEWED A LITTLE BIT OF CAND

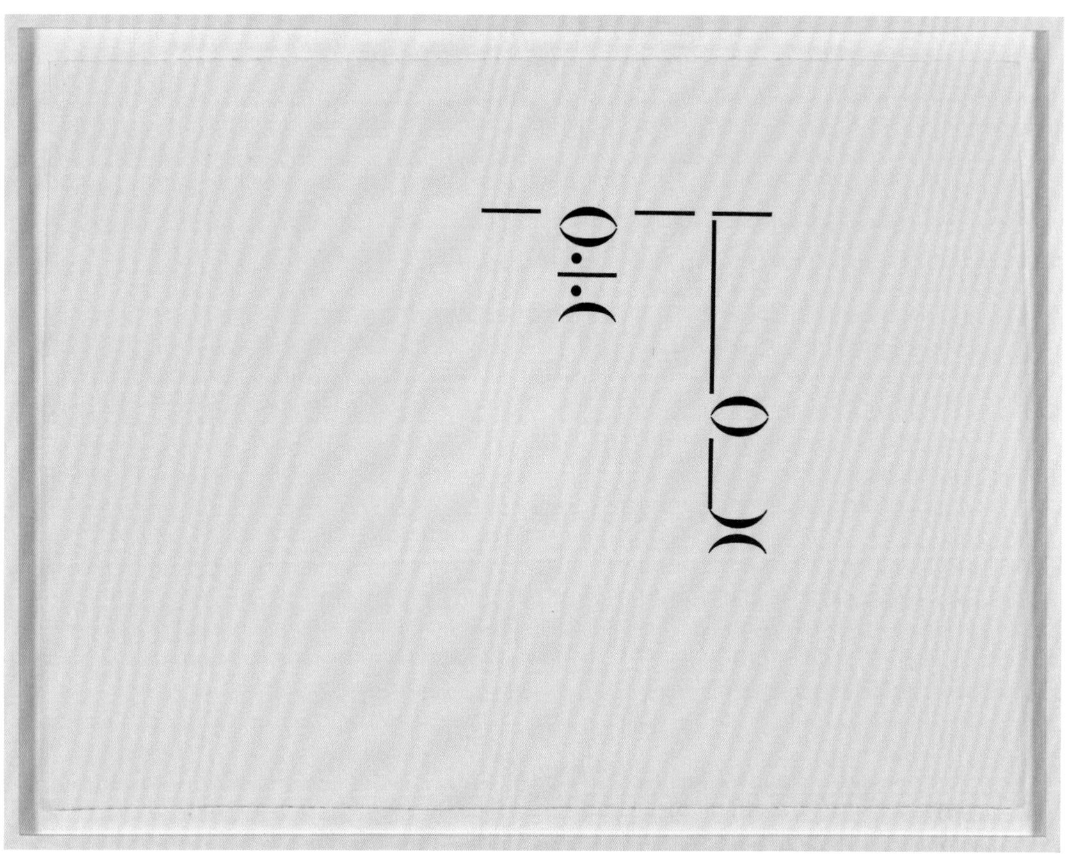

Lisa Lapinski, *Jawlensky/Cage Face*, 2001. Screenprint. 22 x 29 in. (55.88 x 73.66 cm). Museum of Contemporary Art (MOCA), Los Angeles.

meaning is fully exhausted in the brand it signifies and as whose surrogate it serves—as is, say, the three-pronged star of Mercedes—the logo, in her hands, becomes a metastasizing material being, a *creature*, that effloresces new forms, associations, and sensations, from Shaker furniture and Larry Bell to dirty restrooms and shaggy bellies. Is it any surprise, looking back to Lapinski's Winston-Salem visit, that she was so immediately taken by R. J. Reynolds's moldy, plastic-wrapped dromedary monument?

A related set of concerns and procedures are at work in Lapinski's early play, initiated during her student years at Pasadena's ArtCenter College of Design, with the schematically rendered faces of Russian-born expressionist painter Alexei Jawlensky. Built—repeatedly, incessantly—from an elongated central "L" (nose), trio of horizontal or arching lines (mouth and two eyes), and accompanying steep and shallow curves (chin and brow), Jawlensky's decades-old visages, Lapinski recognized, are every bit as effective a logo as R. J. Reynold's camel. And this spiritualist-face-as-one-shot-sign was made, to boot, by a figure who appeared to have "never said an interesting thing in his life"—to be, as Lapinski has noted, about as uncool an artist to work from as possible.[3] So, of course, Lapinski got to work. Much like she would later do with her shaggy dromedaries, she began to explore Jawlensky's face-as-insignia as a seed from which a constellation of forms could grow. It became a quasi-medium.

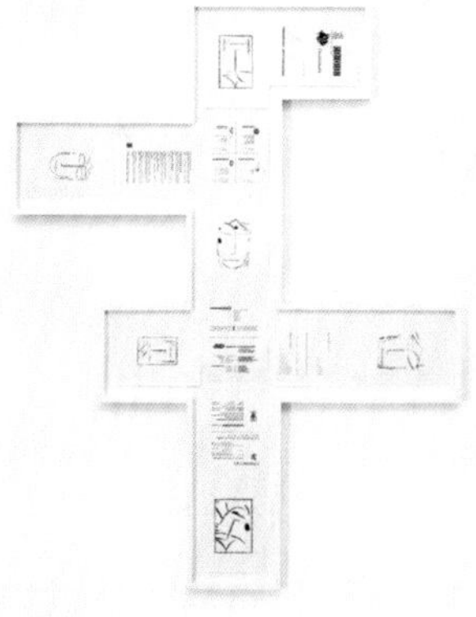

Lisa Lapinski, *Rod Cross*, 2002–03. Screen print on paper. 72 x 57 in. (182.9 x 144.8 cm).

First, Lapinski literalized the schematic quality of Jawlensky's faces by rendering them as a field of typographic characters—simple horizontal and vertical lines, parentheses, brackets, slash marks. These she paired with photographs of blanched female faces in the style of the LA-based illustrator Patrick Nagel, uniting soulful early twentieth-century expressionist and late-seventies *Playboy* favorite in a constellation of emptied-out human forms. Lapinski also brought together, across what appears to be a merger of swastika and Russian Orthodox cross, a set of Jawlensky faces with a selection of sponsor advertisements from the back pages of one of the artist's German museum exhibition catalogues, creating, in *Rod Cross*, a cascading black-and-white tangle of text, image, and line.[4]

All of these elements, Lapinski had perceived, shared formal DNA: Jawlensky's faces were echoed in the spare logos and ad layouts of his museum sponsors, and the form of her own shaped image assembly was in turn derived from the linear networks of the earlier artist's faces—resulting, perhaps not coincidentally, in a strange amalgam of cross and swastika that merged what are arguably the two most successful (and charged) insignias of all time. That art historians have linked Jawlensky's repeated faces to those of Andy Warhol—who merged face, painting, and logo more effectively than anyone, and whose life was marked by both deep Catholicism and maddeningly opaque political convictions—made these ingredients only that much more compelling.

In developing and interweaving such elements—as with her shaggy, odiferous camels—Lapinski was focused on neither structuralist semiotic critique nor poststructuralist analysis of the world's transmogrification into deracinated sign. Her driving interest, rather, was (and is) the material life of signs themselves, blooming and transmogrifying across the spaces, contexts, and periods they traverse. We see this as well in such projects as her reshaping of the anodyne bow of Holly Hobbie—best known as the namesake of a series of ragdolls—into intricately crafted wooden sculptures that recall the digitized attacking forms of *Space Invaders*, or in her multiple placements and alterations—hanging, standing, faceless, caned—of a diminutive chair based on the Swedish children's character Lilla My, known in English as Little My.

Notable in both of these works is not just their immediately recognizable visual form—the subtle aggression of Lapinski's bow-as-invader and the cute-sinister vibe of her frequently faceless Swedish protagonist—but also the impeccable craftsmanship Lapinski brings to bear on both, and the cascade of associations each accordingly puts into play. These go together: Holly Hobbie's and Little My's constellations of association are, in part, Lapinski's very sculptural material, which she makes her own through just such studied and precise craft.[5] Similar to her work with Nagel's women, gendered agency and objectification (a subtly complex word in the context of such carefully rendered objects) are also at work here—reaching from Lapinski's own evident skill with a saw, to Little My's legendarily "fiery and irritable" personality, to the resonances between the name Holly Hobbie and that of the notoriously antiabortion crafting shop Hobby Lobby. (The latter, I should note, was directly invoked in Lapinski's 2017 titling of these pieces' debut exhibition at LA's Kristina Kite Gallery as *Holly Hobby Lobby*.)

Uniting all of the projects I've so far discussed is Lapinski's generatively specific material and semiotic play. Her forms, materials, and references are all chosen and crafted with the utmost precision, and yet they consistently produce, through their interlacing and expansion of elements, a set of meanings and associations that reach far beyond their immediate frames of reference. In this, Lapinski's work has something of the mad discovery and assembly of childhood games about it—of children's ability, as Walter Benjamin described it, to "wander through the world of things like the stations of a journey of whose extent we can form no conception."[6]

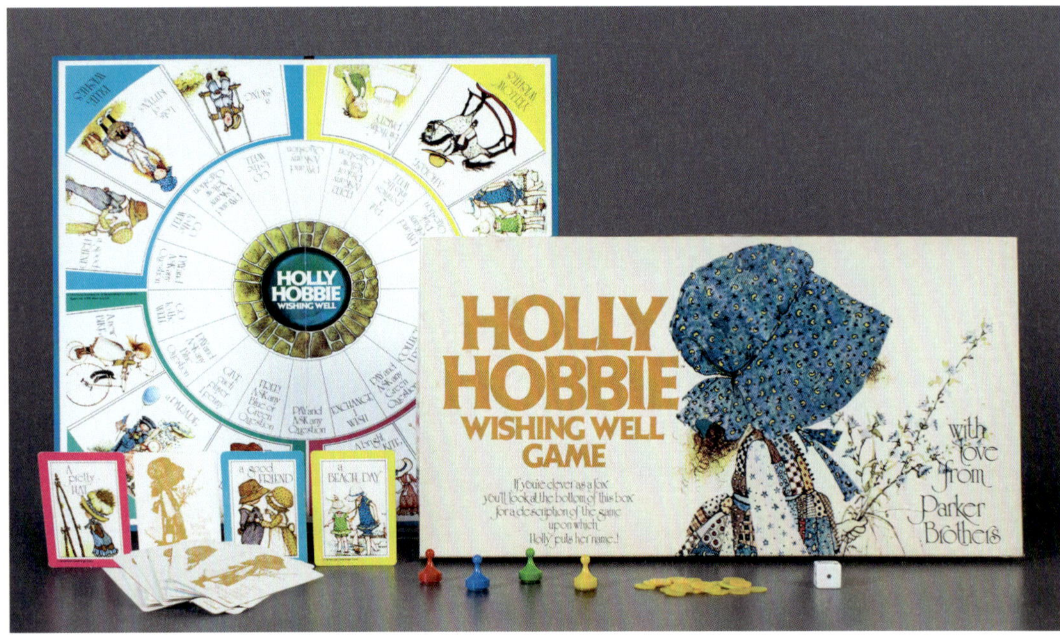

Holly Hobbie Wishing Well game (manufactured by Parker Brothers, 1976).

This imaginative capacity was described by the critic as that of *mimesis*—by which he meant not simple resemblance but the particular facility (abundant in children and premodern cultures but all but lost in modern adulthood) to see in every object and image a potentially endless web of correspondences and connections: the overgrown tree transformed into an ancient castle, the rock into an extraterrestrial artifact, the back of the closet into a forgotten cave.

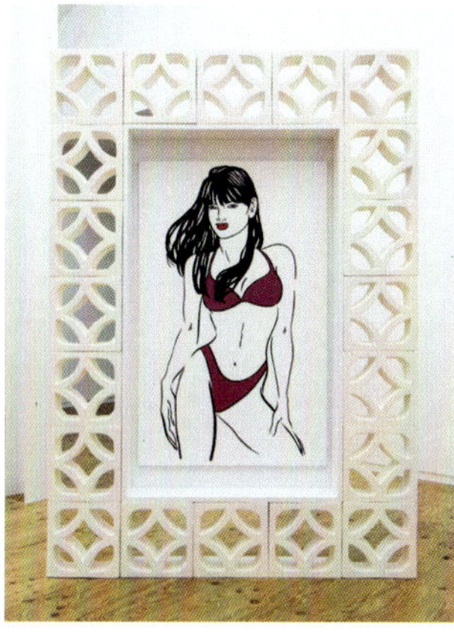

Lisa Lapinski, *Th th th th th Snow White (Plum)*, 2010. Slip cast ceramic, wood, paint on plywood, hardware. 77.6 x 56 x 7.3 in. (197.1 x 142.2 x 18.5 cm).

Or, to return to Lapinski's practice: the bow of a ragdoll become a menacing, culture war–battling space invader; the faces of Jawlensky transmogrified into a meeting of orthodox crucifixes, *Playboy* illustrations, and provincial German transport company ads; and the iconic logos of R. J. Reynolds made to speak the language of dirty bathrooms and Shaker craftsmen. It's no surprise, viewed through this lens, that toys and games repeatedly appear in Lapinski's work, or that she titled her Kyoto show at which one of the *Tobacco Camels* first appeared *Th th th th th Snow White*, after a line from a story by her then not-quite-three-year-old daughter, in which a seemingly endless chain of exchanges lead, with many steps in between, from Tinker Bell to Elmo to Captain Hook to Pinocchio (as well as, of course, to the sleeping princess herself).

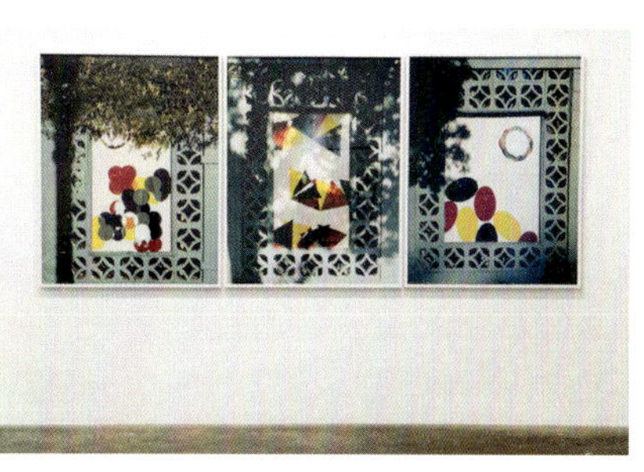

Lisa Lapinski, Untitled, 2007 (detail). Chromogenic prints on paper. 50 x 40 in. (127 x 101.6 cm).

The potential weave and impact of Lapinski's work reaches far beyond my quick list of connections above, just as do the implications of Benjamin's mimetic theory. As Miriam Hansen has described the latter, "the mimetic is not a category of representation [for Benjamin] ... but a relational practice—a process, comportment, or activity of 'producing similarities' (such as astrology, dance, and play) ... [and] a mode of access to the world involving sensuous, somatic, and tactile, that is, embodied, forms of perception and cognition."[7] It is, we could say with an eye to Benjamin's interest in such ancient practices as reading entrails or tracing the patterns of the night sky, a form of generative participation in—or relation to—the world by which its objects, images, and forms start to talk together, to become animate with the stories they tell and the spaces, associations, and experiences they invite us to inhabit.

This idea of the world's forms—its signs and things—as an ever-expanding set of conversant and inhabitable beings seems a particularly apt lens through which to view Lapinski's work, whose combination of material precision and expansive selection thus comes into focus as a means by which to take part in, and help shape, this particular embodied exchange. Arguably Lapinski's most frequent interlocutors in this process are Nagel's women, and most specifically the Nagelesque bikini girls she transformed beginning in 2007 into a mobile band of painted-canvas-and-screen-block monuments.

Lapinski's work with these figures began decades ago, in the outlying LA enclave of Altadena. As she drove down Lake Avenue one day on her way to Pasadena, she saw five bikini-clad women—each made to mimic a generic Nagel girl and set in a Plexiglas box surrounded by screen block—staring out at her from a local swimwear shop, an impression that so struck Lapinski that she felt compelled to fetch a disposable camera and capture the group on film. She essentially *never* took pictures, she has stressed to me, making this urge strangely significant, almost uncanny; the set of Altadena women, she recounts, "was the only thing I wanted to photograph in the entire world and it was a momentary feeling."

On film these figures at first remained, their unprinted negatives tossed into a drawer—at least as Lapinski recalls it—until she happened by the same building around eight years later. By then the structure had become a Montessori preschool, its earlier Nagel girls covered over by a set of abstract compositions—bikinis be gone!—and their framing blocks painted a sickly green. But as Lapinski recognized, these girls were in fact still there, not so much covered over by as *entombed within* the building's façade redesign: they remained lodged in their Plexiglas boxes beneath the new Montessori abstractions as a kind of latent, materially present signifying force, their real form having come to match her own submerged images back on those tossed-away negatives.

And so she set out to let their ghosts speak, to invite them to wander once more. Printing her photographs—a decade late—and hiring the renowned LA sign painter Norm Leich, Lapinski had the gaggle of figures reproduced and reset in new screen block, to be displayed (and photographed again) in front of her and her neighbors' homes. And then the group hit the road, joining *Tobacco Camel* at her 2010 exhibition at Kyoto's Taka Ishii Gallery, the set of awoken "sleeping beauties" they formed echoed in her titling of that show (with help from her daughter)

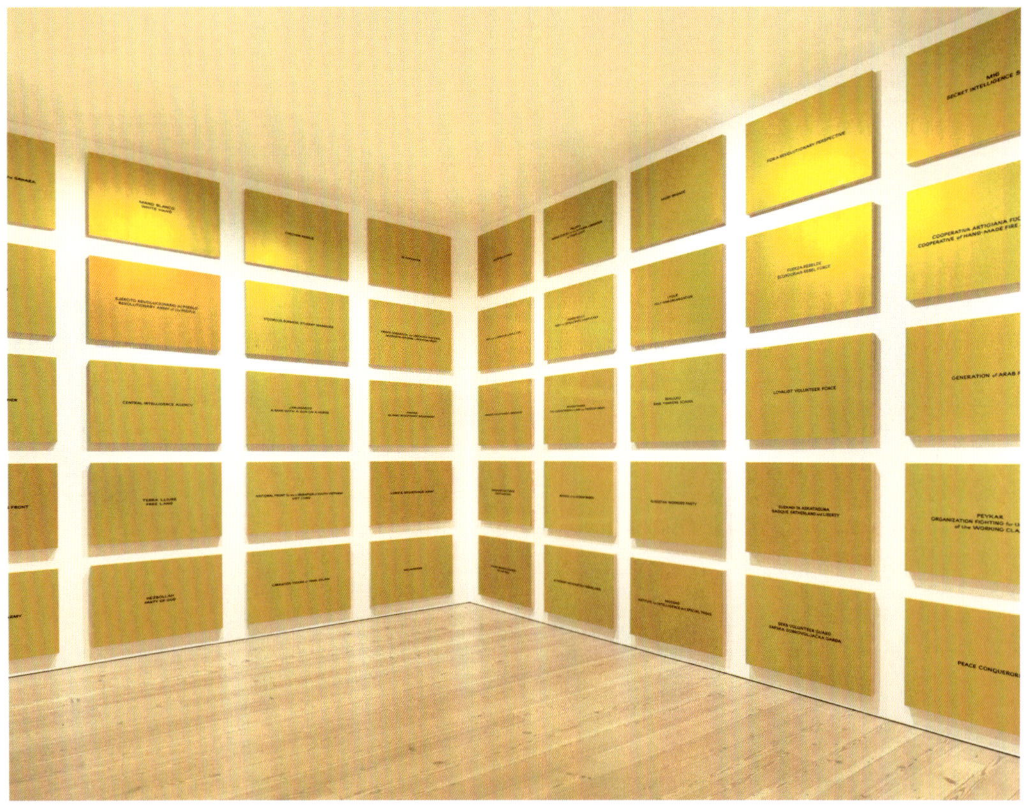

Daniel Joseph Martinez, *Divine Violence*, installation view, 2008. Whitney Biennial 2006, Whitney Museum of American Art, New York. Enamel and oil on 92 panels. Overall: 153 × 275 × 187 in. (388.6 × 698.5 × 475 cm).

in reference to Snow White.

There's other voices we could add to this assemblage—such as those of the organizations that fill Daniel Martinez's *Divine Violence*, also painted by Leich and hanging for weeks across from Lapinski's girls in his studio, as if engaged in a kind of secret communion; or Lapinski's own teenaged, ruffled-bikini self, whom she came to see as an unsuspecting prefiguration of the Altadena group; or again Warhol, whose 1982 *Eggs* paintings are almost perfectly matched by the tumbling multicolor ellipses that filled one of the Altadena Montessori's new abstractions. And this is not to mention Jawlensky, R. J. Reynolds's camel, Holly Hobbie, and Little My (along with all their associated references, suggestions, and echoes), who further extend the interweaving exchanges Lapinski's colloquy puts into play.

Rather than voices in conversation, though, Lapinski's sequence of referents and forms is better viewed through Benjamin's metaphor of stops on a journey—for which exchanges, linkages, and unexpected turns are equally constitutive. Even more fitting, in fact, is the critical framework established by her own daughter more than a decade ago: that of voices in conversation (in Lapinski's case, those of camels and bows and bikini girls and Swedish children's characters) as themselves expansive and inhabitable nodes of experience, each growing and mutating as it connects with the next, as if momentary stops on an open-ended itinerary.

So just how, after all, *do* logos smell? That I can't really say—but you may want to ask Alexei Jawlensky, who I'm pretty sure I saw right around the corner, sharing a smoke on his way to the beach with Patrick Nagel and Little My.

KIKI AND BOBO. OH, THEY ARE ALREADY THERE. KIKI AND BOBO WERE WAITI

1. Here and elsewhere, details of Lapinski's work and its genesis are taken from a series of May 2021 conversations with the artist.

2. As quoted in "Tobacco," Perfume Society, https://perfumesociety.org/ingredients-post/tobacco/. Accessed May 27, 2021.

3. The comment is Lapinski's, in conversation—though she's quick to add that Jawlensky surely *did* say interesting things, just that none of them appear to be recorded in his published statements.

4. Particularly significant for Lapinski was the purchase of *Rod Cross*, at the opening of her 2003 exhibition *Analysandom*, by her teacher Mike Kelley—whose enthusiasm for the work, now in the Mike Kelley Foundation for the Arts, was an important early confirmation.

5. For the barest sense of these associations, look up either figure on Wikipedia.

6. Walter Benjamin, "The Lamp," in *Walter Benjamin: Selected Writings*, vol. 2, pt. 2, 1931–1934, ed. Michael W. Jennings, Howard Eiland, and Gary Smith (Cambridge, MA: Harvard University Press, 1999), 691.

7. Miriam Bratu Hansen, *Cinema and Experience: Siegfried Kracauer, Walter Benjamin, and Theodor W. Adorno* (Berkeley: University of California Press, 2012), 147.

R MR. CAMEL. SO THEY LOOKED IN THE SUNNIEST, SUNNIEST PLACE BUT

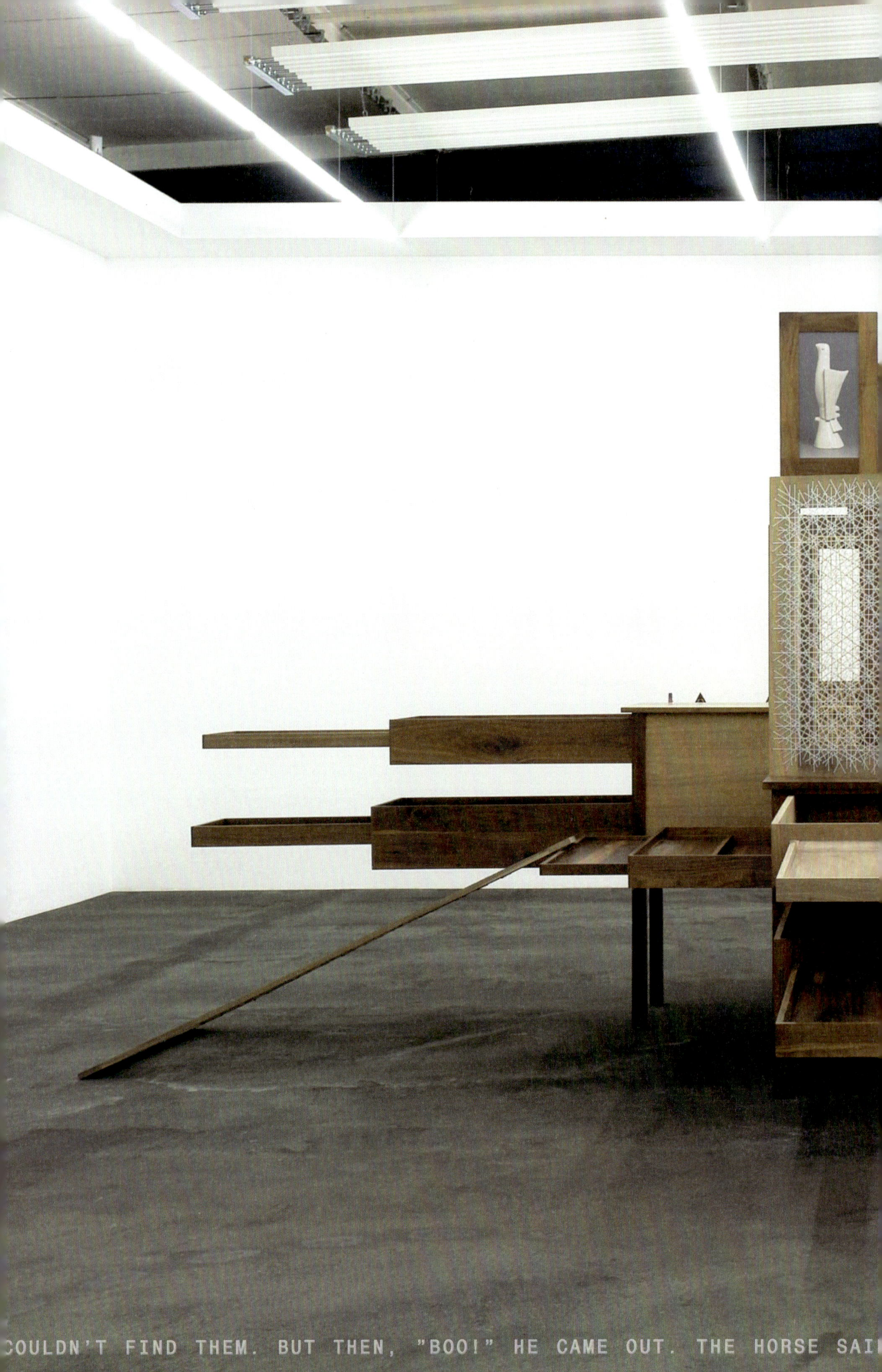

COULDN'T FIND THEM. BUT THEN, "BOO!" HE CAME OUT. THE HORSE SAI

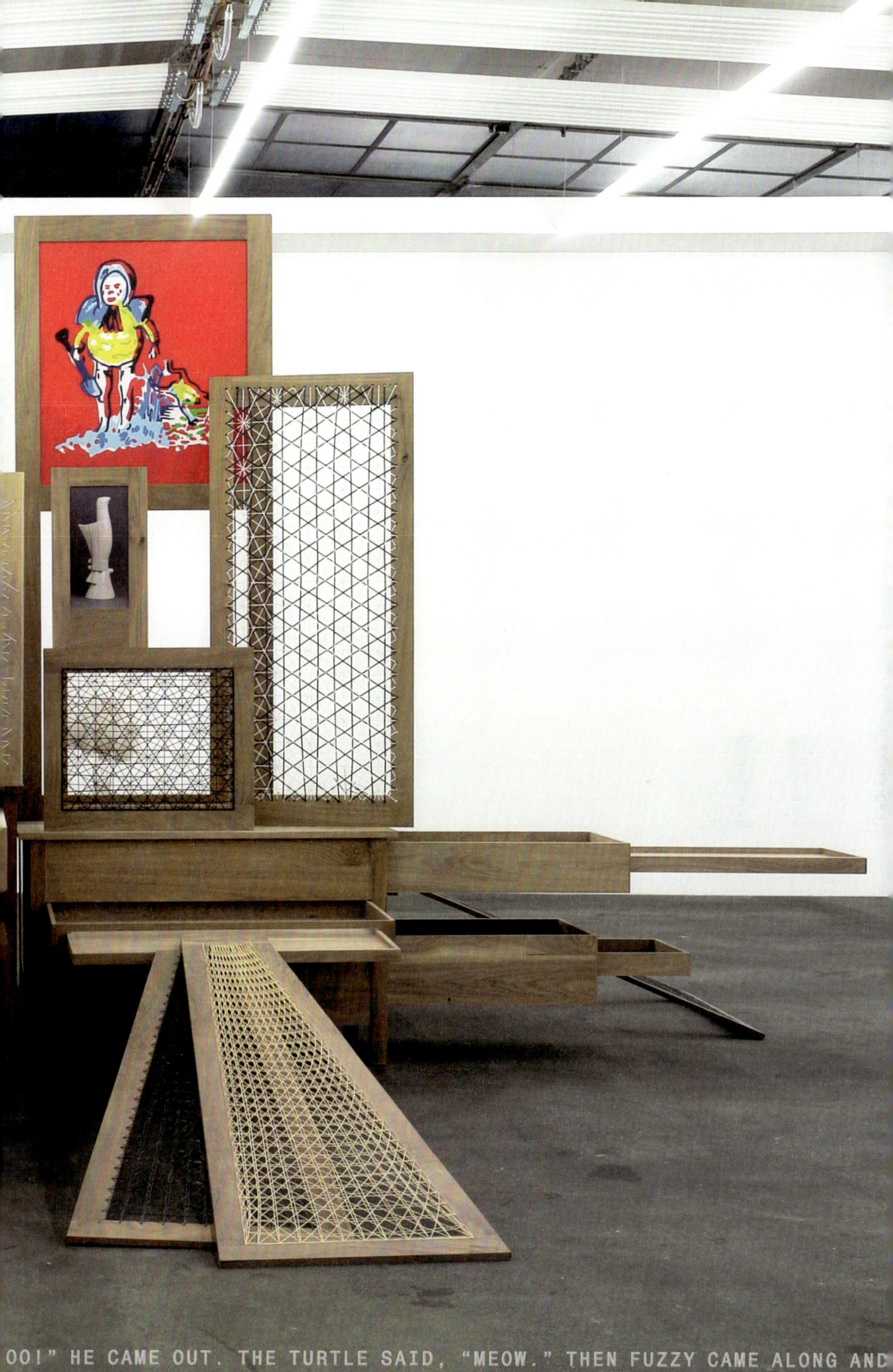

OO!" HE CAME OUT. THE TURTLE SAID, "MEOW." THEN FUZZY CAME ALONG AND

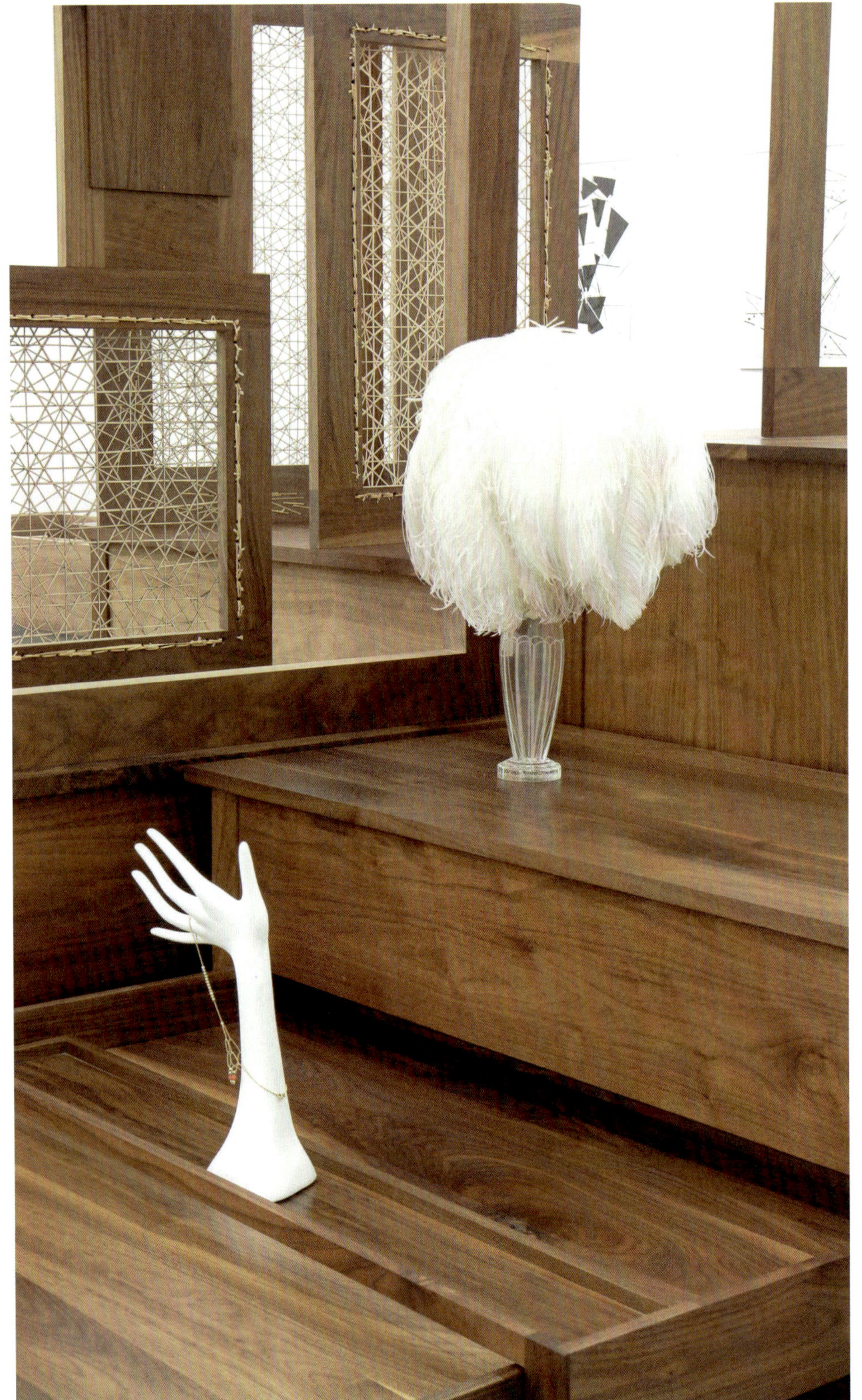

previous spread

Nightstand, 2005
Walnut hardwood, polyurethane, acrylic paint, panel and canvas, photographs, caning, glass, feather, hat form, hardware, found objects (jewelry display hand and bracelet)
Dimensions variable

Nightstand, 2005 (detail)
Walnut hardwood, polyurethane, acrylic paint, panel and canvas, photographs, caning, glass, feather, hat form, hardware, found objects (jewelry display hand and bracelet)
Dimensions variable

OFY AND ZOE, HUEY, DUEY AND LUEY. THEY CAME WITH…WHAT IS DONALD'S

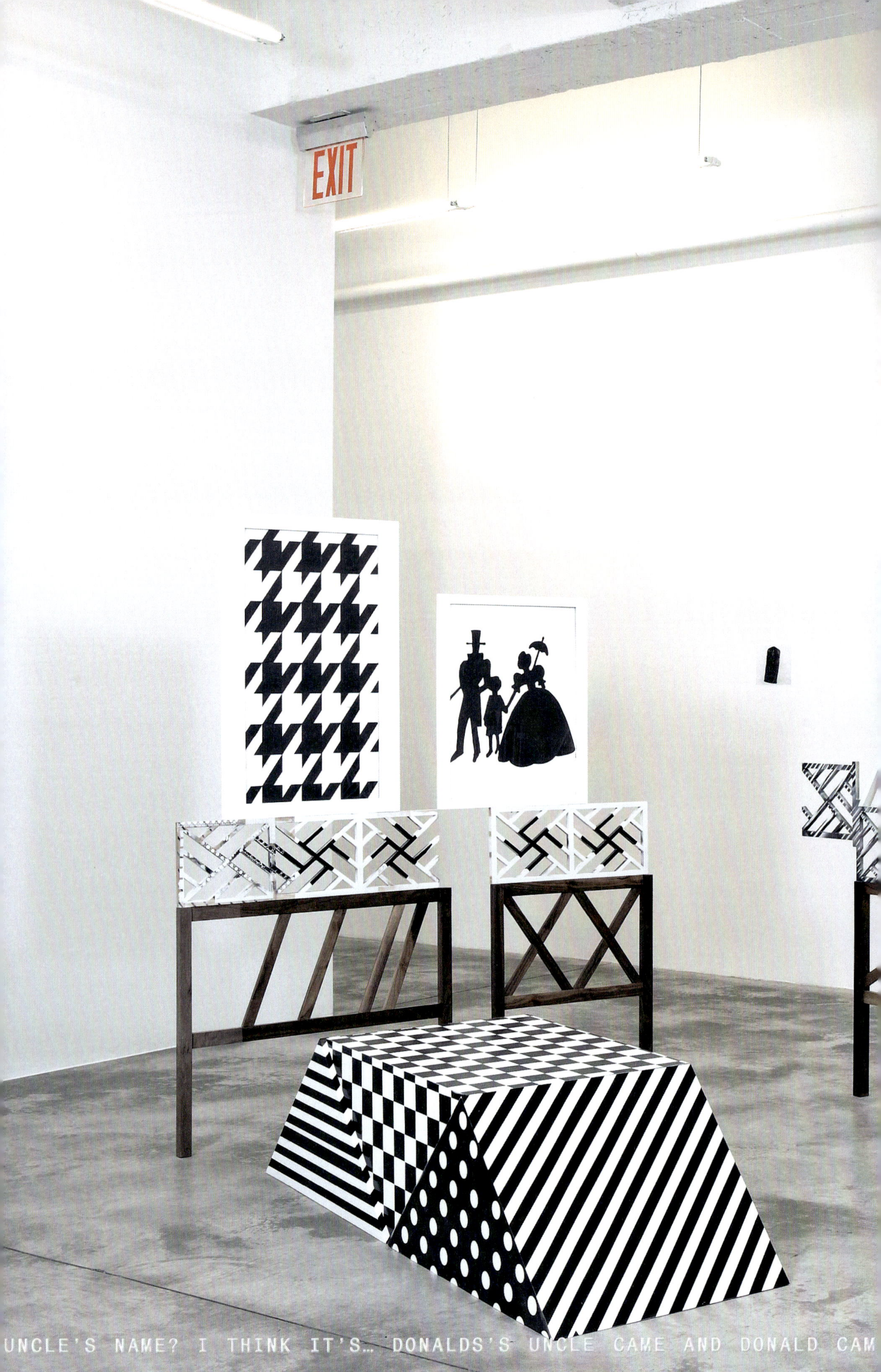

UNCLE'S NAME? I THINK IT'S… DONALDS'S UNCLE CAME AND DONALD CAM

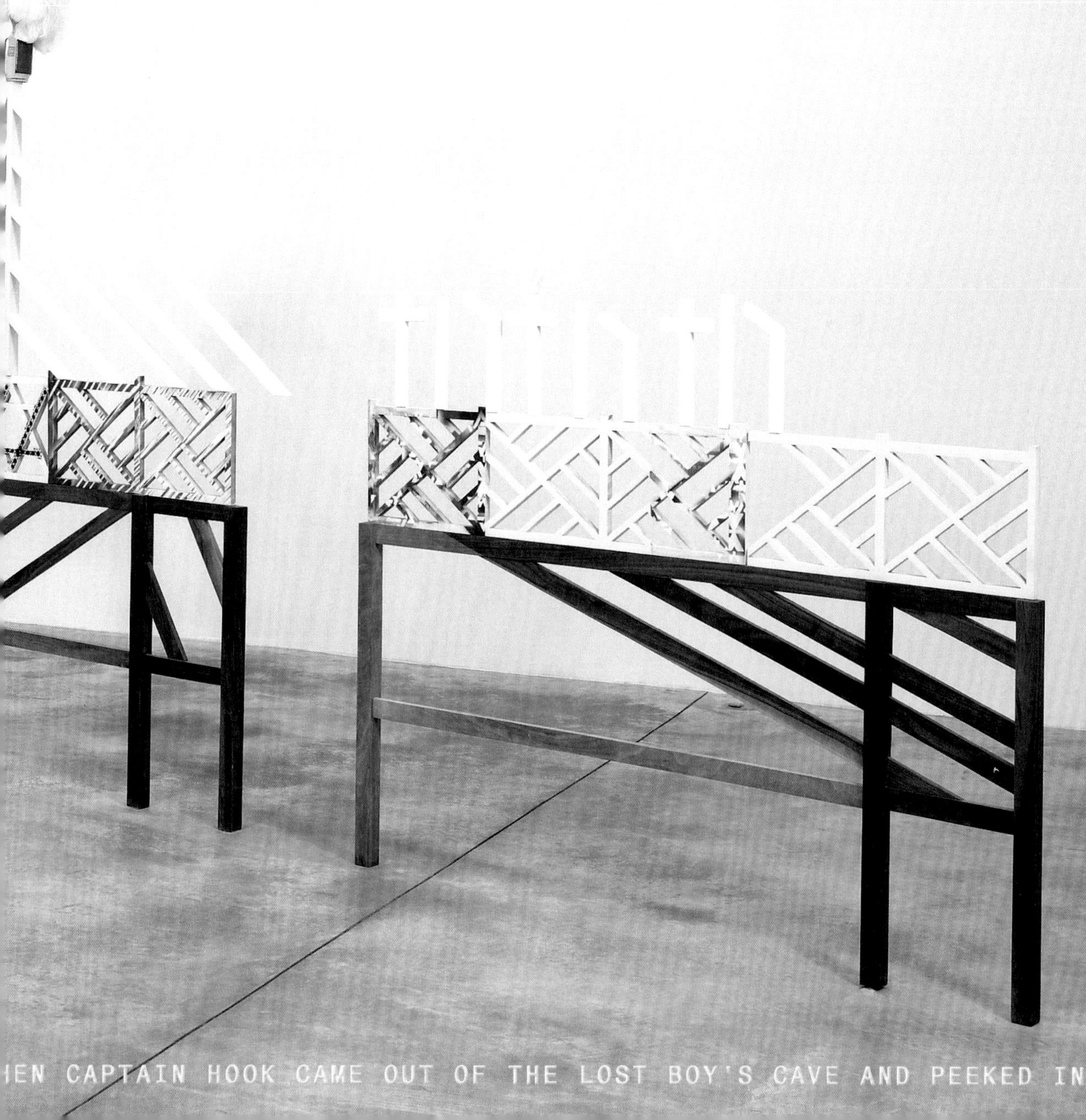

HEN CAPTAIN HOOK CAME OUT OF THE LOST BOY'S CAVE AND PEEKED INSIDE

previous spread

Christmas Tea = Meeting, Presented by Dialogue and Humanism, Formerly Dialectic and Humanism, 2007
Walnut, poplar, Baltic birch plywood, acrylic paint, paper, board, steel, feather, and found Soviet-era vase
Dimensions variable

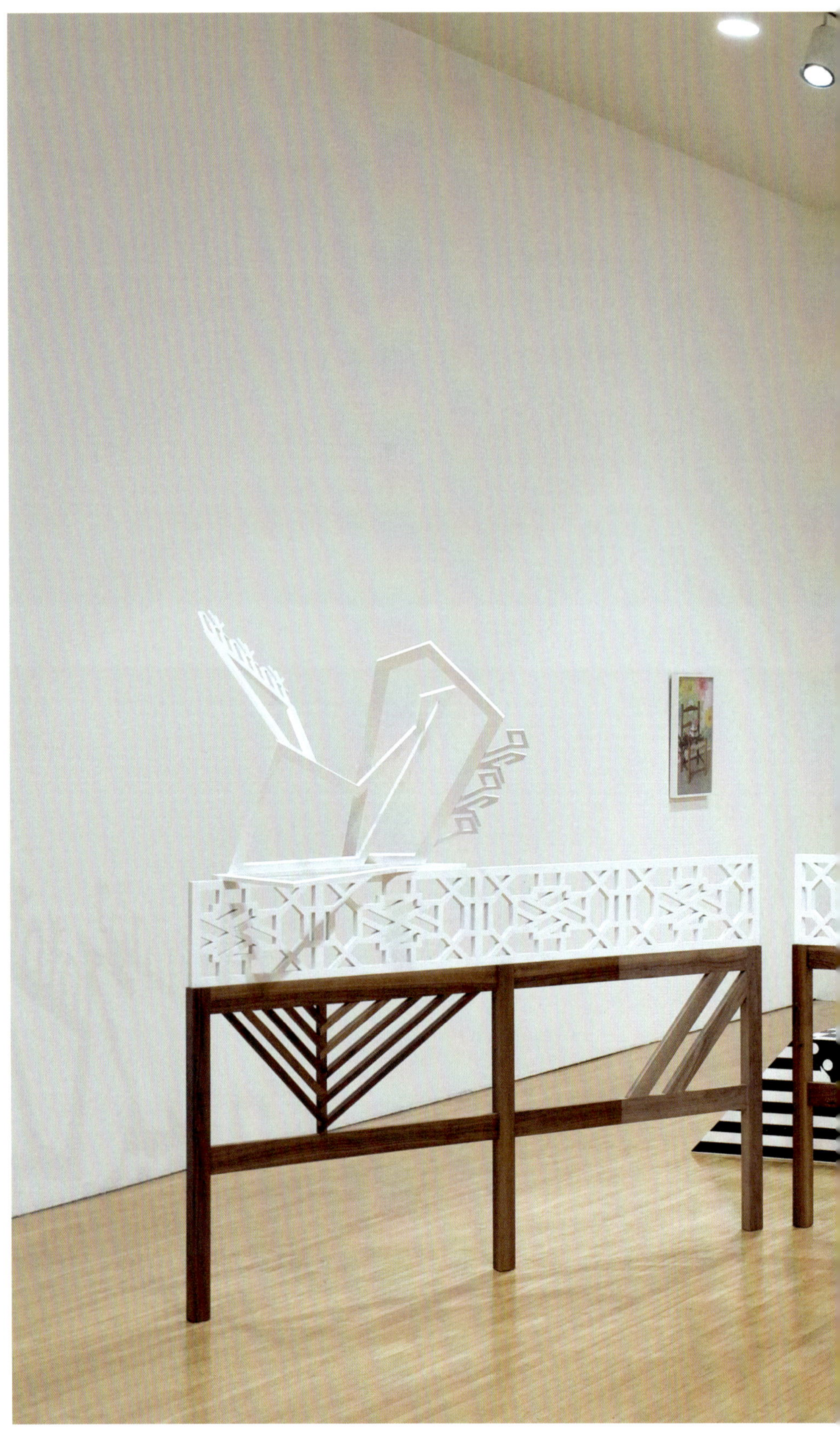

THE CAVE AND SAW WHAT THE CROCODILES DID. THEY WERE HAVING A PICNI

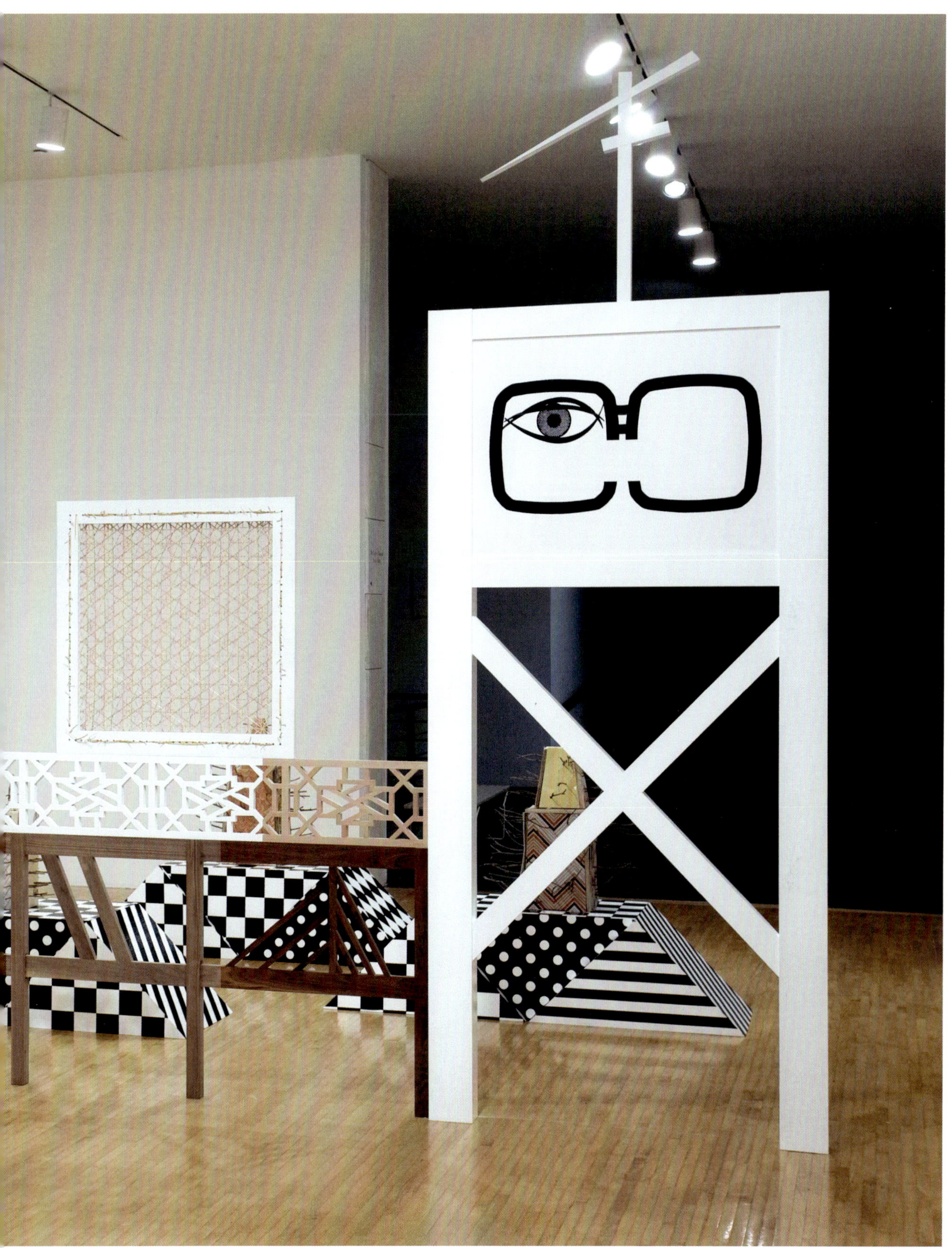

Monty Python Precedes Dungeons and Dragons, 2008
Walnut, beech, poplar, acrylic paint, cane, canvas on board
Dimensions variable

TH WENDY AND CHOMPING ON SOME PICKLES! “WHY ARE YOU CHOMPING ON THE

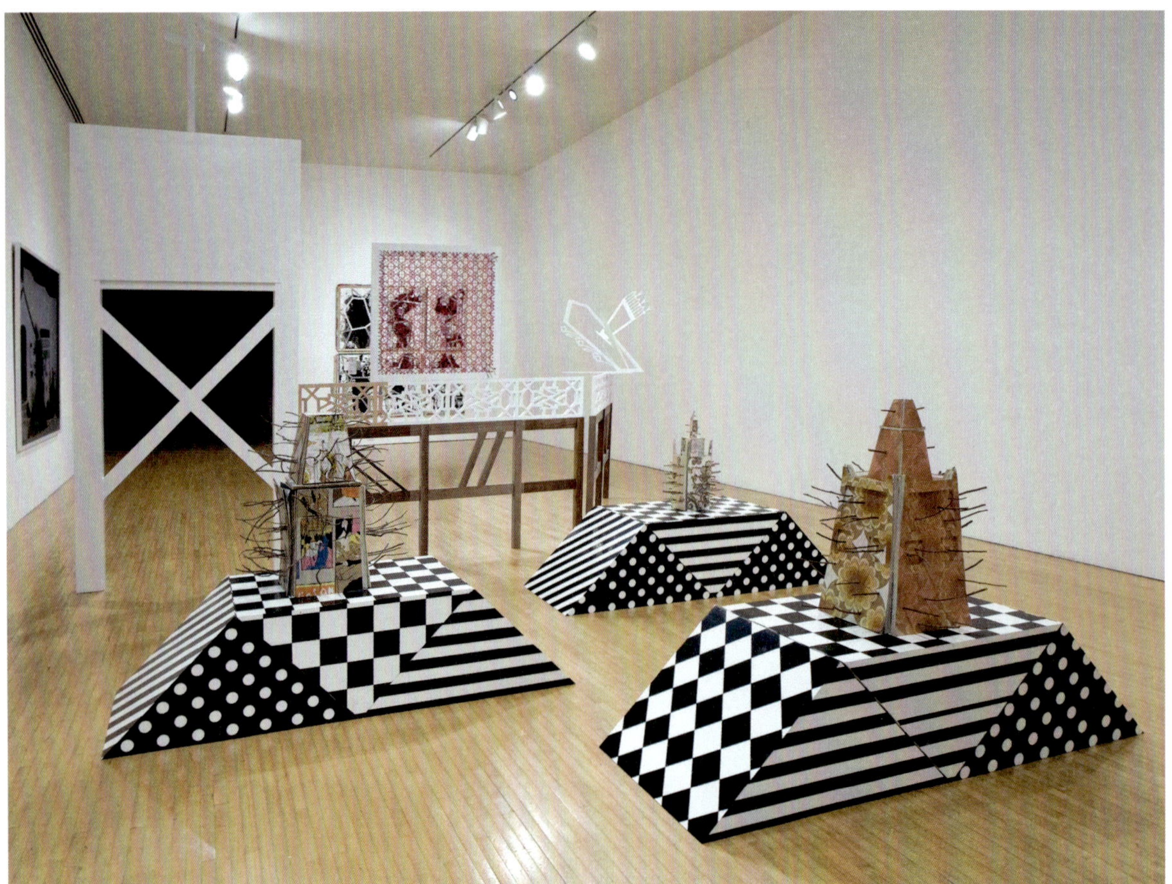

Mosque of Boré, 2001
Wallpaper, adhesive, sticks, clay
28 x 29 x 29 in. (71.1 x 73.7 x 73.7 cm)

Mosque of Mopti, 2001
Wallpaper, adhesive, sticks
23 x 13 x 13 in. (58.4 x 33 x 33 cm)

Mosque of Sankoré, 2001
Wallpaper, adhesive, sticks
23 x 13 x 13 in. (58.4 x 33 x 33 cm)

Three Stands for Mosques, 2008
Plywood, Bondo and paint
Each stand made from 3 triangular blocks
(9 triangular blocks total)
6 triangular blocks: 17 1/2 x 35 x 25 1/2 in.
each (44.5 x 88.9 x 64.8 cm)
3 triangular blocks: 17 1/2 x 35 x 24 in. each
(44.5 x 88.9 x 61 cm)

SISTER'S PICKLES?" WE'RE SHARING THE PICKLES WITH WENDY'S SISTER.

The Fret and its Variants
Installation view,
Museum of Contemporary Art
(MOCA), Los Angeles,
June 26–August 25, 2008

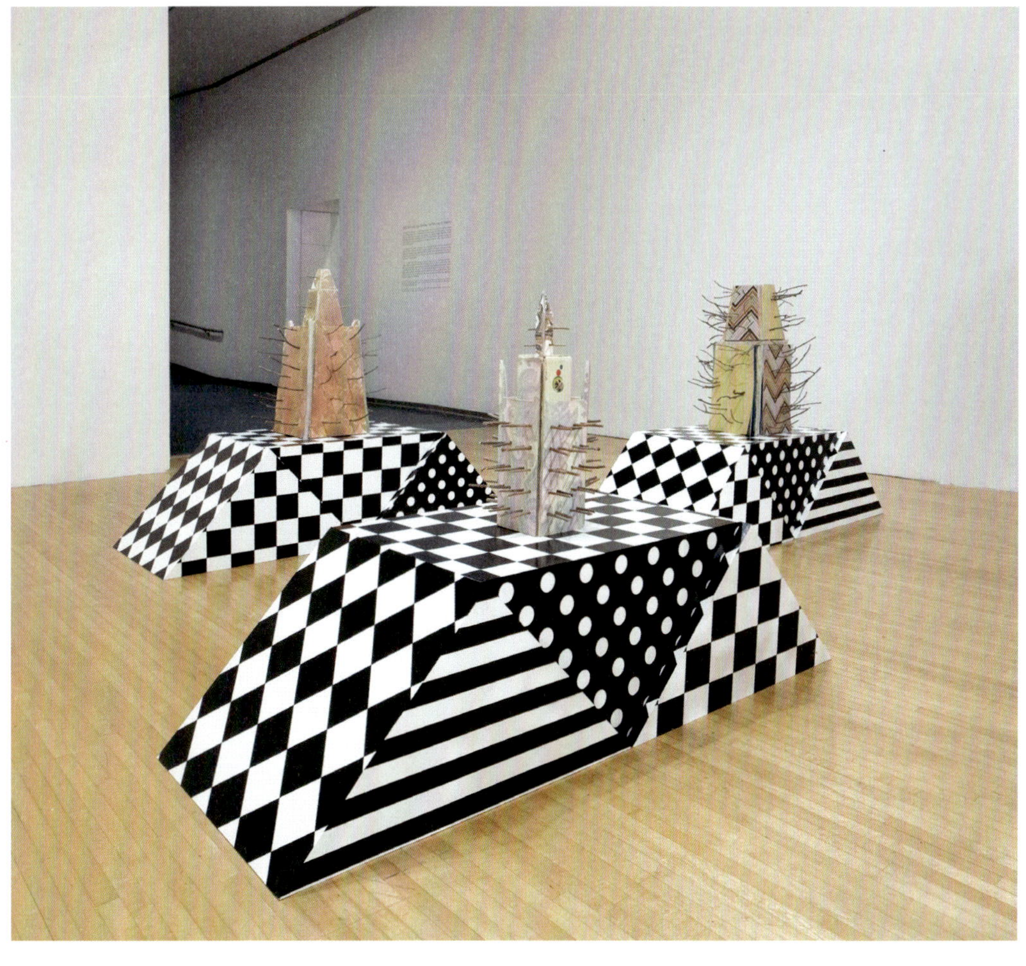

APTAIN HOOK LEFT. HE PEEKED INSIDE THE CAVE. IT'S A BIG ONE. IT'S

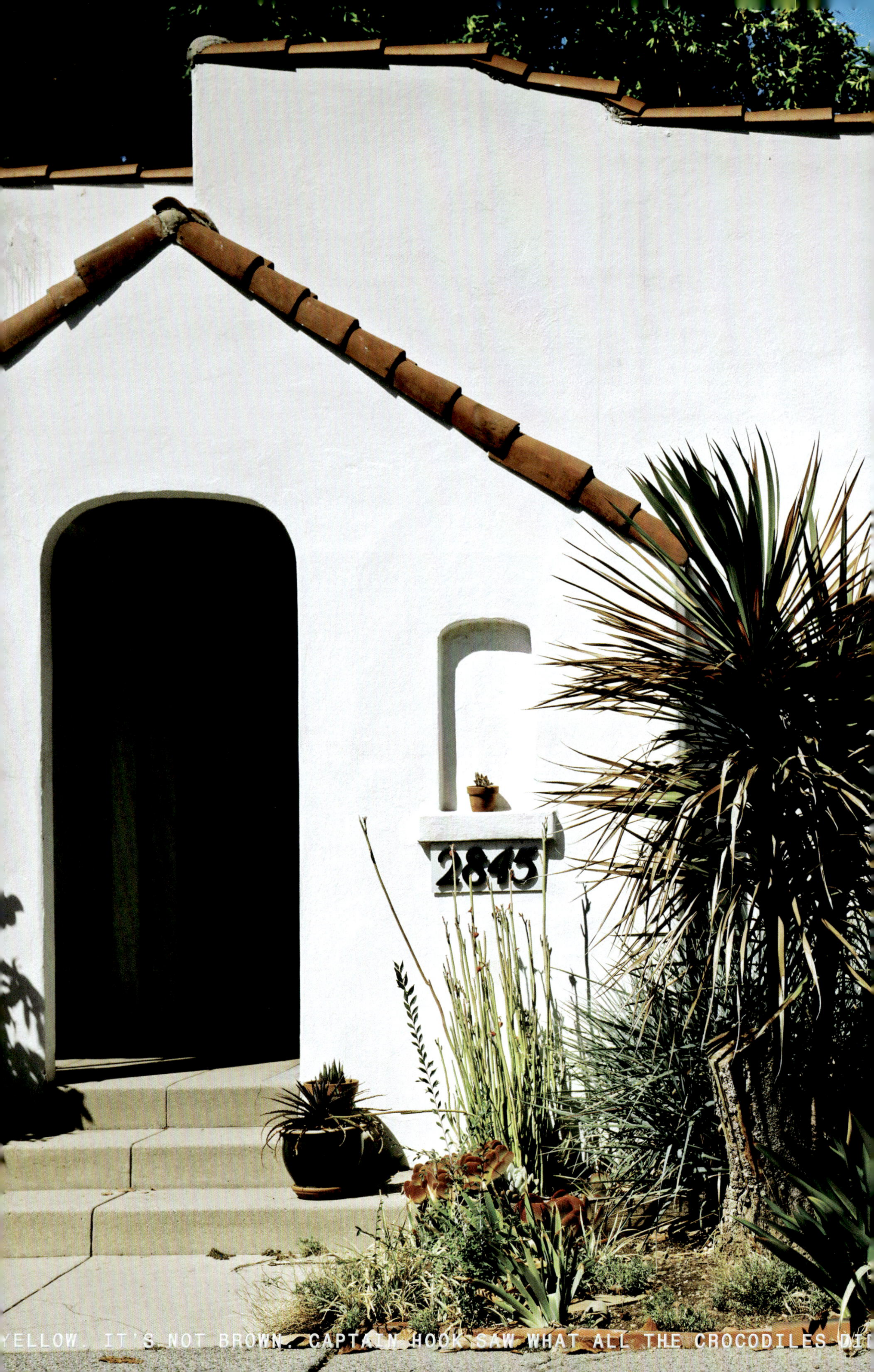

YELLOW. IT'S NOT BROWN. CAPTAIN HOOK SAW WHAT ALL THE CROCODILES DI

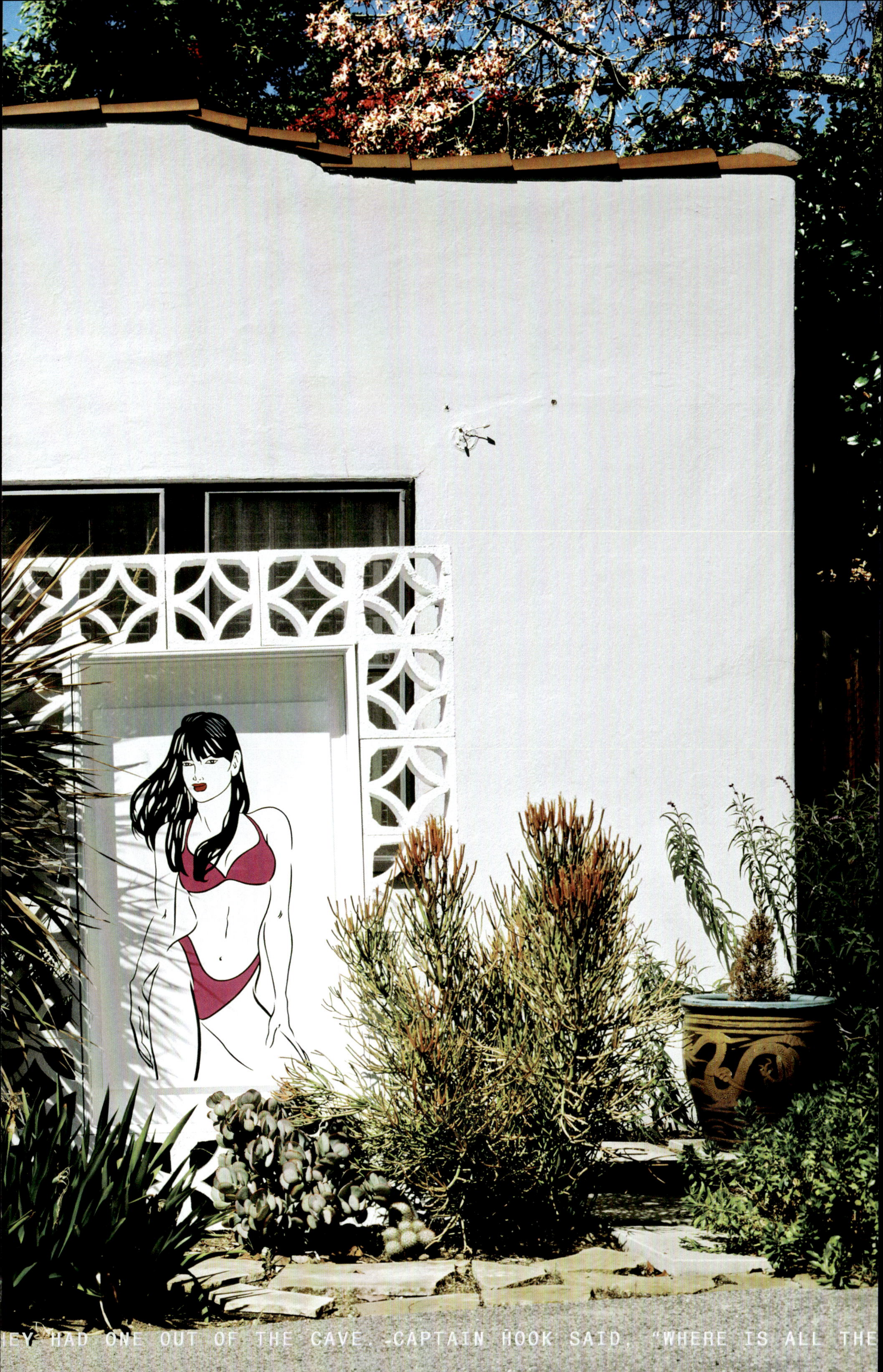

HEY HAD ONE OUT OF THE CAVE. CAPTAIN HOOK SAID, "WHERE IS ALL THE

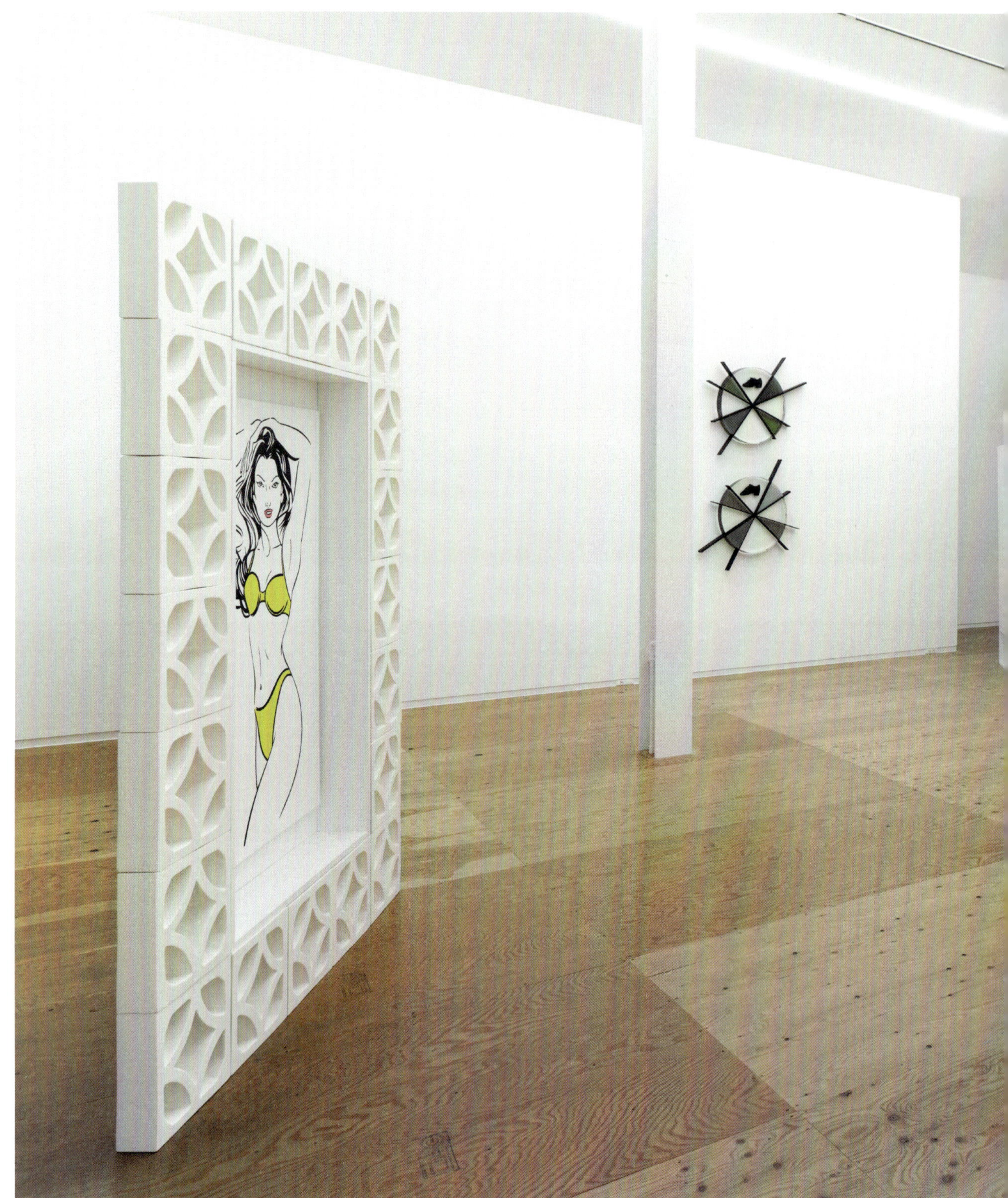

previous spread

Untitled (from *Linz Wedding Song* series), 2007–08
Chromogenic print on paper
69 1/16 x 90 1/4 in.
(175.5 x 229.2 cm)
Edition of 3

CROCODILES?" HE WAS WONDERING WHERE ALL THE CROCODILES WERE. ONE

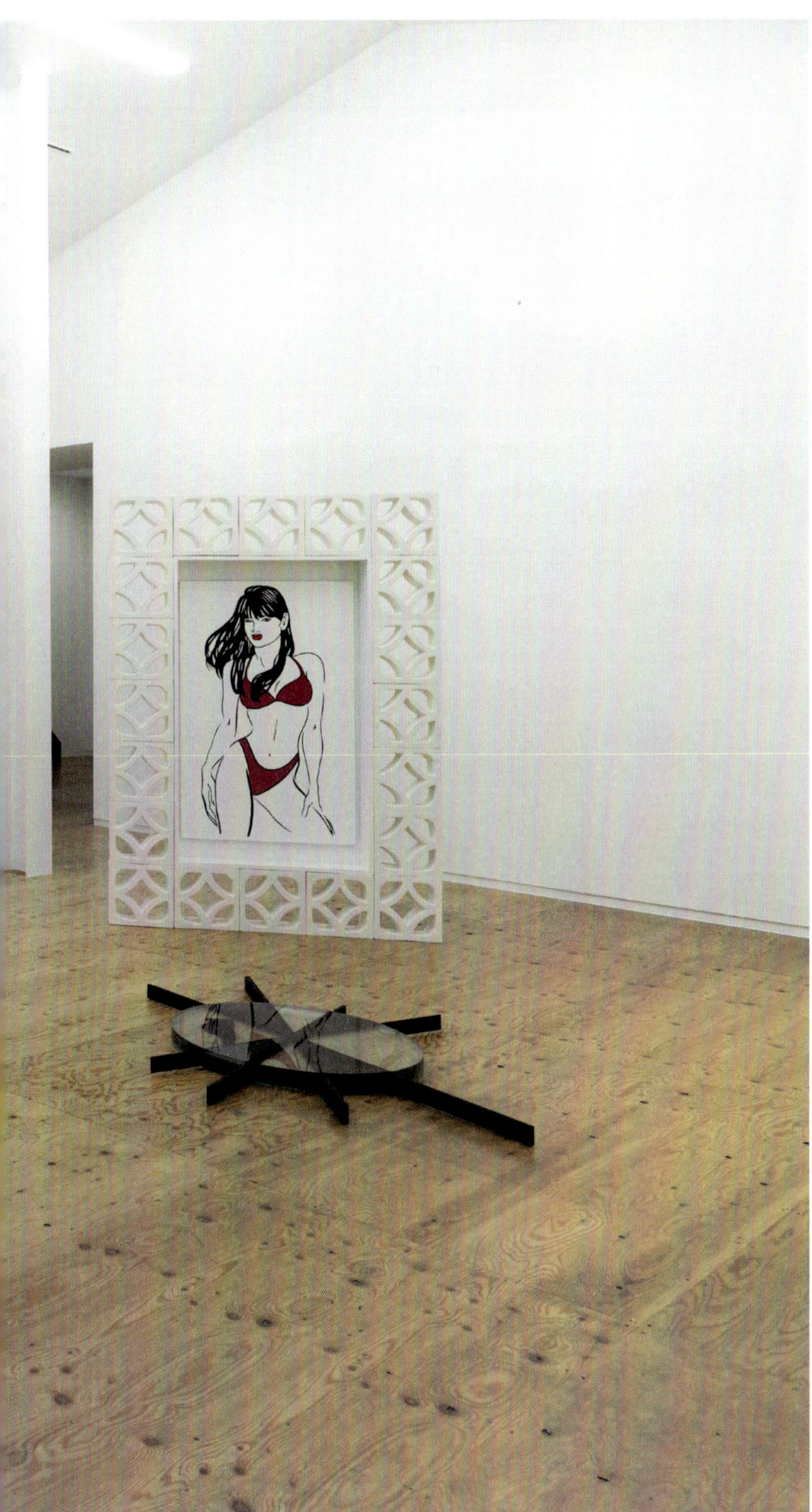

Th th th th th Snow White
Installation view, Taka
Ishii Gallery, Kyoto, Japan,
November 6–December 11, 2010

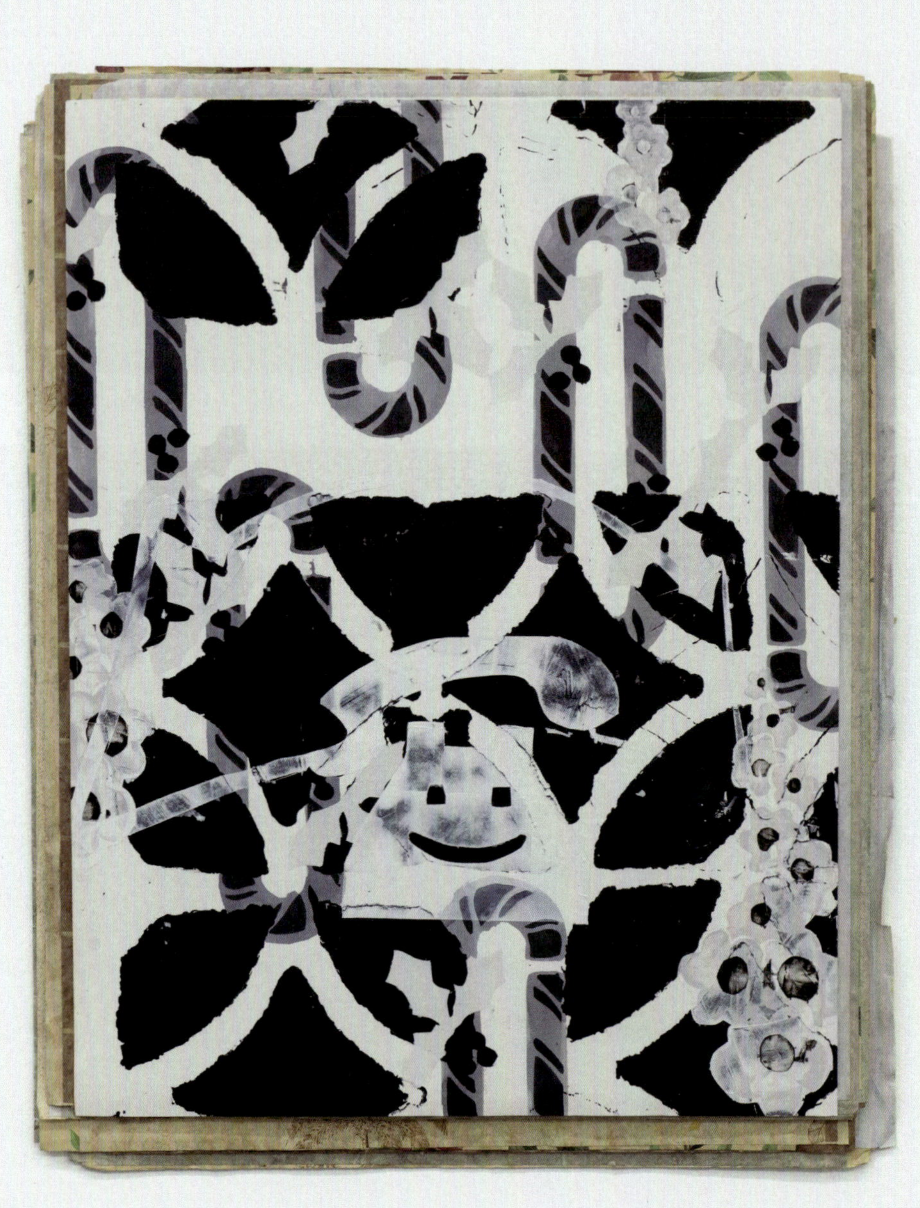

A LITTLE PICNIC SNACK. ONE DAY, TINKER BELL WAS SICK ALL MORNING.

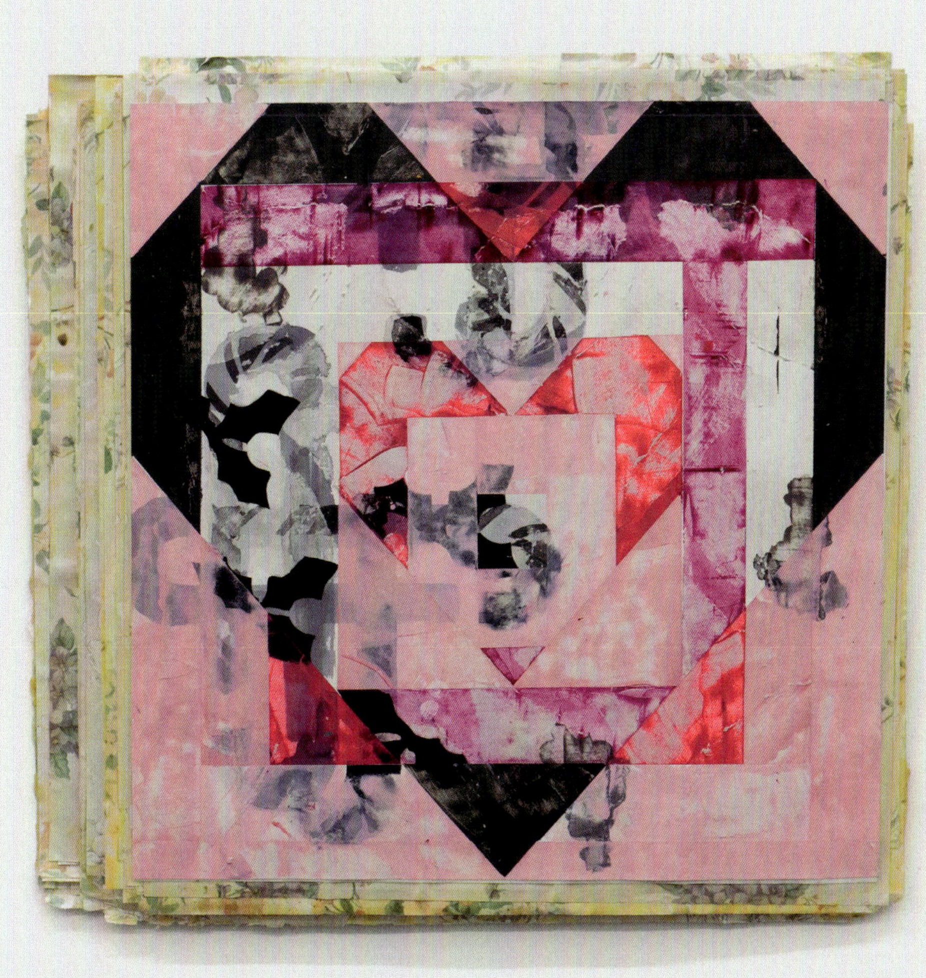

INK TINKER BELL HAD TO HURRY TO PETER PAN. SHE HAD TO ASK PETER PAN

previous spread

Untitled (from *Call Zone* series), 2010
Wallpaper, glue, wood, metal hardware, acrylic paint on paper
29 x 23 x 1 1/2 in.
(73.7 x 58.4 x 3.8 cm)

Untitled, 2010
Wallpaper, glue, wood, metal hardware, acrylic paint on paper
25 x 25 x 1 1/2 in.
(63.5 x 63.5 x 3.8 cm)

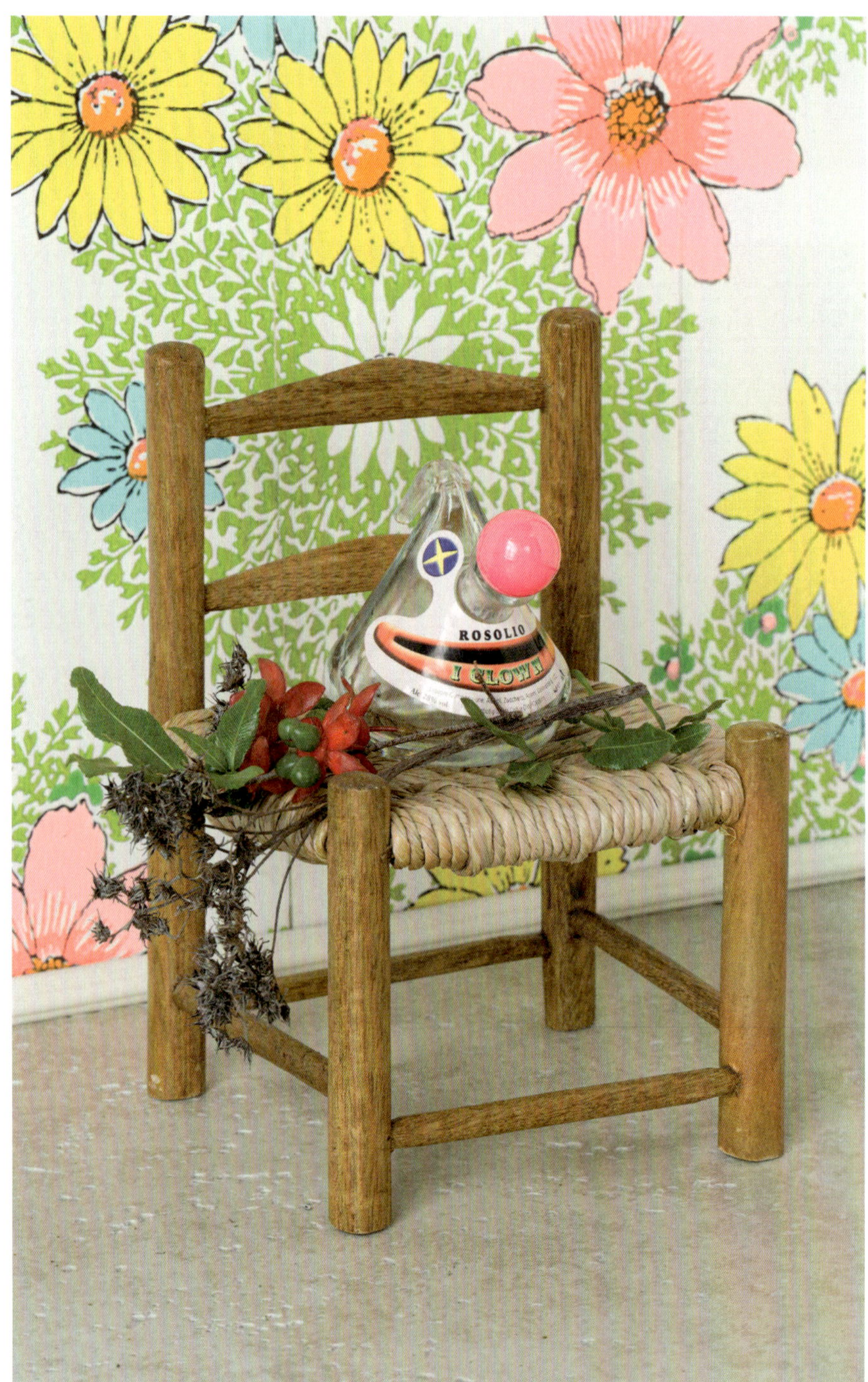

from left to right

I Clown (Version A), 2008
Chromogenic print on paper
24 x 16 in. (60.9 x 40.6 cm)
Edition of 5; 1 AP

Moomin Chair Room, 2010
Wood, caning, acrylic paint, glue, wire, spools, found chair
Dimensions variable

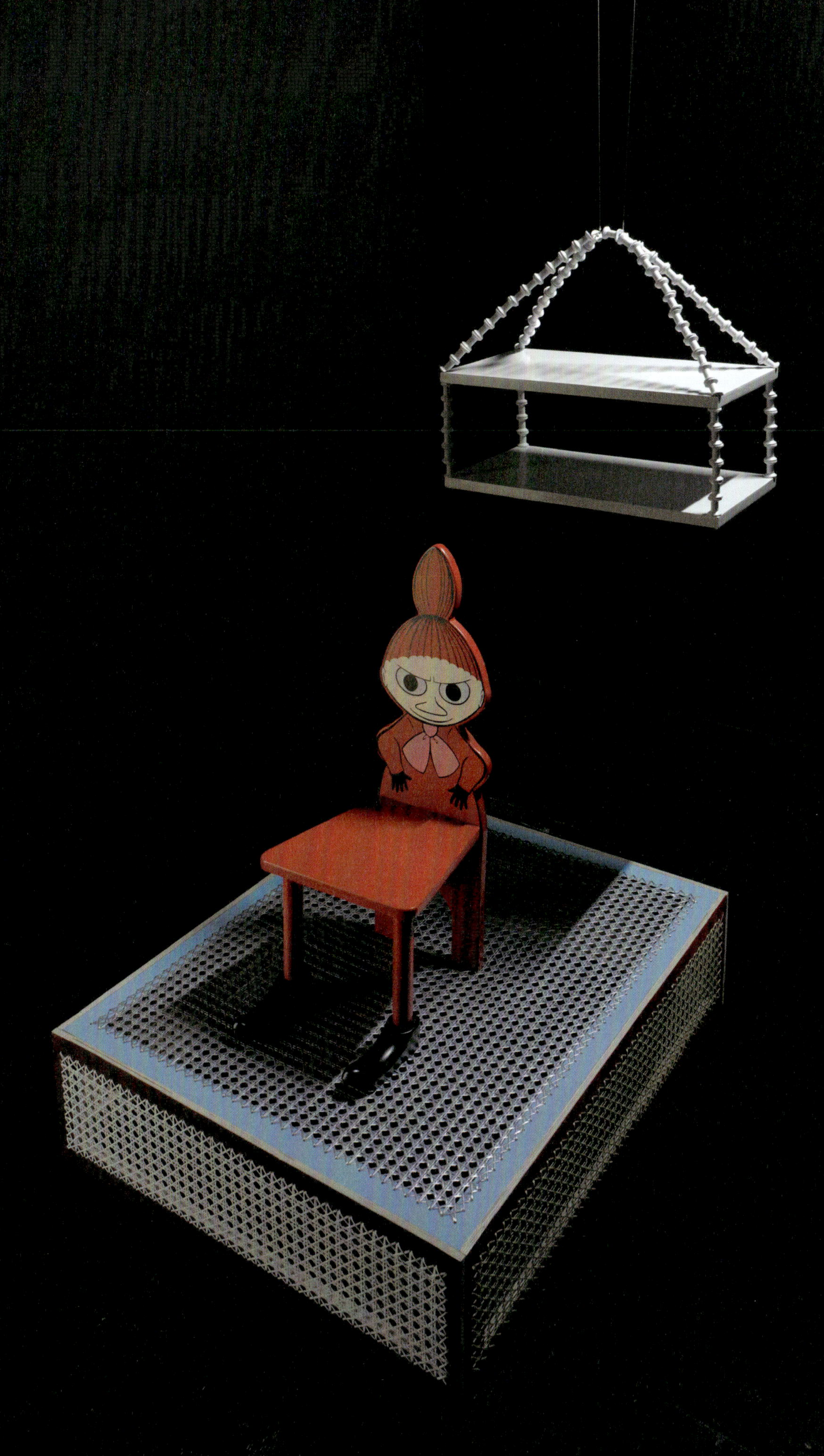

ERE. THEN RABBIT CAME BOUNCING UP. HE WAS SO HAPPY. HE CAME BOUNCING

Lisa Lapinski & Viola Schmitt

In Conversation

* * *

This email conversation between Lisa Lapinski and Viola Schmitt took place over the course of 2019. Lisa and Viola have been in dialogue about Lisa's work for several decades. In this discussion, they dialogue about Lisa's practice and what informs her process.

VIOLA SCHMITT

My first question is very simple: When you make individual pieces (say, the Little My chair works), do you already think of them in context (i.e., do you think of potential combinations)?

LISA LAPINSKI

No, it's not that I have a context that I am trying to fill in. The Little My Chair is a good example to start with. About a decade ago, I was flipping through a Japanese interior design book about children's rooms in Stockholm. It was all in Japanese. I couldn't read the text, but I was looking at all the photos of these Swedish children's rooms with all of these beautifully designed toys and furniture. I was just flipping through it casually. I don't know how I got this book—it is not the type of thing I would usually be reading. I got to one page, which had a picture of a child's room like all the other pictures of children's rooms in the book except there was this tiny personified chair. Her expression was unreadable to me. Maybe she was angry or maybe determined. It was hard to tell if she was young or old even though she wore a top bun. I did not know who she was, but it seemed to me that she had to *be* something. It was like I was looking at a Snoopy chair, but I had never heard of the cartoon strip *Peanuts*. She seemed to question everything in the room, and then everything in the book, and then context itself, and then my own existence, but not chairs themselves.

I know this sounds peculiar, but when I met Little My Chair I had a feeling that I had only experienced once before in my life. I am so hyped up all the time. I am like a chihuahua, Viola. I don't think I experience feelings as often as most people do. I was perplexed by this feeling and thought to myself, "Oh, okay, I am having a feeling and I have had this feeling before, but only once in the late 1980s. I need to pay attention."

VIOLA

I have two follow-up questions. They are both connected to something I want to find out more about, namely, this complexity in your work, which

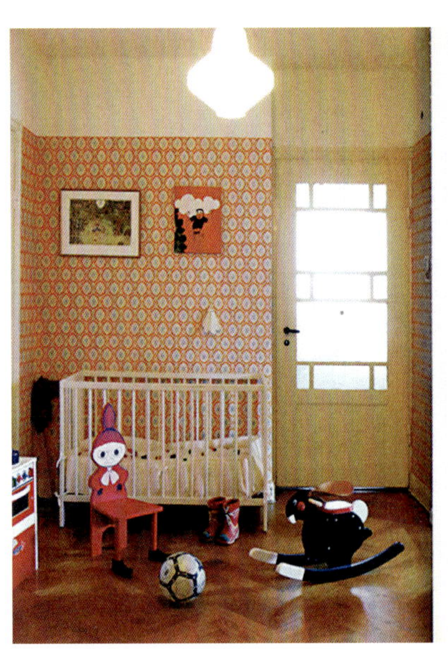

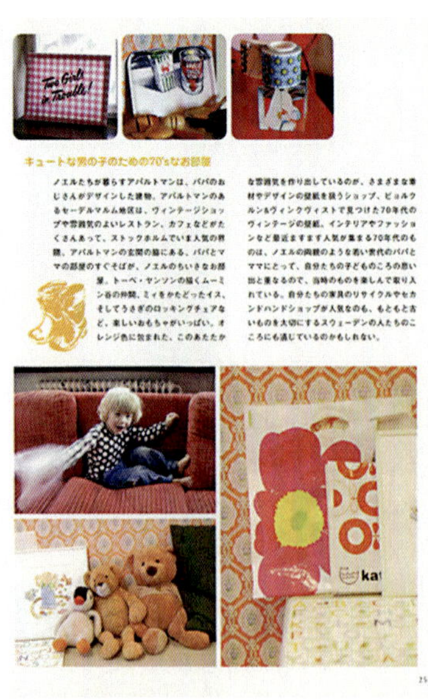

キュートな男の子のための70'sなお部屋

ノエルたちが暮らすアパルトマンは、パパのおじさんがデザインした建物。アパルトマンのあるセーデルマルム地区は、ヴィンテージショップや雰囲気のよいレストラン、カフェなどがたくさんあって、ストックホルムでいま人気の界隈。アパルトマンの玄関の脇にある、パパとママの部屋のすぐそばが、ノエルのちいさなお部屋。トーベ・ヤンソンの描くムーミン谷の仲間、ミィをかたどったイス、そしてうさぎのロッキングチェアなど、楽しいおもちゃがいっぱい。オレンジ色に包まれた、このあたたかな雰囲気を作り出しているのが、さまざまな素材やデザインの壁紙を扱うショップ、ビョルクルン&ヴィンクヴィストで見つけた70年代のヴィンテージの壁紙。インテリアやファッションなど最近ますます人気が集まる70年代のものは、ノエルの両親のような若い世代のパパとママにとって、自分たちの子どものころの思い出と重なるので、当時のものを楽しんで取り入れている。自分たちの家具のリサイクルやセカンドハンドショップが人気なのも、もともと古いものを大切にするスウェーデンの人たちのこころにも通じているのかもしれない。

Spread from *Paumes*, on children's room "Stockholm."

JP. AND THEN ARIEL CAME SWIMMING TOWARDS THEM. SHE WAS SO HAPPY S

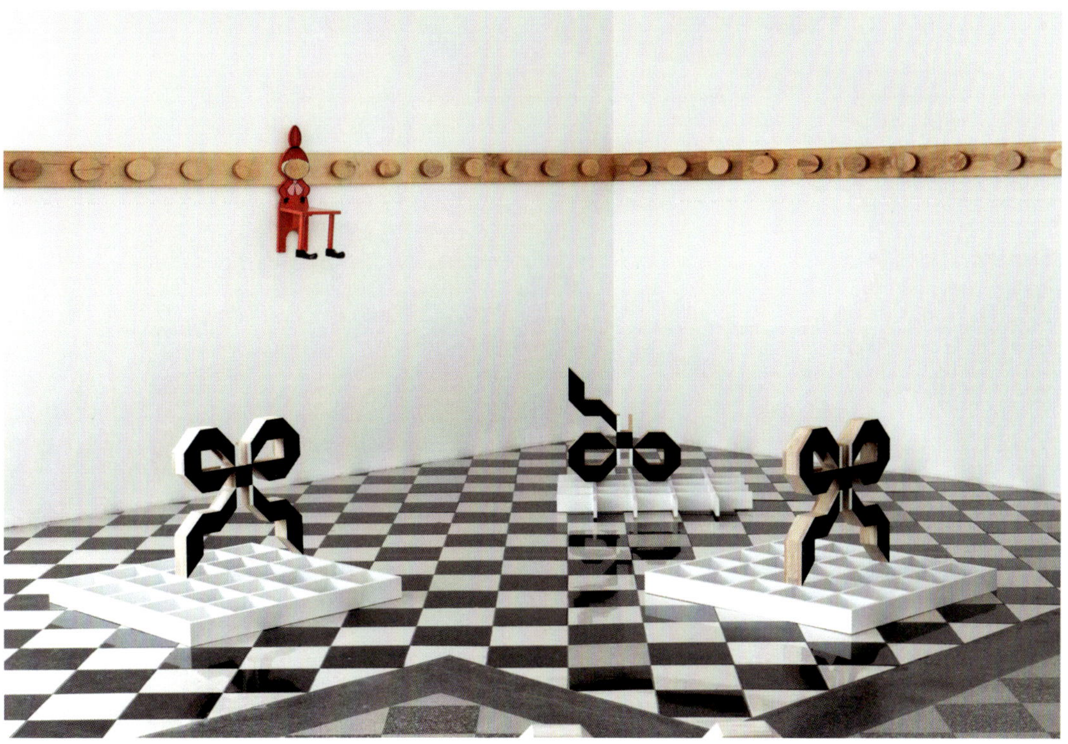

Holly Hobby Lobby, installation view, Kristina Kite Gallery, Los Angeles, September 9, 2017–November 4, 2017.

I find very hard to grasp (and the fact that I find it so hard to grasp is, of course, one of the things I find interesting).

The first is, given that you do not project a context, as you just explained, when you make an individual piece, how do you go about combining it with other pieces? So, in the case of the Little My work in *Holly Hobby Lobby* (which is a particularly good example), it somehow counteracted the sculpture on the floor both formally and in terms of content. It almost seemed like they were made for each other. So, how do you decide how to combine the individual pieces?

LISA

I want the works themselves, as they are being made or as they are conceived, to create the logic for why and how they are together. Again, Little My Chair is a good example. She first appeared in an exhibition titled *Th th th th th Snow White,* which was presented at Taka Ishii Gallery in Kyoto in 2010. She appeared at the exact midpoint of my two decades of art production, and as a readymade. I would say strict readymade because I did not alter her at all, but maybe I shouldn't say strict because I *did* make things for her. I made her a special colorful caned base and I made her white shelving, which was made from wood spools and which hung empty behind her. The shelving felt a little mysterious, almost like a dream object. So it feels wrong to call her "strict" when I assisted her with a dream object.

She was there because I thought the other pieces, "the bikini girls," were probably going to be disliked by just about everyone and I needed something beyond reproach to make up for them or corral them. In my mind, she was, I mean, beyond reproach.

VIOLA

What do you mean "dislikable"?

LISA

The girls were not dislikable in the way Vito Acconci's *Seedbed* might be considered dislikable. This iconic work is so incredibly likable, and was at the time, and I think it has aged so well. I thought the bikini girls would be understood as inferior art and therefore unlikeable for just about everyone and perhaps they shouldn't even enter the public sphere. The bikini girls would fail at first sight; fail to create a feeling of gestalt and they would also fail to persuade or influence people in the long run. I knew it from the get-go and perhaps I should have buried them in vertical graves like the "unseen" in Charlie Kaufman's *Antkind*. There were theoretical reasons why I had to make the bikini girls, and different theoretical reasons that I had to show them, but I was resigned to the fact that people would not find value in them. I needed something that was to

JMPED UP AND DOWN IN THE SWIMMING POOL. THEN JASMINE CAME SWOOSH

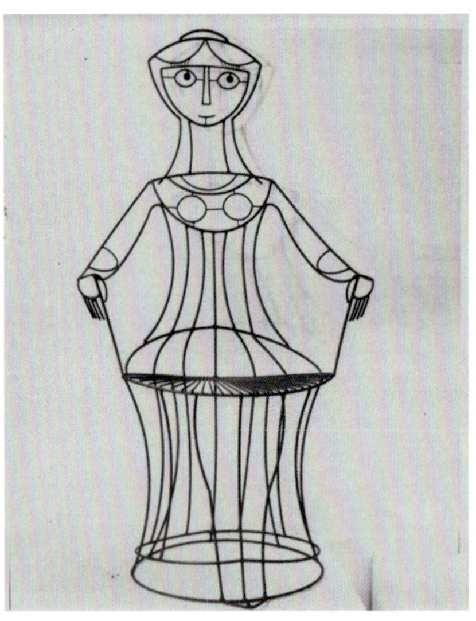

John Risley, *Lady Chair*, 1963. Steel and paint. 50 x 17 in. (127 x 43.2 cm).

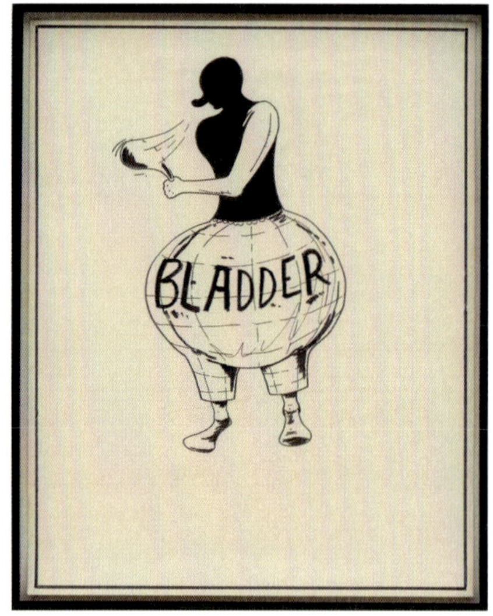

Mike Kelley, *Monkey Island: Travelogue series*, 1982–83. Felt-tip pen on nine pieces of paper. 24 x 19 in. (61 x 48.2 cm).

exist along with them to cut their distastefulness. The Little My Chair served this purpose. This was her beginning.

VIOLA

You already partially answered the second follow-up question. It relates very generally to our perceptual sieve, so to speak, with which we view the world and categorize certain things, but not others and the relation of this perceptual sieve to artistic work. I know it is very hard to describe what exactly the relevant feature is of those things that we *do* follow up on, but since you gave such a precise description of what caused this in the case of *Little My Chair*. Say you come across some object or idea that stands out for you in some way (which means, you notice it and reflect upon it consciously)—do you think you could classify which properties cause you to decide to use this object or idea?

LISA

First of all, I am happy you used the phrase "perceptual sieve." I am guessing that is a translation from German or some kind of phrasing from philosophy of which I am not aware. But I love that you used the term sieve. Because all of the caning and screen blocks, which are constants throughout my work over decades, are literally sieve-like, but I also consider it a perceptual sieve. The work is straining solids from liquids and creating finer particles of perception. It's like I am shoving a huge idea through a strainer, and at the end there is only a small angry chair left.

Let's stay with the chair for a moment. When I saw it in the book in the *children's room "Stockholm,"* published by the Jeu de Paume, I knew I would use it if I could get a hold of it. I didn't know what it was. I had never heard of Tove Jansson or Mooomintroll when I first saw the chair. I mentioned that I had a feeling I had only experienced once before in the late eighties. As a philosophy student, I was going through a MOCA catalogue which had pictures of all sorts of art in their collection, and when I got to this drawing by Mike [Kelley], *Monkey Island: Travelogue* (1982–83), my heart stopped because it seemed to be questioning all the other works in the rest of the book, but not the idea of art itself. This work seemed to be affirming art at the expense of all the other works, which is what Diedrich [Diederichsen] would later argue about Mike's work, calling Mike a universalist by being a provincialist. So, when I saw Mike's drawing it was a very important moment for me, and I never felt anything like it again until this little red chair. I was confused, and thought to myself, how can I be having this important feeling, *the* feeling with this fucking chair? It made no sense. So, of course, you become obsessed with thinking about the properties of the chair. Is it some aspect, or combination of aspects making me feel this way? She has these funny shoes, and a top bun, and an indiscernible expression. As I said before, it is hard to determine if Little My Chair is young or old, which is curious. The chair was personified, but of course, I had seen many personified chairs. She is in a category of chairs that includes John Risley's "people chairs," which were designed in the 1960s. None of her properties explained *my* feeling. But I felt she had the potential to be blowing something up quietly without anyone noticing.

VIOLA

I think this will be a non-linear conversation because I want to get back to various and different points you just brought up. I actually made up the term "perceptual sieve." As far as I know it's not a technical term at all (although you never know, there might be some German philosopher who used it—there are so many). But I really like your explanation of shoving a huge idea through a strainer to get the small angry chair. I think the reason I have been so interested in this issue is that this function (the shoving) is non-trivial in your case and the characterization you give also bears witness to this.

Getting back to your answer to my earlier question, I think your answer made something clear to me that I couldn't put my finger on in the past. Whenever I have seen your shows or pictures of your shows (and this also extends to the period before I knew you), I have always been touched by them. I mean touched not in a sentimental-reactionary-is-feeling-the-sublime type way, but rather in the way that I am touched by something that needs my help or onto which I project: it needs my help.

So, as stupid as this may sound, there is a weird emotional component to your art, which is *not* triggered directly by the objects in it (i.e., the tobacco camel, the rat column, *Little My Chair*, etc.), but by something more abstract. Now, I realize what it is: it is almost like the different pieces are protecting each other (e.g., *Little My Chair* protecting the bikini girls), which also means that they are in need of protection. Now, given this, I noticed that this "protection" idea might be even more prevalent: You do not only protect the bikini girls from mistreatment, you also protect several components that you use for your work from being brutalized by a blunt reduction to the obvious (where "obvious" can also include easy irony). Here is a particularly obvious example: for a long time, I have been thinking about the fact that you are probably the only artist I know who can reference Wittgenstein (e.g. *Goose Fair* and *Christmas Tea = Meeting, Presented by Dialogue and Humanism, Formerly Dialectics and Humanism*, 2007) without being annoying. I have always wondered how you did it, but now I realize it's probably a protective mechanism. Do you think that this is an adequate description, and if so, could you describe how you perceive the threat that the works need to be protected from?

LISA

I feel connected to the present moment in time more than I felt connected to my own, which would have been the early 2000s, when I started my career. I find it funny and disconcerting that you got to this question so quickly. No one has ever asked me this question and it was *the* question for me when I began making art. Issues of risk and protection were there at the very beginning for me. I decided to become an artist while standing in front of Haim Steinbach's work *Untitled (bronze statuette, Wakamba Gourds*, 1989*)* at the opening of Ann Goldstein's *Forest of the Signs* exhibition at MOCA in 1989. I was an undergraduate philosophy student at UCSD, and I thought to myself,

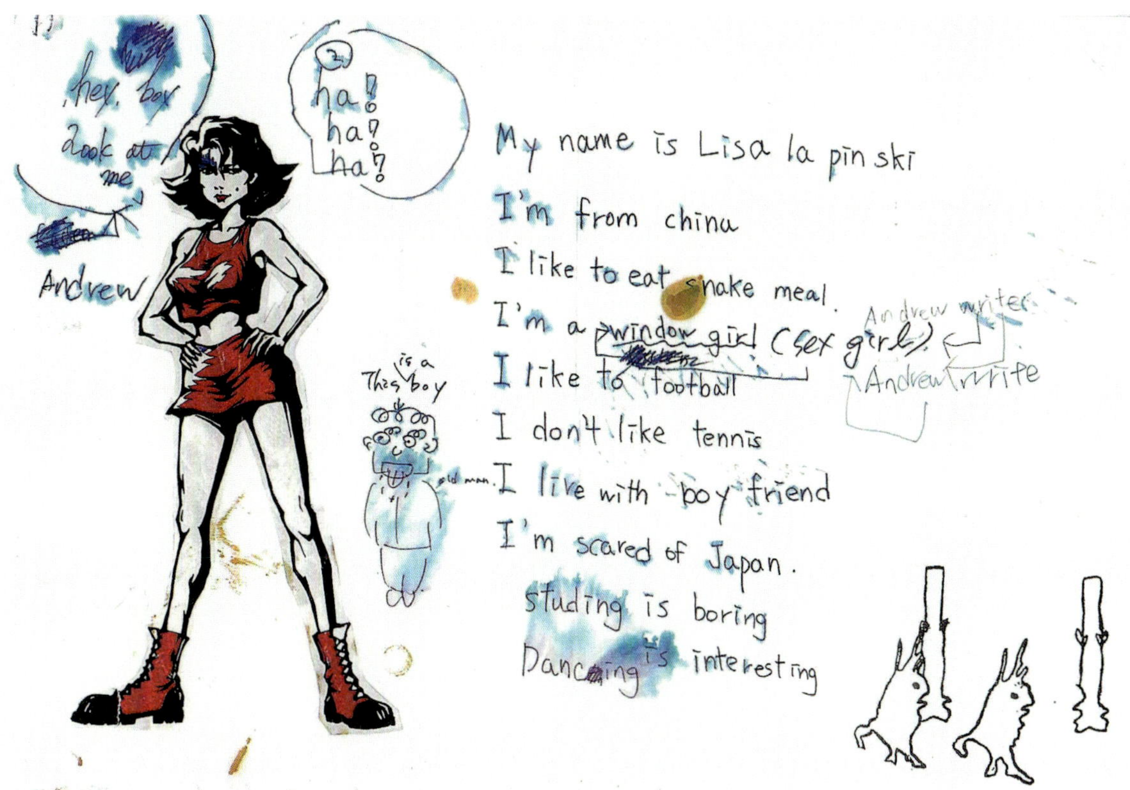

Lisa Lapinski, invitation for *Diagram for Neutral Love* (verso) exhibition, ArtCenter College of Design, 1999.

LLY PINOCCHIO CAME. THEN WENDY CALLED OUT, " IT'S TIME TO DO ROLLER

"Oh this is philosophy and I could do this as a job." It was like I was seeing myself for the first time. I had a very personal and intimate experience in front of this second-generation conceptual artwork. It was not something I was told anything about or taught. I thought I knew what it was, what I was looking at, and its implications all at once. It was like a gestalt experience. I felt Haim's work was a very risky enterprise and my experience of it felt risky and emotional. Later when I read everything there was to read by, on, or about Haim I was mostly drawn to an interview he did for a catalogue for a two-person show with the Italian artist Ettore Spalletti at the Guggenheim. In that interview, he explained that he "invented" the shelf like someone invented the tuba so he could throw himself into the world of objects. He speaks specifically about risk - that the shelves allow him to take risks in the world. I can see how people could look at the shelves and see the very opposite of risk, read them as a kind of artistic signature that protects the artist, but I did not experience them that way at all. To me, it was an endgame which threw the viewer into an abstract experience of pure risk. "Why wasn't everyone running from the room in terror?" was my experience of his work when I was young, which I realized was not everyone's. A decade later, when I was in graduate school, Haim came to visit ArtCenter, and one of my fellow grad students scribbled "Lisa ♥ Haim" in the corner of the poster advertising his lecture. It was very embarrassing, and I debated in my head whether I should rip it down, but then I had to admit it was true, and pretty funny, and so I left it.

One of the very first projects I did as a grad student at ArtCenter related to my dad. He had a very serious case of arthritic psoriasis, similar in kind and degree to the main character in the television show *Singing Detective*, which was written by the British television writer Dennis Potter, who also had an extreme version of psoriasis which covered his whole body. My dad developed psoriasis when he was twenty-seven before I was born so I had never known him without it. In grad school, I was reading an essay by Mark C. Taylor about *Singing Detective* in which he talks about psoriasis as a metaphor for truth in contemporary society. He explained that the psoriatic body is not able to determine the difference between itself and the outside world. The person's body is creating skin at an accelerated rate, desperately trying to create a border with the world, which it cannot sense. A medical site online described the "flakes [as] the result of your overactive immune system speeding up the rate at which your skin cells grow, causing skin cell buildup." While someone without the disease might change their layer of skin every few weeks, the person with psoriasis builds up skin in days or hours, and that is why the scabs form. The excess skin is always fluffing off. I remember as a child seeing little bits of my dad's skin on the floor, and my mom vacuuming them up.

ArtCenter is in Pasadena, so I was living in LA at the time. I would travel down to San Diego to visit my parents and secretly collect the bits of dry diseased skin while my parents were sleeping. I would bring this material to my studio in Pasadena and make art with it. I think I needed to start making work from an extremist position, and with a material that was so psychologically charged it would be almost impossible to work with. At the time I thought the choice of materials had to be a radical decision and could be anything. My dad's body was unable to see where he started and where the world began and so it produced this material, which I turned into an art material. Today I feel like this as a proposition in itself is enough. At the time, I worked very hard to figure out how to actually use the skin to make art. But, I always thought this material was produced by a protective measure gone terribly wrong.

VIOLA
What did you use the material for?

LISA
I made different works with the skin but they had been tentative, and I was stalled. One day Mike Kelley was in my studio at school and he suggested that I mix the skin with paint medium, which is a fucking insane suggestion, but it was made by him in a calm matter-of-fact kind of way. So, I went to the art store and bought some clear paint medium and mixed it with my father's dry skin bits, and the smell was disgusting, like a dead body, and I threw up. It struck me what I was doing, and I knew I couldn't do it anymore.

After that I plastered a single layer of an individual sheet of wallpaper and then another single sheet over that one until they built up into a block that got so heavy it peeled off the wall. It was like I was acting out the psoriasis with the wallpaper. I was acting out protecting myself from everything that was beyond the walls of my studio. I felt severe anxiety being at ArtCenter at that moment and the only thing I could do was act out an overactive immune system. I put the block of wallpaper in our

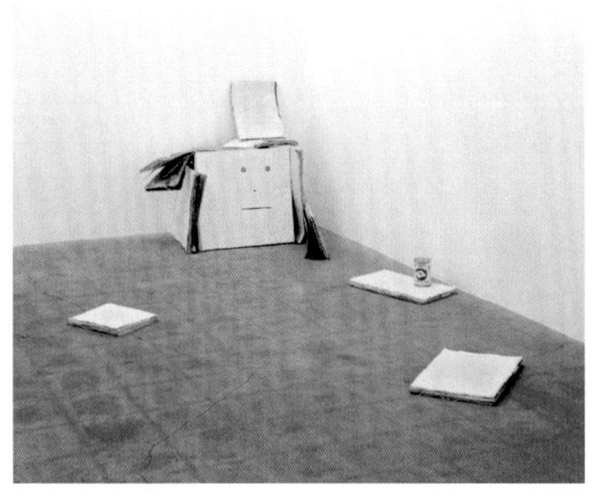

Lisa Lapinski, *[Clown Type] face*, 1999.
Wallpaper, Xerox, staples, canned hearts of palm, paint.
Dimensions variable.

SKATING." MINNIE SAID, "OK, WE'LL DO ROLLER SKATING." SO THEY PUT garage for something like six months where it grew mold and got dirty. I then cut it up into panels and made *[Clown Type] Face*. So yes, the question of what counts as extreme risk and extreme protection is at the very start of my work.

VIOLA
What about the can?

LISA
The can in this piece says "California Girl Hearts of Palm," and there is an icon on the can of a surfer girl. They are tubers from Brazil I found in a shop on Hollywood Blvd.

VIOLA
The psoriasis link is so excellent. Sorry for exploiting this analogy, but I think there was no way for me in this context to avoid it: Some autoimmune diseases are such that they are overly active, so they destroy anything that comes into the body, and they also turn onto the body itself because they are blinded by their overactivity, so they are really aggressive. So, going back quite bluntly to the art analogy, I think that some of your works are not only defensive-protective, some seem aggressive-protective, like the thorny mosques (this one architectural feature of mosques being overemphasized), so here the artwork itself is aggressive and going after the potential viewer, which of course it cannot do because it is a small and inert artwork. This made me think of the actual human audience for your artworks because the little mosques seemed to me like they want to get into a fistfight with the audience.

Do you ever reflect on potential causal links between your artworks and the audience's individual internal states? Do you distinguish those from your own? Do you hate your audience?

LISA
I had been traveling around outside the country for many years, most of my twenties, before I returned to the US to get my MFA. In Warsaw I worked as an assistant for a philosophical journal published by Warsaw University, and after that I taught English at a power components factory in Elblag, Poland, then I taught at a turbine factory in Budapest. Then I left Europe for South Korea where I taught at small language schools in Suwon and Seoul. Finally, I went back to Europe and taught the employees of Portugal Telecom in Lisbon. This was in the 1990s. I was moving around a lot, but always managed to find real jobs and apartments in each city.

When I got to ArtCenter in 1997, I wasn't coming from an undergraduate art program or any kind of art milieu. I didn't know any artists or even what an art studio class would be like. My work to that point had been developed in isolation. I had made collages when I was an undergraduate philosophy student, but I think I started making work in earnest in Budapest in 1992. I guess this would be the time that many LA artists my exact age, Diana [Thater], Laura [Owens], Frances [Stark], Pae [White] would have been in grad school at ArtCenter or Cal Arts in LA. I was living in this huge apartment on the seventeenth floor of a tall communist housing block on the Buda side near the Aquincum Roman ruins, within walking distance of the Vasarely Museum. You would look out the window and just see massive communist-era concrete apartment buildings. That was all. I started making artwork alone there. I developed long and intricate stories around my work, however slight or half-baked they were visually, in part, to assure myself of the meaningfulness of these works when I was without social context. I think those stories or theories about my early works could be described as me being ready to get into a fistfight. The works always felt like powerless outsiders ready to take someone on, even when it didn't make sense anymore given my position or involvement. I don't think I hated or hate my audience, but my works were definitely prepared to fight the audience.

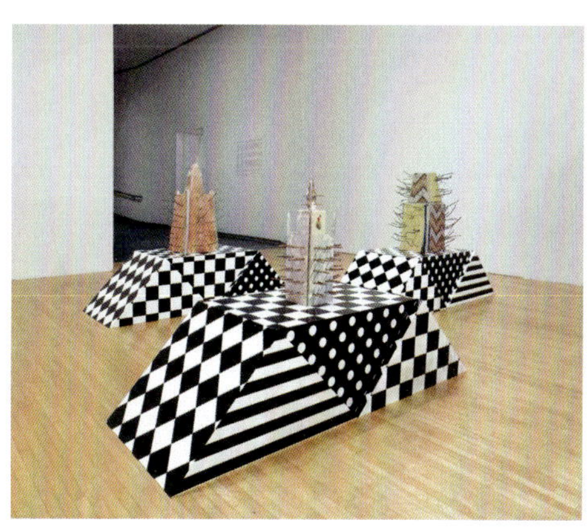

Lisa Lapinski: The Fret and Its Variants, installation view, Museum of Contemporary Art (MOCA), Los Angeles, June 26–August 25, 2008.

VIOLA
Could you specify the threat?

LISA
There is a way in which I am always performing a nascent phase, and during that first phase of development, there is the chance something will be snuffed out before it gets a chance to develop fully and become something important. In the beginning, the work needs to be protected or needs to protect itself. I don't even think you can say I have mature work. I keep asking myself how to start over and over again.

Over twenty years ago in school, I had a studio visit with the art historian Norman Bryson and he said that all of my work was "regressive reductive," and I was a little taken aback so I started to mess with him during the visit. I asked him what he meant, and then after he explained "regressive reductive,"

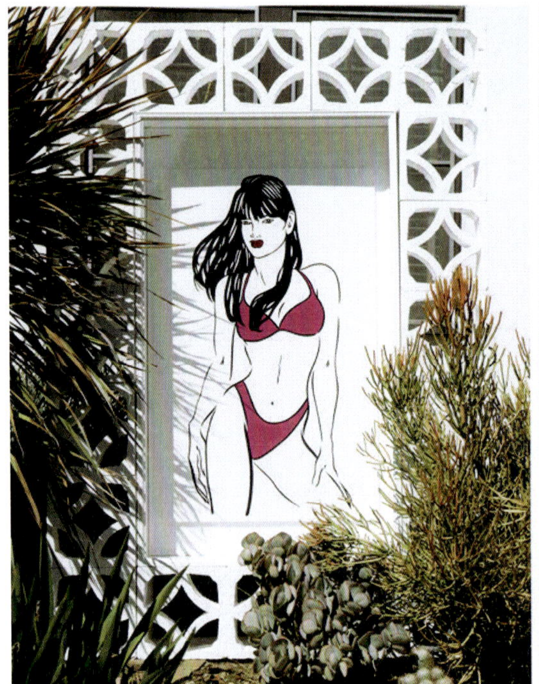

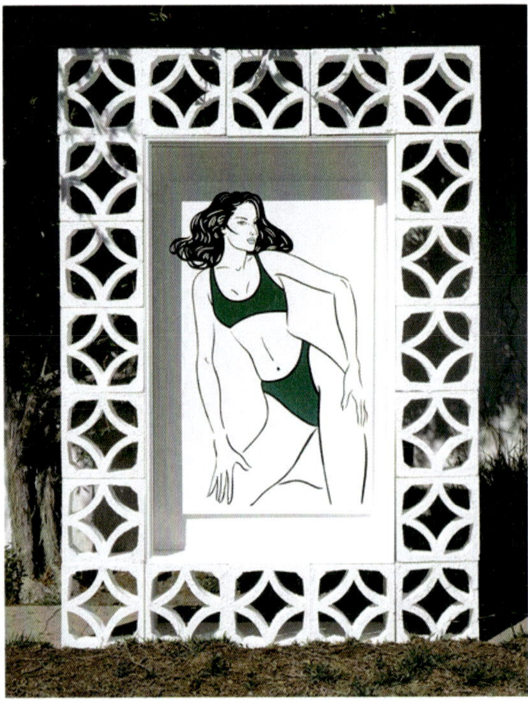

Untitled, 2007. Chromogenic prints on paper. 50 x 40 in. (127 x 101.6 cm).

I asked him what that explanation meant, so he tried to simplify his language. But I asked him again and again what he meant like a child who keeps asking "why" until Bryson simplified his language to an absurd degree and became noticeably upset and refused to continue. I remember that he was wearing a black leather outfit and I was making him speak in baby talk. He probably thought I had some kind of problem but I thought it was the funniest thing ever. I was prepared to completely embarrass myself. I am telling you this as a story now, but I almost felt like this exchange with Professor Bryson was a work of art.

VIOLA

I don't know whether I would apply "regressive reductive" to the thorny mosques because to me this term has an anti-intellectual connotation. Could you say more about how the mosques came about?

LISA

The only sculptures I ever made with the psoriatic build-up wallpaper method (it seems strange to call it a method, but yes, a method), were *[Clown Type] Face* (a self-portrait), a stool, and the mosques. I started the mosques in the summer of 2001. I was researching Rimbaud's biography, and specifically the period when he had quit writing poetry and was living in Harar [Ethiopia]. He wrote to his mom and asked her to send something like thirty books on trades and techniques, which included everything from well digging, to steamboat captaining, to forging weapons (a one-man colony?). I was going to make a sculpture that used all the trades and techniques that Rimbaud had wanted to learn from the books bought by his mom, but I couldn't do it in the time frame and was beginning to panic. My first show was scheduled to open at Richard Telles in LA in November. I was reading about Harar as it was at the time Rimbaud was there, and I found out that it had a snow-white mosque with two snow-white minarets. So, I started making the mosque works out of the layered wallpaper. What you said about those works not being actual mosques is really important. I took apart the outside of an actual mosque and repeated the form on all sides of the sculpture and added sticks to represent the logs that often protrude from these structures (and yes, this seems really aggressive to me now, too).
I was taking aspects of the typical mosque structure, simplifying them, and combining them to form little defensive potentialities.

I was in my studio in Boyle Heights making these mosque works listening to the radio on 9/11. Will [Fowler] was with you in Austria, right? I didn't understand what was happening, and I took my car to go buy linoleum flooring at this outlet on Washington Blvd. The linoleum flooring outlet had thousands of rolls of linoleum in this warehouse and an old grainy TV installed high up on a wall.

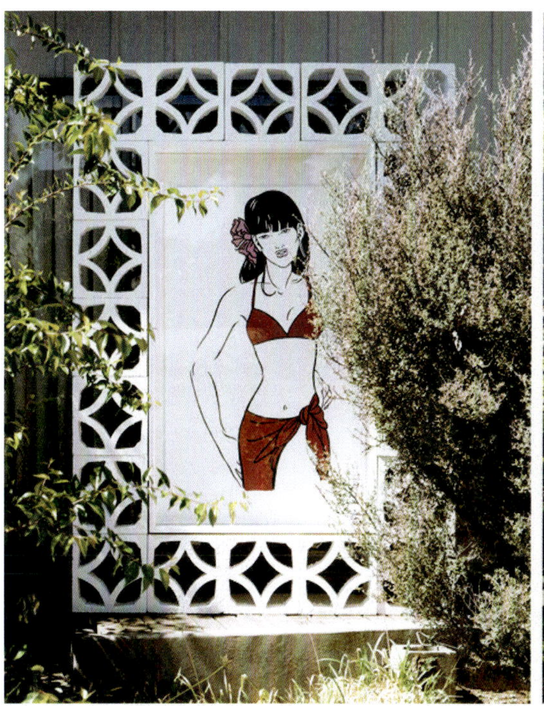

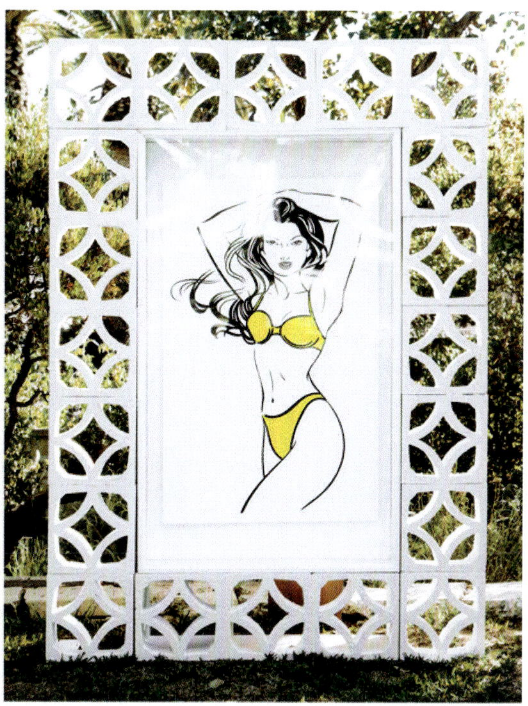

Untitled, 2007. Chromogenic prints on paper. 50 x 40 in. (127 x 101.6 cm).

It felt like the TV itself was in the sky. I could see the video of the planes crashing, but the program was in Spanish so I couldn't make out what was going on. No one was watching and so I thought it might not be so serious, although it looked serious.

VIOLA

I don't think I knew you and Will in 2001. Will might have been with Martin [Prinzhorn] in Austria on 9/11. I was on a plane to New York that day with Anne Speier. The plane had to land in Newfoundland, where we spent an entire week. The head of Hugo Boss (the clothing company) was on the plane, and while everyone else was very nice and supportive, he seemed to use this period to make money, selling Boss underwear to the other passengers (we couldn't get to our luggage).

There are a couple of things I want to pick up from what you said, but I'll start with your point of not having mature work. I think this is very important, this quest to start over and over again. I think you defy one of the real dangers, namely, the idea that there is anything like a narrative, i.e., something that is coherent that goes on. This presupposes that certain things have been fixed and have been established because there is a narrative through which the works assume meaning. You essentially take an anti-lazy position here, which must be very exhausting for you, but also for the audience because they cannot take the easy way out by contextualizing it through your other work. At the same time, while there isn't a general narrative, there is some connection between the individual works you made at different points in time. I was trying to put my finger on what this connection is, apart from the more abstract properties we discussed before (like the works protecting each other, the juxtaposition of different pieces in a show that prevents easy irony, the artworks being outsiders that are ready to fight, etc.). I sense there is a connection in terms of the actual shape and material makeup of the pieces, but I just went back and looked at a number of them and it is really unclear how to root this intuition in reality because the materials, shapes, and techniques of the individual works are in fact completely diverse. So, I was wondering whether it is a more elusive formal property that might be at the root of this intuition. So, here is my question: So far, the formal features of your work were always functions of certain attitudes (e.g., in our discussion of the mosque sculptures, or the psoriasis link with the wallpaper pieces). Are there also features that result from pure formal decisions, by which I mean you simply think that something shouldn't look like *this* but should rather look like *that*, without reflecting on why this is the case? This isn't supposed to sound like such decisions are morally inferior to those triggered by conscious access to other content.

LISA

Why don't we call this "intuitions of form"? It might be my definition of art. Probably one of the most beautiful things to experience as a human, right, is intuition of form, and I think that is what I am always trying to do. I just want to put myself into a state where I am intuiting forms. It seems like a good way to spend one's short time on earth: making things without reflecting on why you are making them. But I don't separate that out from meaning or even irony. The meaning in my work, which does involve irony, is still there and driving things even if I am not reflecting on it.

I get nervous talking about some other kind of experience called "purity of form separated out from everything else." There is an essay Diedrich Diedrichsen wrote in 2014 called *On Surplus Value in Art* which I keep coming back to lately. In it he discusses the German word *Mehrwert.* There is the everyday use of the term, which means pay-off, and a different meaning Marx uses, namely, the value added by labor. I think the only actual Marx quote Diedrich includes in his essay is a description of *Mehrwert*: that which "transforms every product of labor into social hieroglyphics." To briefly summarize one point from the first section of a not easy essay, he suggests there are two types of audiences: One audience is conditioned to expect a punchline from the artwork. He calls them "punchline fetishists." He has this great discussion on Dali and Kippenberger withholding punchlines, and Kippenberger's withholding of the punchline being a punchline in itself. So, this is one kind of art *Mehrwert*. Then there is the audience who believes that they are experiencing something that cannot be captured in words. They have a "reactionary desire for total immersion." So, let's call them reactionary desirists. This is a second type of art *Mehrwert*. I want something like Kiekergaards's "second immediacy" from my art. An idea which suspends logic and is based on irony in a very Kierkegaardian way. It posits an immediacy *through* reflection. And this is where I disagree about my work not being ironic.

And now that I have set out these conditions for my response, I will actually answer your question. My work is flat. Don't you think it is barely sculpture? I mean, it sometimes makes an L-shape, but not even in a classical minimalist L-shape way. It is flatter than that. Sometimes the plane gets curved a little. When I started, I never set out to make sculpture. I am not sure what I was setting out to make. It was other people who called me a sculptor and I remember laughing when someone first used that word to describe me to my face. It was in grad school. I ended up teaching sculpture because I needed to fit into a genre to literally survive, have food, pay for baby formula, but then I found out that I really enjoyed theories around space, and that sculptors and their problems were really fascinating. Even if I wasn't one of them, my problems aligned with theirs. I found that I really cared about the concept of space in my nonsculptural anxiety-ridden way.

VIOLA

Speaking of flatness, in various works you use the black-and-white patterns on the flat surfaces. Why?

LISA

I titled a recent work *Black Cat Portal*. It is a miniature portal I made for a group show at Kristina Kite Gallery in LA. A sign with the band Kiss's logo is part of the piece. It is based on a sign from a bar or strip club or something in a strip mall named Kiss in West Houston. The name of the show was *The Going Away Present* and included forty-nine artists and sixteen writers, all of whom made work for Bruce Hainely, who was leaving LA for Houston. Will and I were the only ones saying hello and not goodbye, and for us, it was a welcome to Houston present.

Black Cat Portal is related to the flatness of some obscure works by the Futurist Giacomo Balla. Balla designed and fabricated furniture for his children's room. One piece of the furniture has cut-out half circles above triangles that look like diagrammatic kids, but all of the furniture has a similar design.

I have talked a lot about grad school and my early work in this interview. I think I keep going back to the late '90s because I have really never been asked about this time in my life, and although I have said some of these things before, I have never had the opportunity to say them in print.

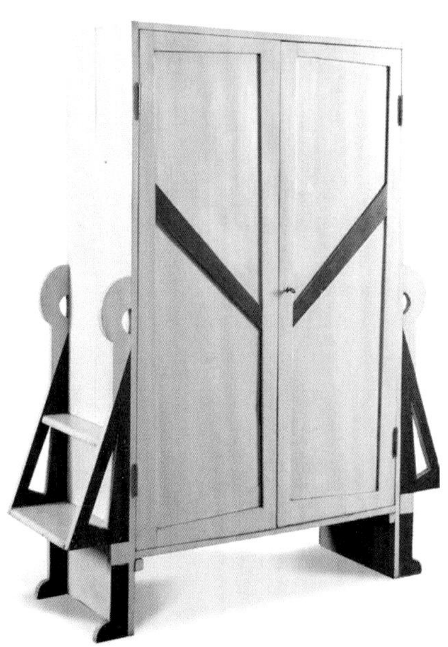

Giacomo Balla, child's wardrobe, 1914.
Painted wood. 63 x 52 x 16 in. (159.5 x 131.5 x 40.5 cm).

MIKO? HE WAS IN THAT PICNIC STORY. SO CHIP AND DALE WENT FOR A WA

When I was a grad student in Pasadena, I was photocopying some diagrams from a metallurgy book at Kinko's. I think this was 1997 or 1998. An older man who worked behind the counter looked at these diagrams and said they reminded him of a psychological test he had once taken in the 1960s. I said, "You mean the Rorschach Test? They ask you what you see in an abstract ink blot." I was startled that he did not know the name Rorschach. That was somehow startling. He said yes, that was it and that he took it as part of a job interview for IBM. He said they told him he didn't get the position because he had seen a paisley instead of an amoeba in this one ink blot. Now, that cannot be how it happened, but it is how he remembered not getting a job at IBM. I got the feeling this was kind of pivotal in his life. I thought, you see the scientific (an amoeba), and that means you will be a good IBM employee or psychologically stable, but if you see the decorative (the paisley) you must be aberrant in some way.

THE WARM, WARM SUN ALL THE WAY TO THE CAFÉ. SO NOW WENDY CAME FOR

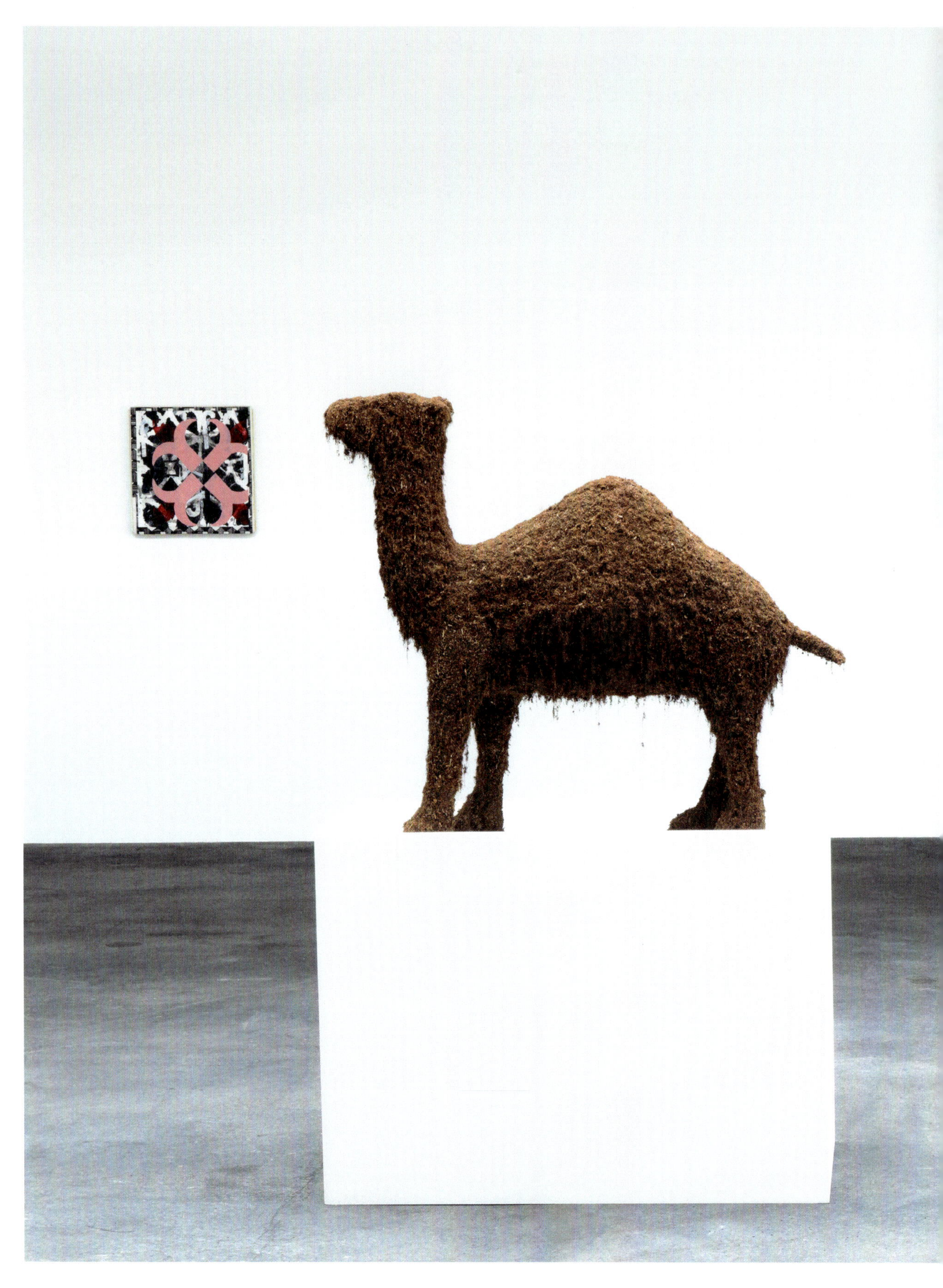

SOMETHING. PETER PAN SAW WHAT THAT MIKO DID. HE GOT SNOW WHITE BA

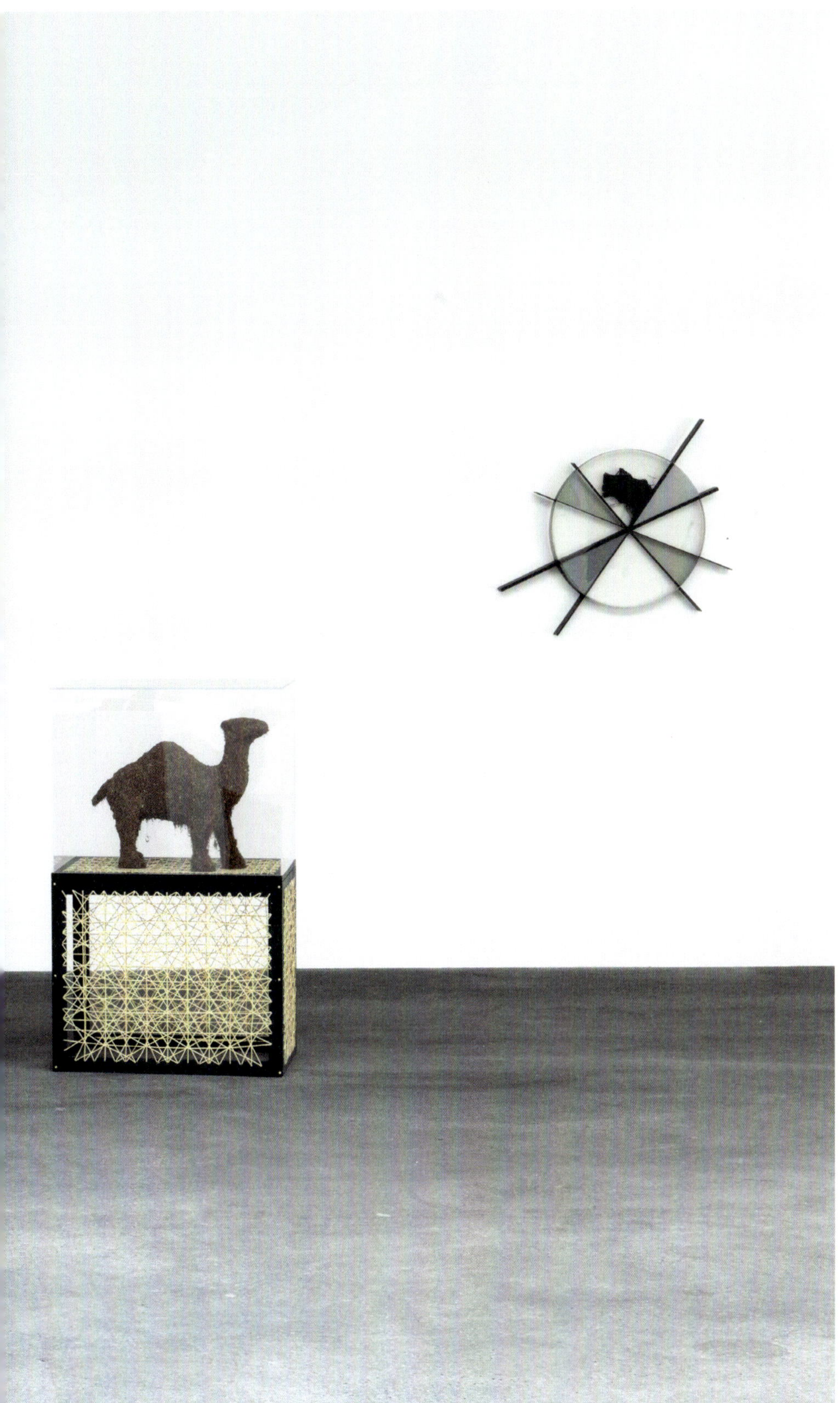

Lisa Lapinski
Installation view,
Johann König Gallery,
Berlin, June 9–July 9, 2011

following spread

Lisa Lapinski
Installation view,
Johann König Gallery,
Berlin, June 9–July 9, 2011

ERE. SOFTLY: "CAN YOU SAY "THTHTHTHTHTH SNOW WHITE?" NOW KIKI AND

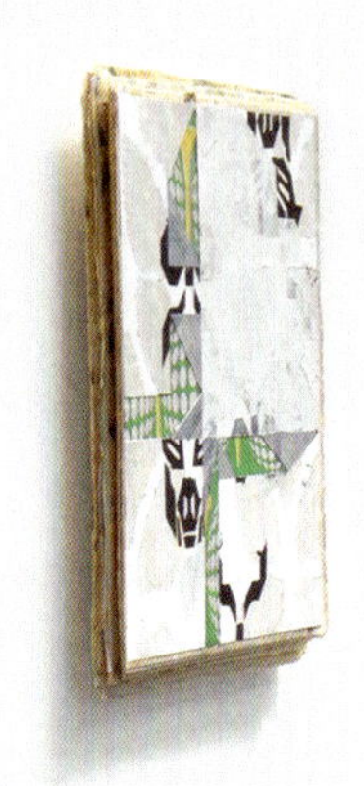

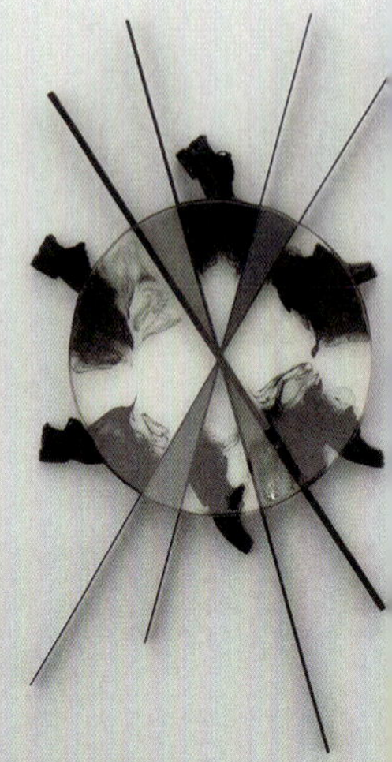

BOBO CAME ALONG AND DONALD WAS RIDING ON THEIR BACK AND DONALD W

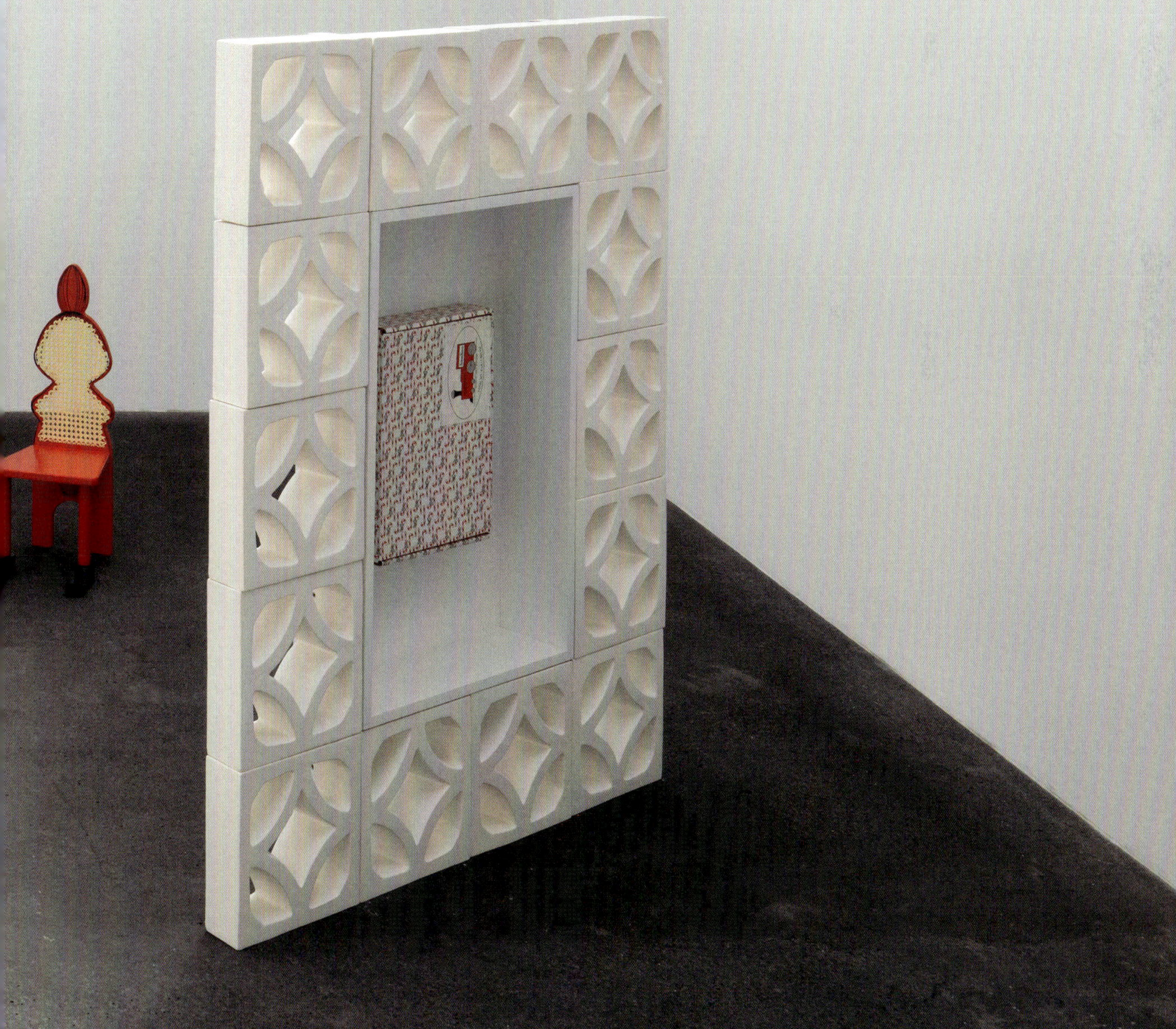

DING ON THE BACKSEAT OF THEIR BIKE AND THEY GOT FIRECRACKERS AND

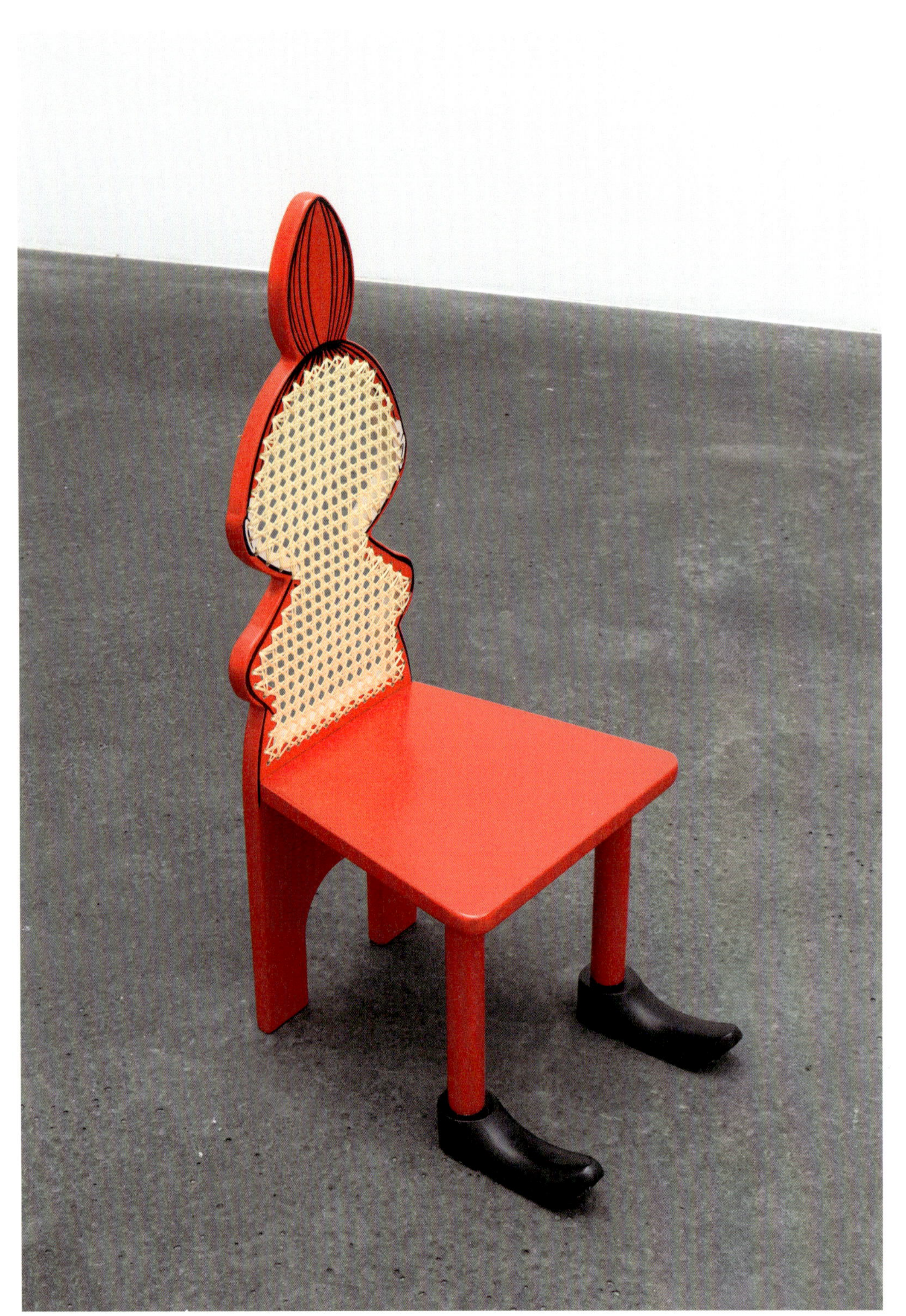

WENT TO SEE SNOW WHITE. SO SLEEPING BEAUTY CAME RIDING ON HER BI

Little My Chair 2, 2011
Found chair and caning
15 x 11 x 30 in.
(38.1 x 27.9 x 76.2 cm)

Disk #3, 2011
Epoxy paint, steel, shoe,
metal hardware
45 x 26 x 2 in.
(114.3 x 66 x 5.1 cm)

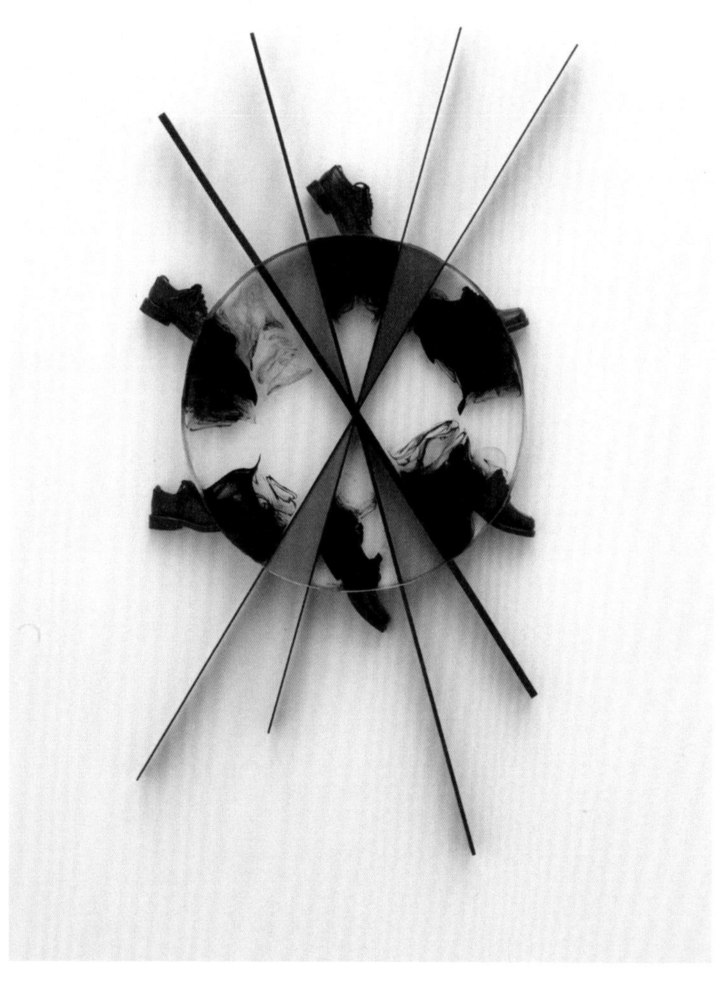

TH THE PRINCE ON THE BACK OF HER BIKE. THEN CINDERELLA CAME ON HER

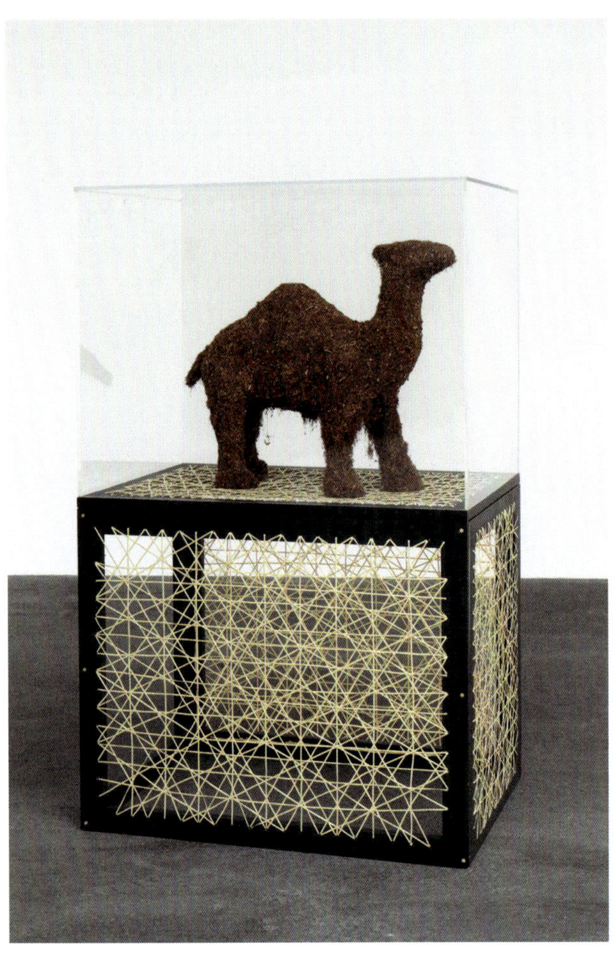

Small Camel Sculpture #3, 2011
Plexiglas box, tobacco, adhesive, taxidermy foam, caning, wood, acrylic paint
27 x 19 1/2 x 40 in.
(68.6 x 49.5 x 101.6 cm)

Small Camel Sculpture #2, 2011
Plexiglas box, tobacco, adhesive, taxidermy foam, caning, wood, acrylic paint
78 1/2 x 27 x 23 in.
(199.4 x 68.6 x 58.4 cm)

BIKE. THIS TIME CAPTAIN HOOK CAME. NOT REALLY CAPTAIN HOOK. CAPTA

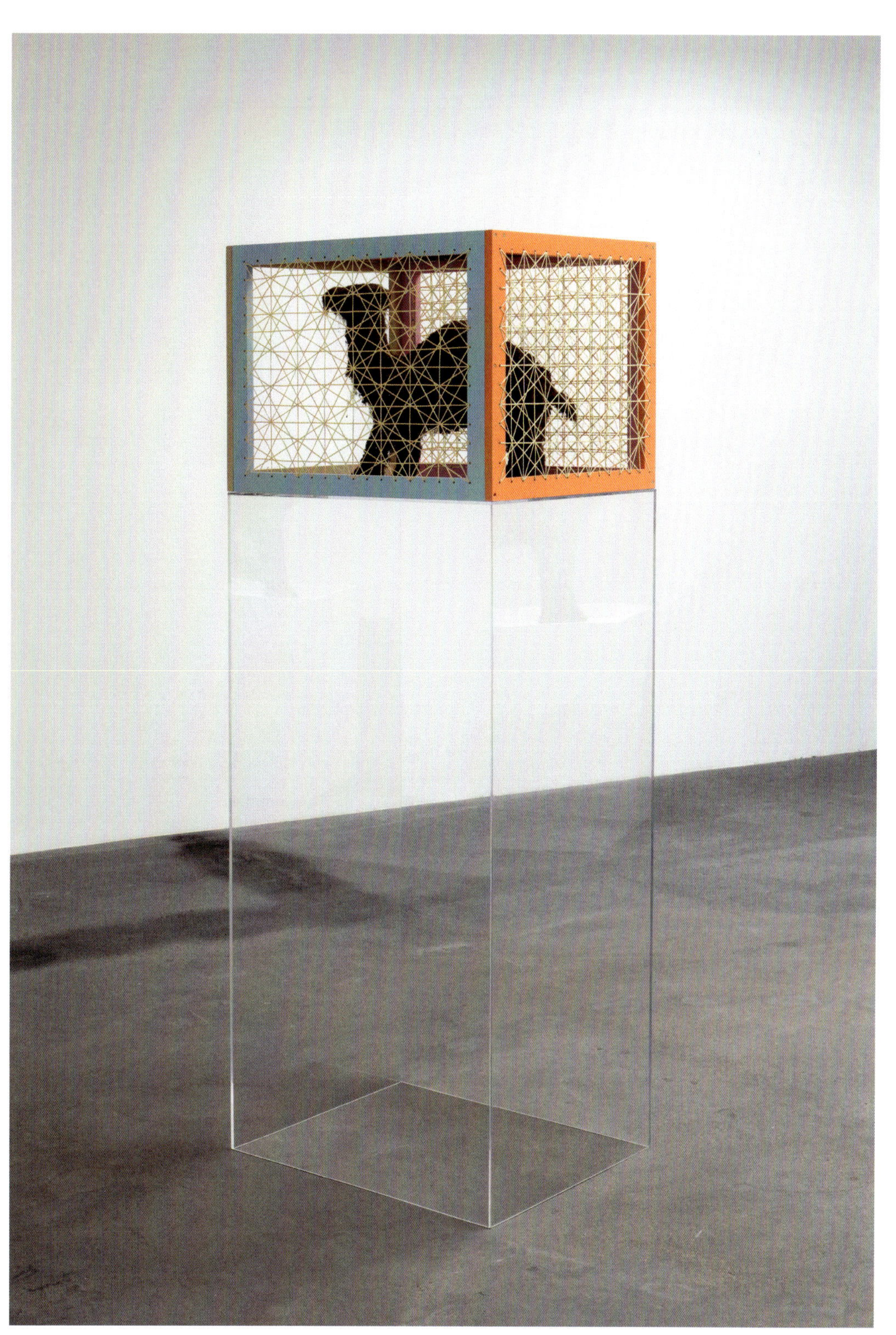

OK STAYED IN THE CAVE. HE STAYED IN THE LOST BOYS CAVE. ALSO, THE

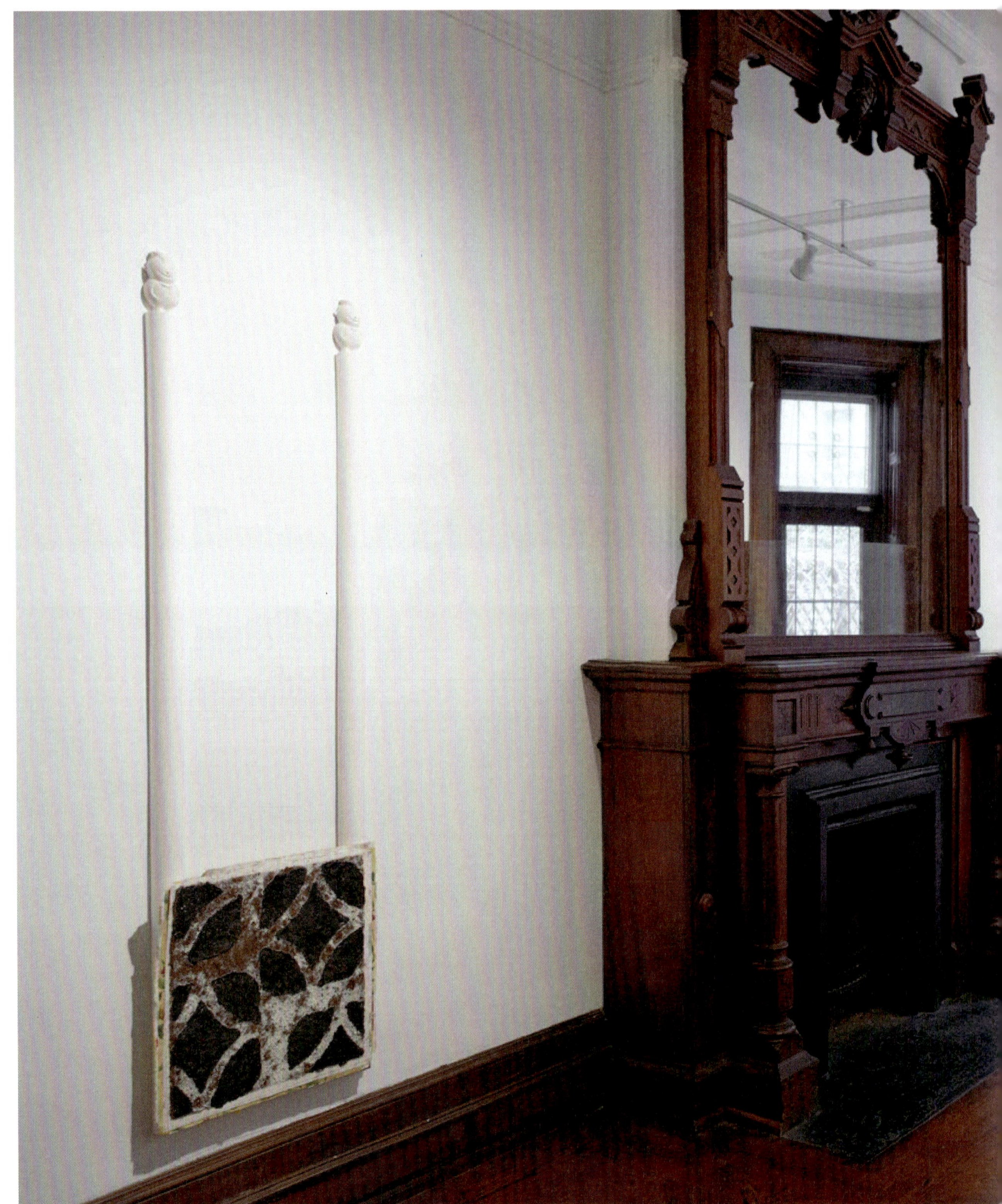

Trieste
Installation view, Marianne Boesky Gallery, New York, March 2–March 30, 2013

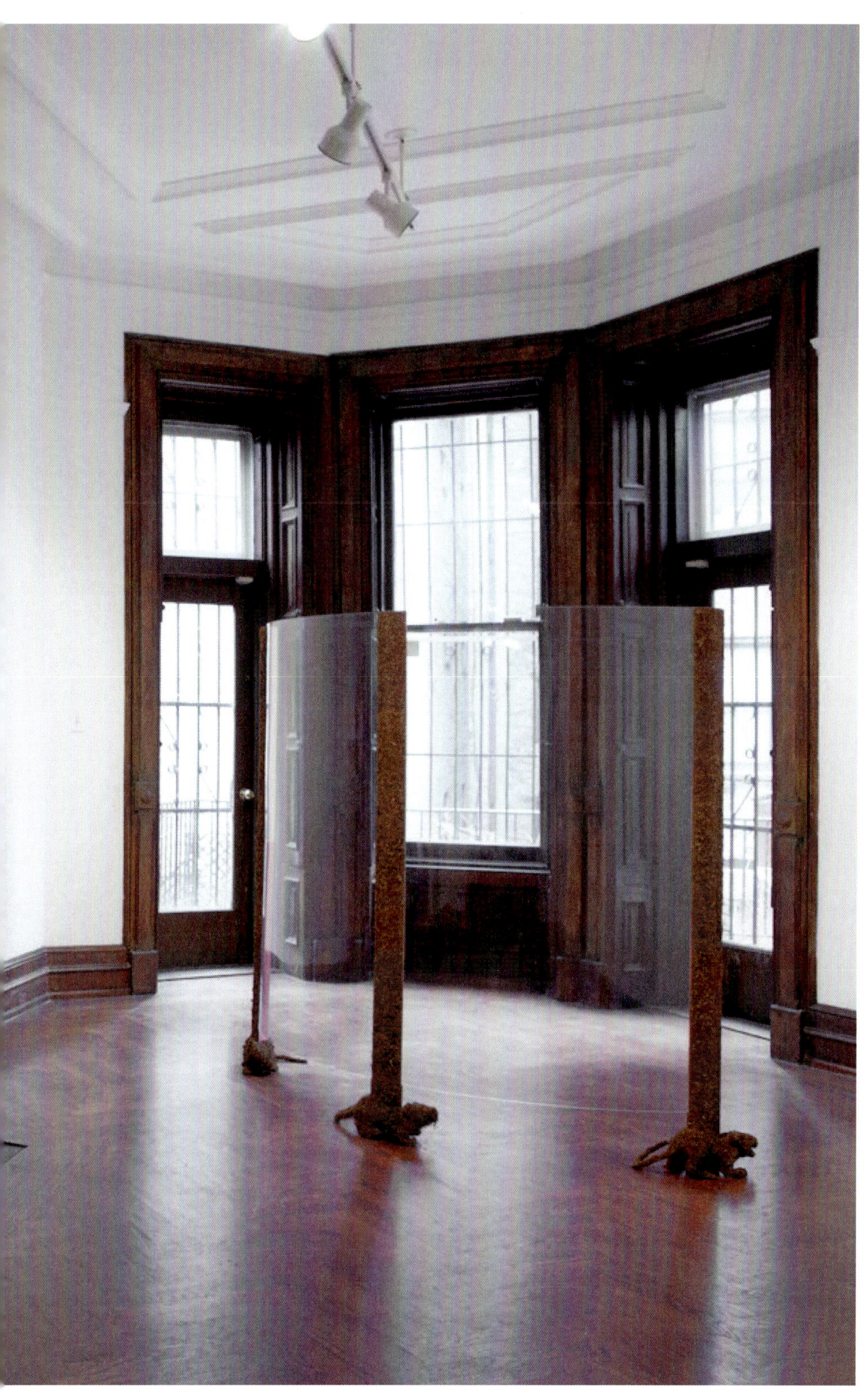

EY CAME ON A BIKE. THE DADDY AND THE MOMMY PUT THEMSELVES ON PETER

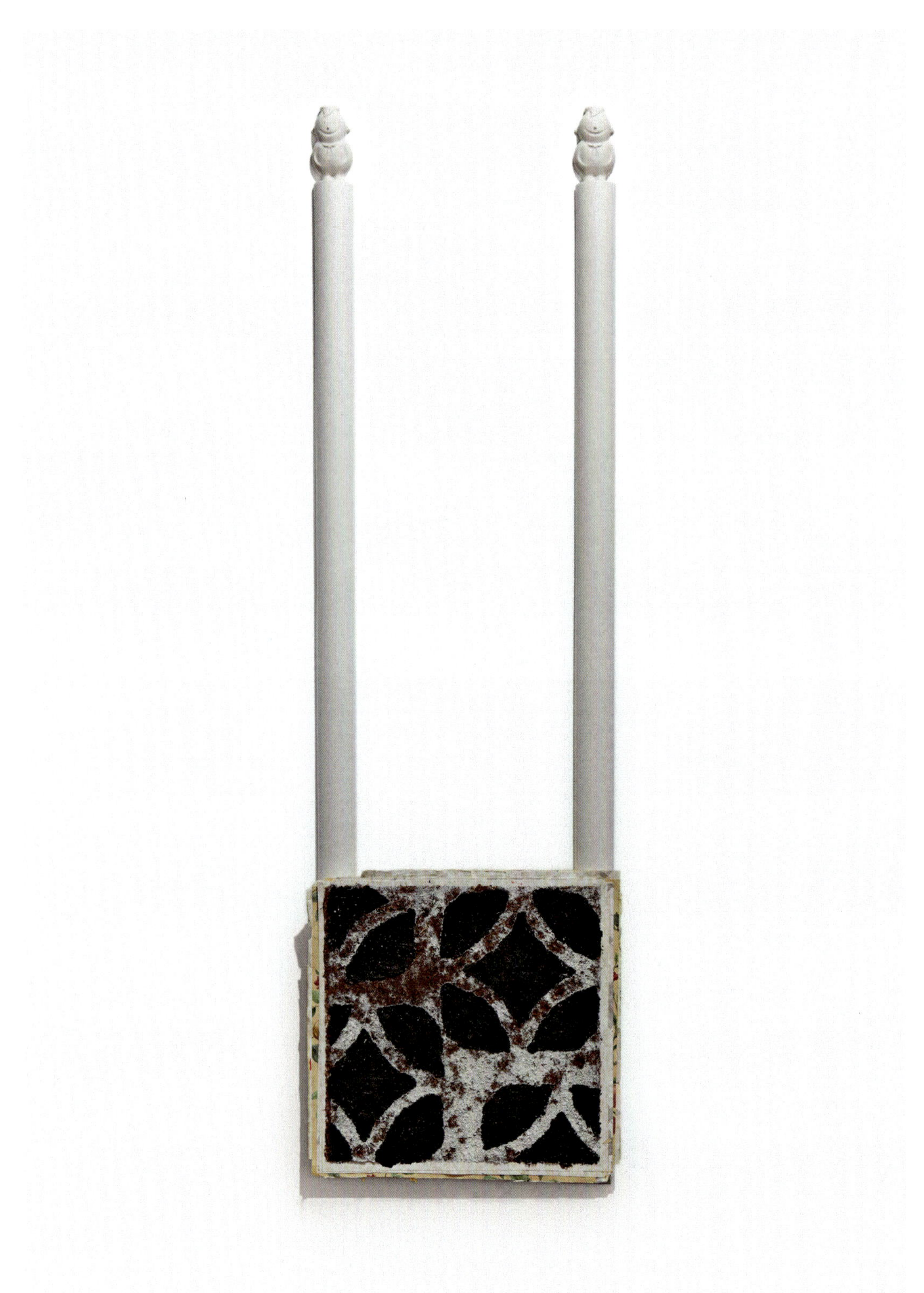

PAN'S BIKE BECAUSE THEY WANTED TO LEAVE THEIR OWN BIKES AT HOME.

Bring on the Philosophy
Ask us (the Philosophy club)
the deepest darkest Questions
But not to hard!

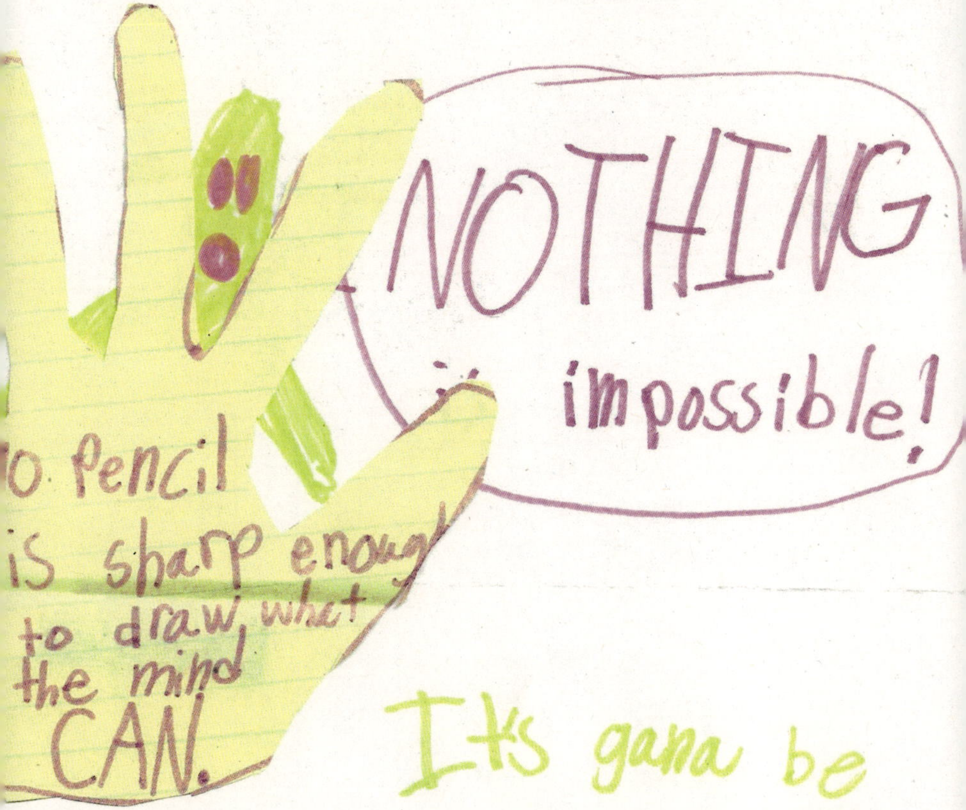

NOTHING
is impossible!

o pencil
is sharp enough
to draw what
the mind
CAN.

It's gana be
EPIC!

Philosophy has

This coul

no limits

be PHILOSOP

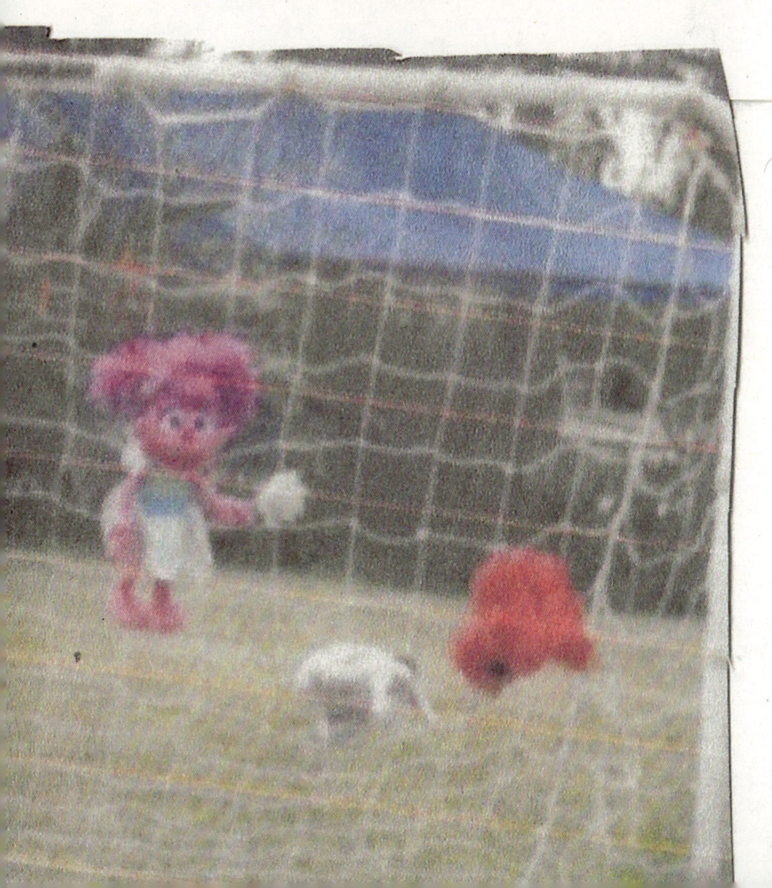

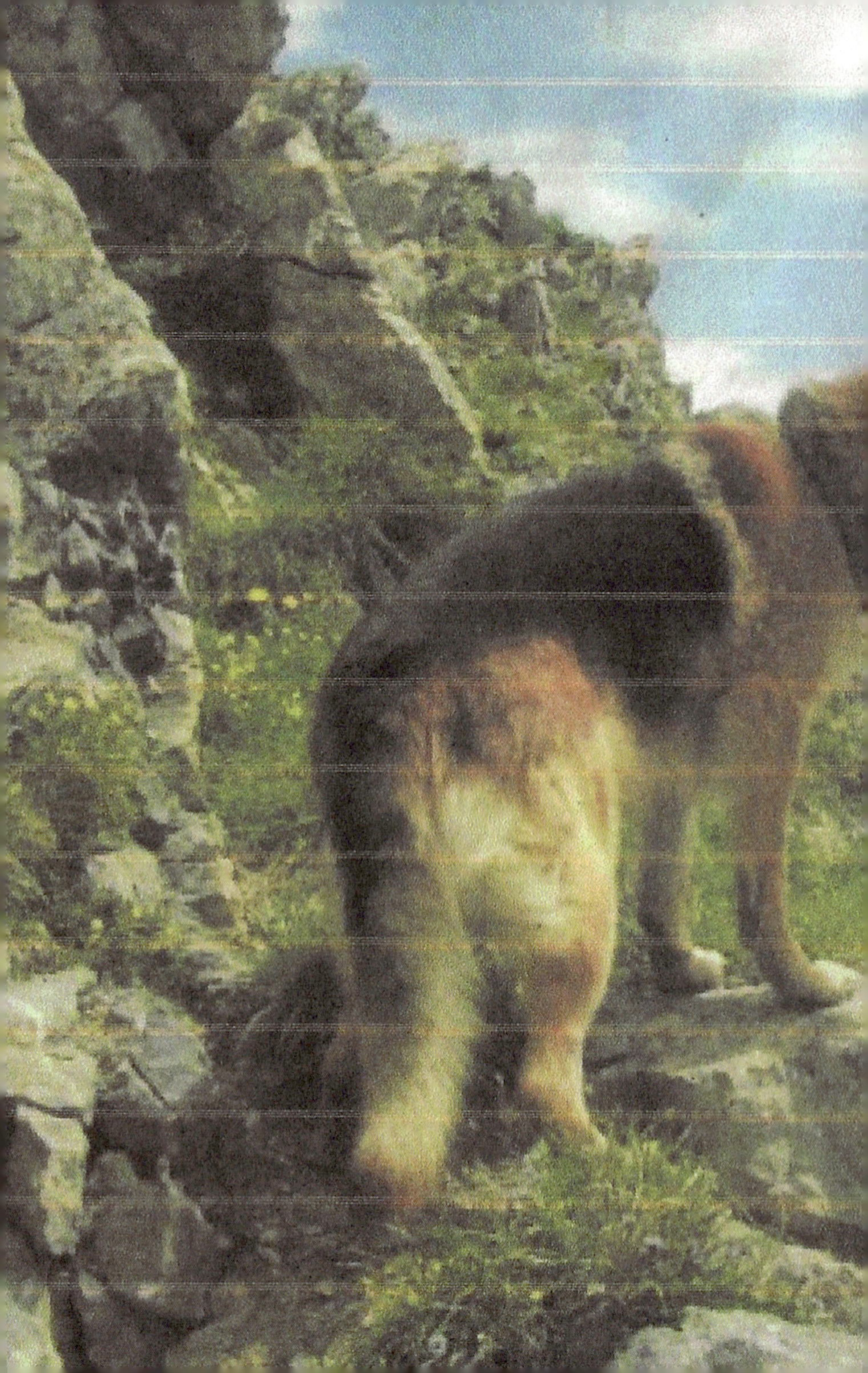

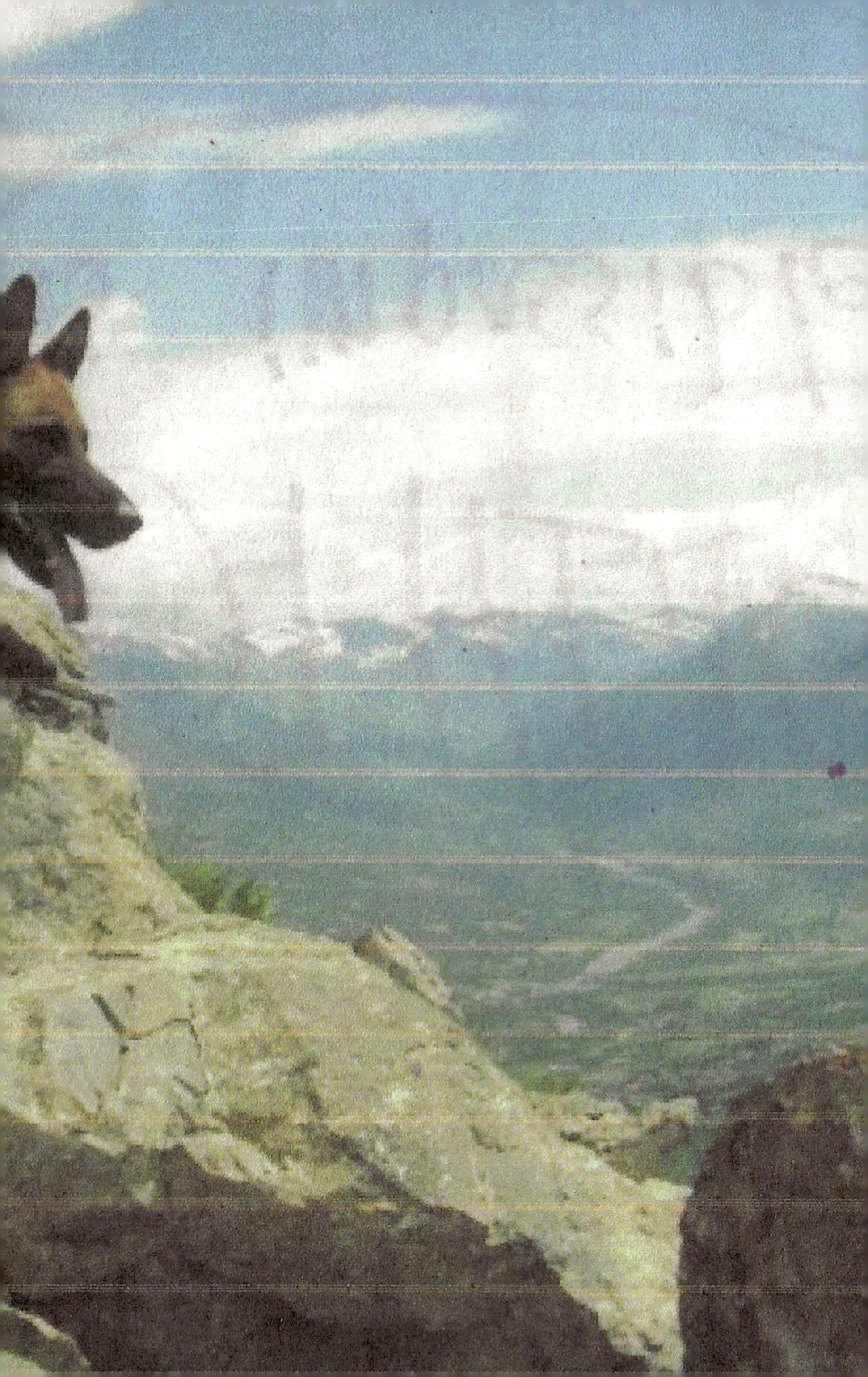

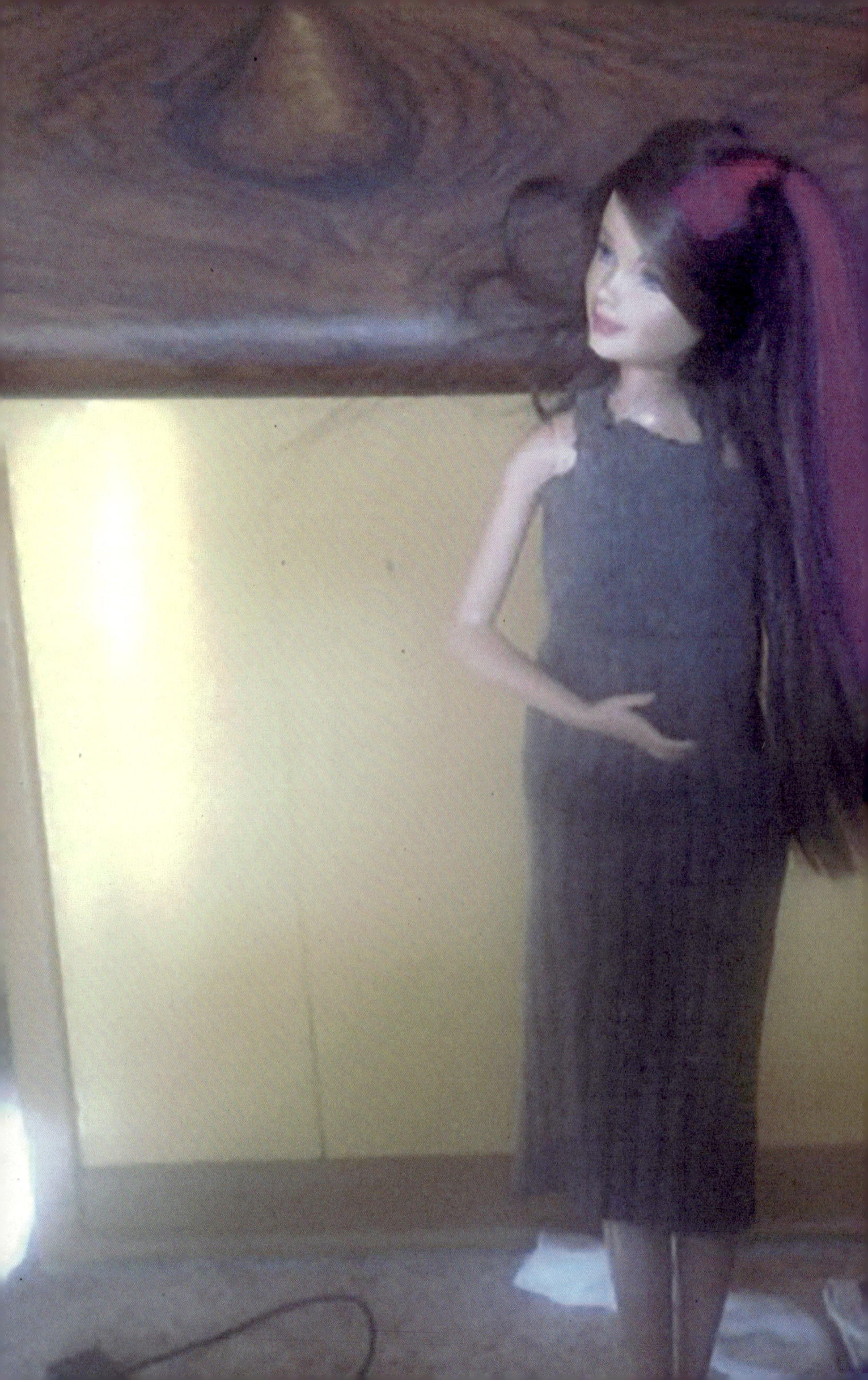

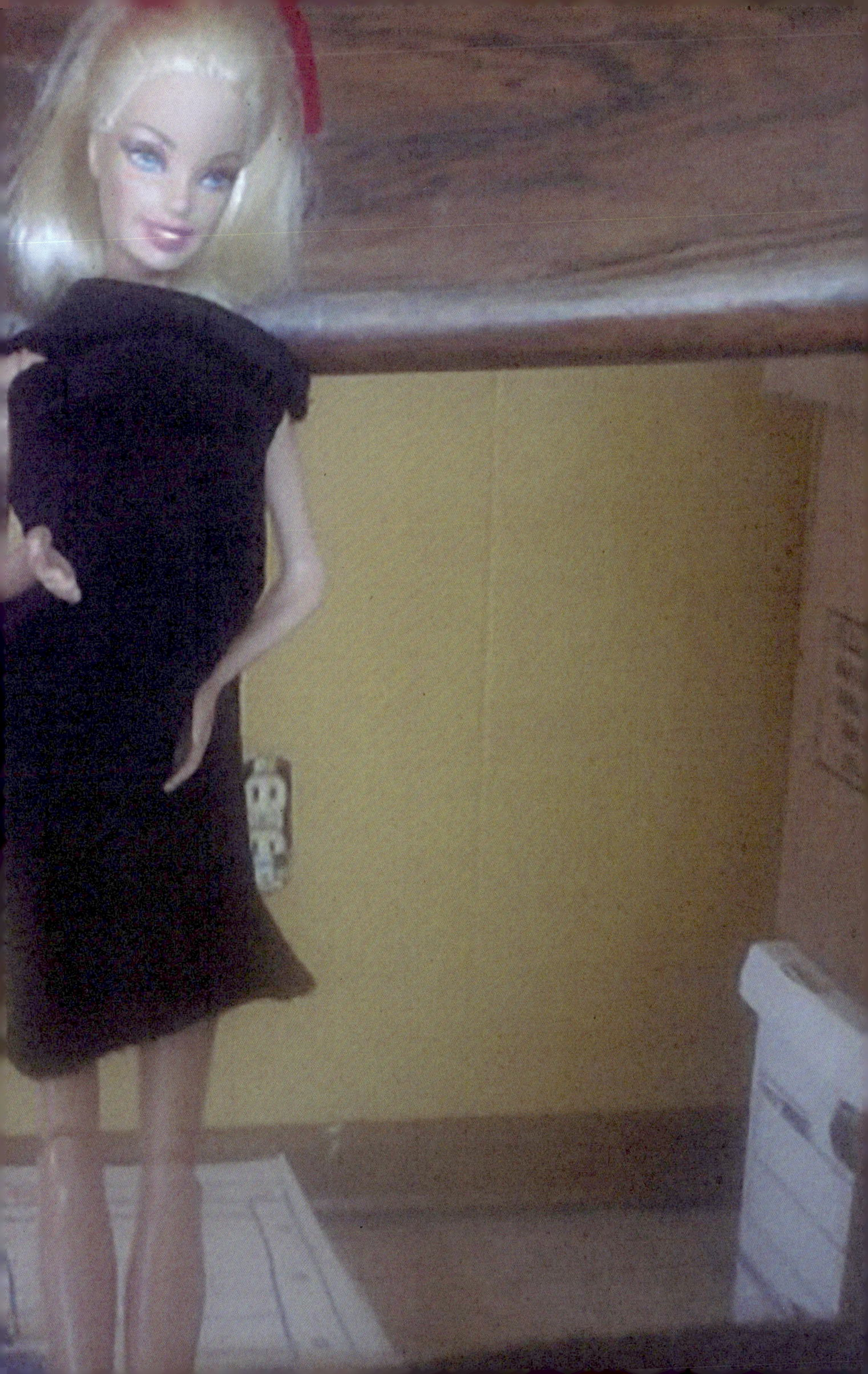

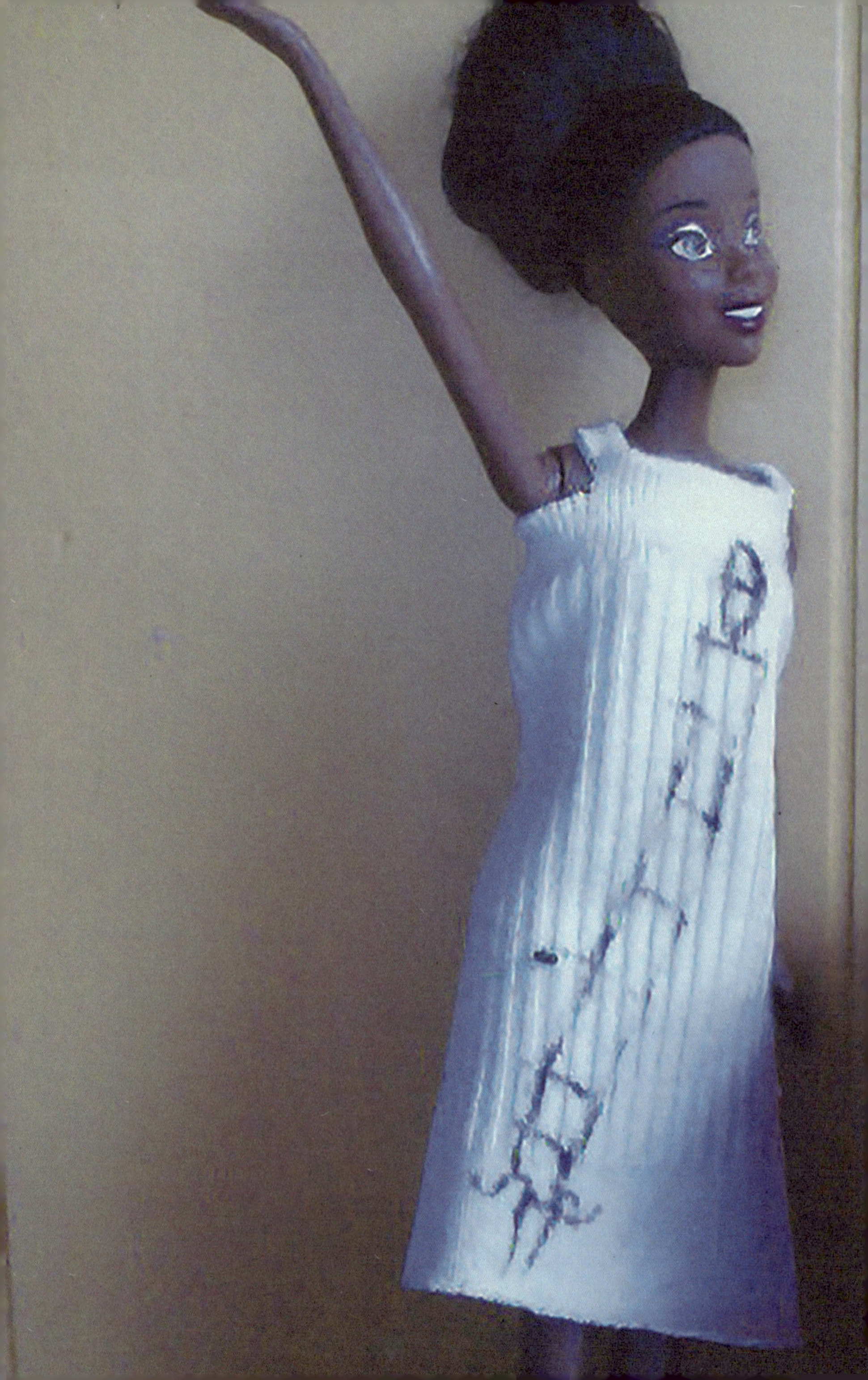

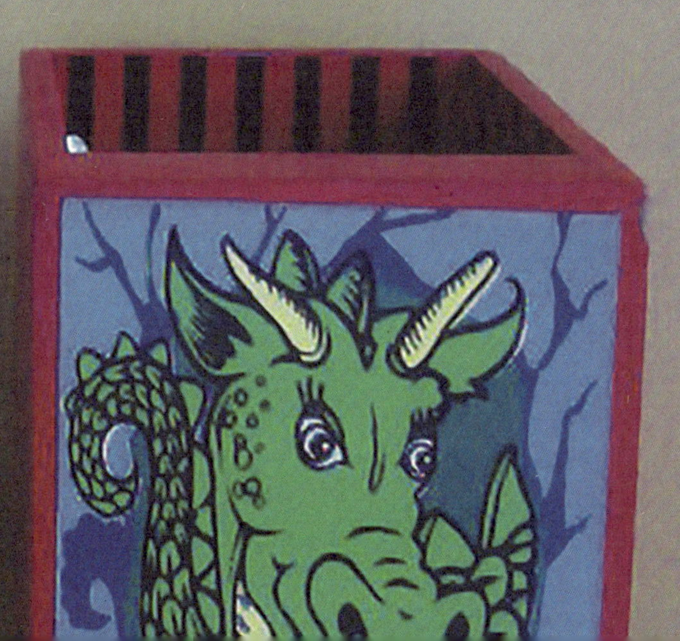

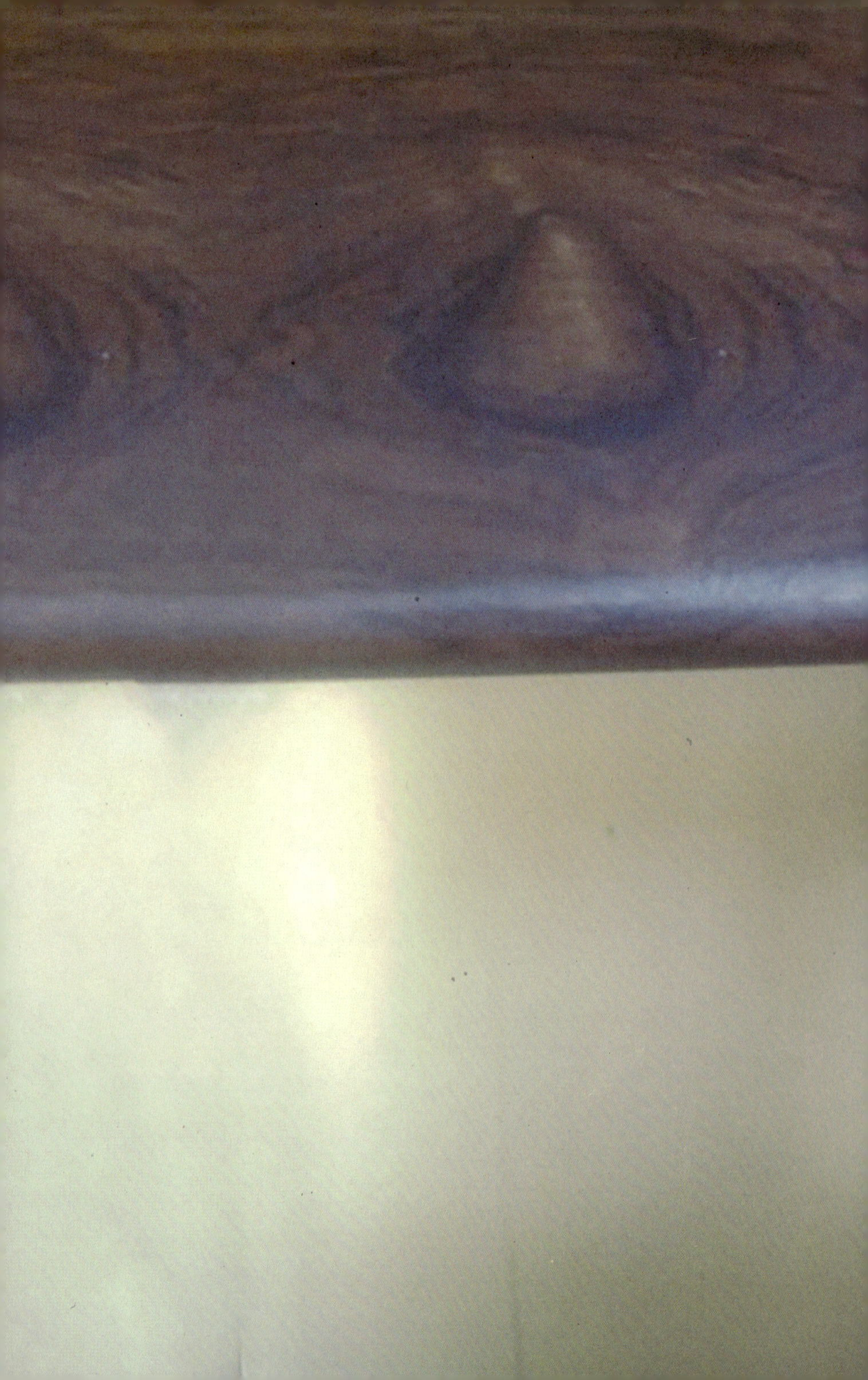

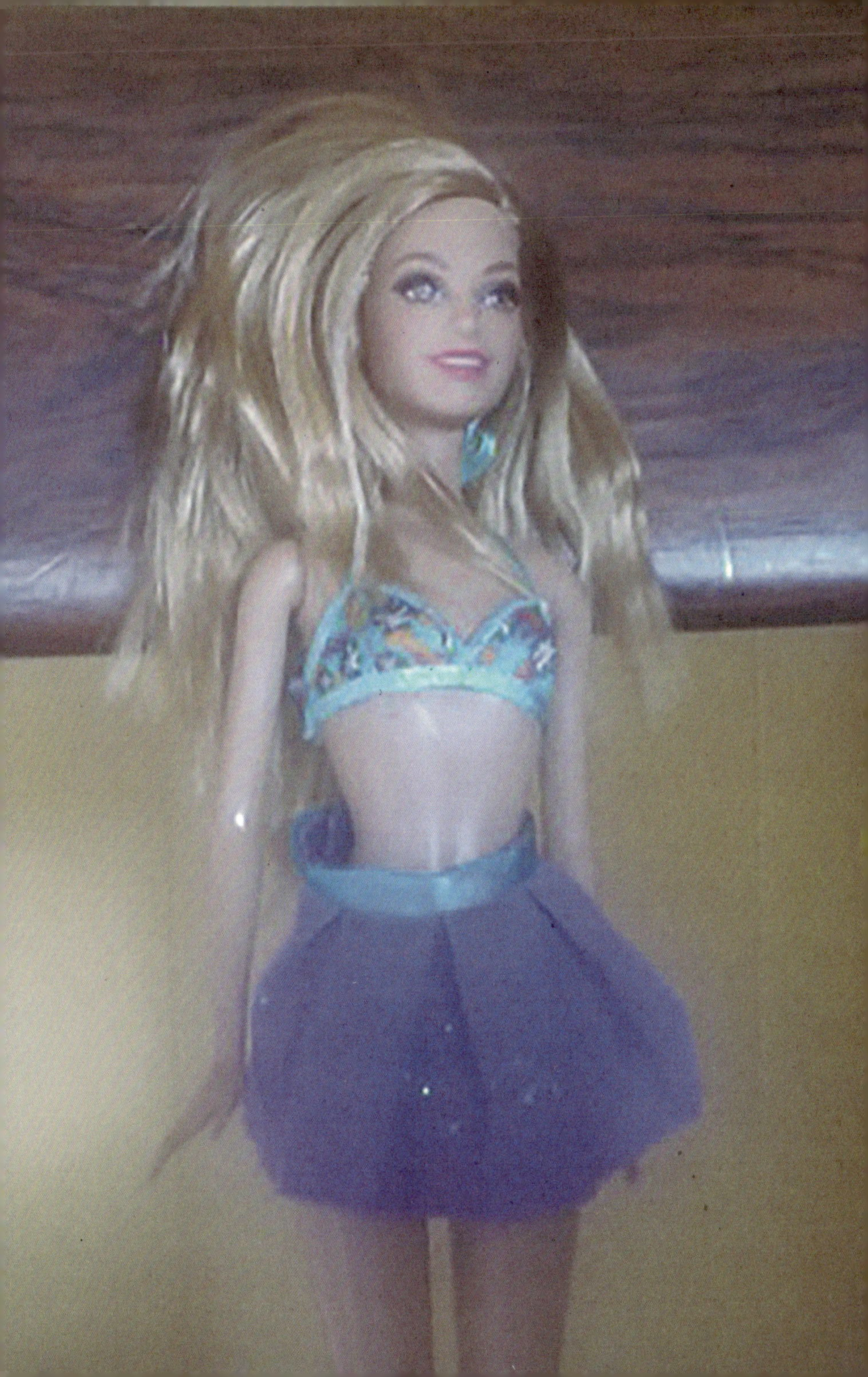

Is free will a question?

Lisa Lapinski

Artists are always trying hard to look like they have the power or right to act, speak, or think as they want without hindrance or restraint. Many, including me, seem to believe that they possess a higher form of freedom than other people by virtue of their involvement in creative acts. But the artists I know rarely appear free in their lives. Artists do represent and perform freedom for the public, in a way. Looking "free" is a big part of an artist's job description. An artist has to appear to be freer than the average person in the way porn stars have to make it seem like they enjoy sex more than the average person. But I am not sure artists are privileged human beings who get to act as they wish any more than people in other professions.

In 2003 Morgan Fisher's future wife, Margaret Honda, worked as a special collections assistant at the Getty Research Institute. My husband, Will Fowler, had the same position at that time, as did several other local artists, and I had been on the staff myself just two years earlier. The job involved fetching rare books and archival materials from the Getty's sizable vaults, carting them upstairs for visiting researchers, and discreetly watching over the reading rooms as those visitors worked. For an artist, it was the kind of job that could be exciting in that it brought you close to magical and unique items, such as Denis Diderot's *Encyclopédie,* Dieter Roth's *Poetrie,* or Clement Greenberg's love letters to Helen Frankenthaler, even if you were merely delivering these items to someone else.

One day I went to visit Will at work and noticed a man working at Margaret's desk. I saw him from behind. I stopped and considered the scene, for which I devised no explanation. After asking around I came to find out that Morgan Fisher, the experimental filmmaker and artist, came every day and worked on a film at Margaret's desk, and that he often ate lunch with Margaret and the rest of the special collections staff before returning to his work at Margaret's desk in the afternoon. At the time I wasn't sure how someone could be making a film at a desk in a library. Although amused by the scene of Morgan at the desk, I hadn't understood it. When else would you see someone working at their girlfriend's desk in the middle of her workplace without raising some eyebrows? There are rules. There is a list. The only other time I had observed something like it was when I was a teenager in the mid-1980s. If you worked the evening shift at Baskin-Robbins and your manager wasn't around, your boyfriend could come in and sit at a table and study for your entire shift. Morgan working on his film at Margaret's work desk felt like that to me. Morgan has a polish and sophistication that make him seem more adult than most people, and a manner that feels like it belongs to a more adult period of history, but he was exhibiting a kind of freedom I had only experienced in my youth. I thought about Morgan at that desk many times, years after seeing him there, often at moments when I felt trapped as an artist.

Morgan seemed to me freer than your average citizen. He seemed like David Hammons or Cady Noland, artists who have made unexpected career choices and whose lives appear not only to be unencumbered by the demands of a professional art world, but to call those demands into question. As I got to know Morgan better, I came to believe he was freer than either of them: he seemed less self-conscious. His freedom was less performed, like it wasn't being presented as his work to be bought and sold by the art world. If someone spoke about freedom in the abstract, which does not happen often, I would automatically picture Morgan at that desk at the Getty. At a certain point, that image became a symbol for freedom, replacing in my mind Peter Fonda and Dennis Hopper riding their motorcycles on the open road in *Easy Rider*. Jack Nicholson is now standing in the Getty, looking down at a seated Morgan Fisher: "They're scared of what you represent to them ... What you represent to them is freedom. That's what it's all about but talking about it and being it—that's two different things. They're gonna talk to you and talk to you and talk to you about individual freedom, but if they see a free individual, it's gonna scare 'em."

The film Morgan was making at Margaret's desk was *( )*.

Morgan hadn't made a film for nineteen years when he made *( )* in 2003. He made sixteen films between 1968 and 1984 and then took an almost two-decade break from filmmaking. He made other kinds of artwork, but he didn't make films. To make *( )*, Morgan bought 16 mm prints of commercial films. This, among other things, was what he was doing at Margaret's desk. *( )* begins with a left parenthesis, white on a black background, and ends with a right parenthesis. In between is a succession of insert shots culled from narrative films rescued from the resale bins of eBay. Most inserts are considered cinematically unexceptional. Morgan has explained that "directors hate them—they can be really ugly, they can disrupt the rhythm of the film—but at the same time the narrative has to be clear ... sometimes they are not even made by directors."[1] When the leading man reaches for something—a wallet? a gun? a glass of water?—and the leading lady follows his reach with her eyes, how is one to know what she sees in his hand? The insert shot provides the crucial information. According to Morgan, the inserts are servants, doing the invisible drudge work of narrative film. There have been inserts that made a star turn, with elegance, such as Stanley Kubrick's shot of the ax in Scatman Crothers's death scene in *The Shining*. Most are inconsequential in themselves, ushering one moment to the next.

Morgan removed the inserts from all the different prints—he seemed to have purchased mostly films from the 1950s and 1960s—and organized them based on a secret rule that makes it seem like there was no rule at all. It is important that his method not be understood as a form of editing. In *( )* we watch one unedited shot after another. If we find ourselves making connections between shots, it is impossible to maintain our belief in those connections for very long over the course of the film. Not only can we not form a new narrative in the absence of temporal markings—we cannot deduce how the shots fit into their original films. The integrity of their original narratives perhaps remains intact in some other realm, but those stories mean nothing in *( )*. As narrative causality and unbroken action slip away from us, we are at first disconcerted—it is jarring to watch 372 individual unlinked shots—and then our only recourse is to take in each and every shot as a thing in itself. This is paradoxically both sobering and delightful.

The online *Stanford Encyclopedia of Philosophy* tells us: "The term 'free will' has emerged over the past two millennia as the canonical designator for a significant kind of control over one's actions."[2] Morgan wishes to free the hardworking, underappreciated, and apparently run-of-the-mill insert shot from the uninspired menial labor it performs for creative narrativity. He uses the words "servitude" and "instrumentality" in relation to its plight.[3] His language is indebted to both the 1970s conceptual artists, who implemented rules to free themselves from personal subjectivity, and the Depression-era photographers, who wanted to make the unseen seen.

When my daughter Nina was nine years old, Morgan mailed her three questions. They were not unsolicited. After a mother-daughter study session on a boring day without TV, Nina formed a "philosophy club" with her Barbie dolls and announced that they would answer questions for the uninitiated. She designed a foldout pamphlet that read like a motivational poster in an elementary school classroom. Above a photograph of her stuffed animals suspended in the netting of a soccer goal it said, "Philosophy Has No Limits. This Could Be Philosophy." Inside it said, "Bring on the Philosophy! Ask us (the philosophy club) the deepest darkest questions. But not too hard! Nothing is impossible." The philosophy club was meant to be a moneymaking enterprise, but no one actually sent her any questions, except for Morgan, who sent her this in the mail: Is free will a question for philosophy? If it is, does everyone have free will? And if they do, do they all have it in equal measure, or do some people have more of it than others?

What struck me first, what I found kind, touching, and remarkable, was that he started by asking her to consider the boundaries of the discipline. Is free will a question for philosophy? Free will is *the* question in philosophy, so to ask if it falls in philosophy's purview sounds funny to adult ears. But in a gentle manner he suggests to a nine-year-old that she should be concerned with whether this is a concern of hers. What exactly is this new role of philosopher she is trying on with such lightness of touch and with so little forethought? But it is phrased in a way that doesn't question that she has done it. His questions also suggest other questions to a child. If philosophy is not dealing with free will, what is? And if philosophy is not dealing with this free will, then why? Is it that philosophy is too good for free will? To a child and to us, some questions seem to be beneath this elevated branch of knowledge—philosophy might not bother with free will just like it doesn't bother with a lot of things—but no questions seem to be above it.

Then, curiously, Morgan's next question is not "Is there free will?" or even "Does free will exist?" or "Is free will an illusion?" Instead, he asks Nina whether we might measure free will in individuals. Again, these questions suggest further areas of inquiry for Nina and her Barbies. Are there some people whose free will measures zero? Do some individuals have noticeably more free will than others? Is this a fluctuating number within the individuals? Is free will stored up in free will coffers, so to speak, to be spent in the future? How exactly might we lose our free will? If we are measuring it, its length and width and depth, could we therefore speak of it having a shape?

If neurologist Sam Harris were a member of the philosophy club, he might have responded with: "Dear Customer, Thank you for your query. We regret to inform you, Mr. Fisher, that no one has control over their own actions. Free will is an illusion. Our wills are simply not of our own making. Thoughts and intentions emerge from background causes of which we are unaware and over which we exert no conscious control." But Morgan's questions seem to be asking for a different kind of analysis, one that assumes self-control is a real phenomenon. He asks the club to make a comparison that requires, in part, a quantitative analysis of control. The club's hasty answer begins by asking the question Morgan does not: "Does mankind have free will?"

Drunk Hawking by the philosophy club

Yes, definitely. Many philosophers have pondered over the question "Does mankind have freewill?"

Everyone has freewill even people in jail. Imagine you were in a jail cell. We usually think of freewill in relation to rules. You would think we don't have freewill because of all the laws and rules. But freewill is not an absence of being controlled by laws and rules. They are unrelated. People in jail have freewill. They can do whatever they want to do. They can knock their jail mate out. They can pick the lock on their jail cell or they can break out and go mess with the vending machines for the prison guards. It is totally their decision.

Imagine Stephen Hawking. You know who he is. If you don't, look him up in National Geographic. *He is completely paralyzed, but he still has freewill of mind. He technically proved that aliens probably exist. Even though his mind has no control over his body, he is one of the greatest people living on the planet.*

The only example of someone without freewill is someone who is drunk. Imagine you walk into a bar and you see a man and he is holding a giant bottle of Santo beer. He is banging things, including the bartender's head, against the table and acting like a mad monkey. He has no freewill over what he is doing because he is drunk and his mind has gone completely haywire. (P.S. Do not try this at home.)

In conclusion, everyone—no matter where you are or when you are—has freewill except when you are drunk. If you can think of any other examples of not having free will, please send them in!

Barbie Philosophy Club mission statement: We are a group of people who like philosophy and want the world to have philosophy. We answer the questions of the world. The prices have gone up because no one wants philosophy today. We realize this is against supply and demand. Mrs. Graeve would be so mad if she heard about this.

Both Nina and Morgan present us with characters who have varying levels of control over their own actions. Nina's cast includes the Drunk, the Prisoner, the Guard, and Stephen Hawking. Morgan's are the Insert, the Projectionist, the Actor, the Director, and the Naked Lady.[4] Nina and Morgan have similar ideas about what kind of people have lost their free will. For both of them, the opposite of free will is not responsibility but the loss of control over one's faculties or behavior. Nina's example of someone who is less self-determined is a drunk who has gone on a violent rampage. The Drunk has willingly relinquished control over his own actions to Santo beer and, in doing so, no longer has the power or ability to act otherwise. For Morgan, it is the conventional film-viewing audience that has lost its self-possession: "The power films have over us is to deprive us of our will; films hypnotize us. The film system which we are meant not to see fascinates me, and I imagine other people too; and films, what the film system produces for us to look at, hypnotize us. Being fascinated and being hypnotized are two aspects of the same thing: helplessness." In the same interview, he returns to this idea: "It produces something that has the power to hypnotize people, and ... this is a power that people willingly submit to."[5] The viewing audience is helpless, having been placed in a hypnotic trance by invisible narrative techniques. Although Nina's example of unfreedom is wild and aggressive and Morgan's is a sleepy hypnotic state, they are not so far apart from each other. Both the Drunk and the Audience are in states of extreme suggestibility, having given up their autonomy in exchange for a good time.

The Drunk will sober up over time and regain control over his actions. He might be arrested for assault. The courts (hopefully) will hold him responsible for banging the bartender's head against the table. Morgan, on the other hand, wants to help the film audience resist the hypnotic trance by taking narrativity's devices as a subject: "One way to treat a film system as a subject is to make it visible, and that is what most of my films do, mainly by documenting their own production, or at least making them aware of the moment of their production."[6] The insert is a short shot that is intended to be totally and firmly legible and lead the audience from one narrative point to the next. *( )* doesn't have any of those fixed points. The audience tries to draw relationships between the images, but they slide by quickly and become a soundless menagerie of elusive meaning. The audience apprehends each shot with heightened attention but is simultaneously left in a state of suspension. Watching *( )*, the audience is being sobered up very quickly, while never quite achieving such a state.

Nina seems to think humans, as long as they are not drunk, possess radical freedom of choice and action even when subjected to extremely restrictive external conditions. She does not understand freedom as the absence of barriers, obstacles, and constraints—what philosophers call "negative liberty." She seems more like an existentialist. What she describes almost sounds like Sartre's concept of radical freedom, in which everyone has a choice and every act is a free act. To return to Nina's characters, both the Prisoner and Stephen Hawking are given as examples of people transcending the facticity of their individual situations. Hawking might have ALS, which is slowly paralyzing him over decades, but he can still practice science and test the limits of his mind. The Prisoner might be locked up in jail, but he can choose to attack his cellmate. Nina's Prisoner is like Sartre's Hikers, who, stuck on a path blocked by a boulder, may believe they have no choice but to turn back. The Hikers could still choose any number of actions: they could study the boulder, they could lick the boulder, they could talk to the boulder, they could throw themselves off the mountain. For Nina, free will is the exercise of radical choice when under the inevitable control of limiting conditions (or facticity, in Sartre's terminology).

Morgan also seems to have little time for the idea of negative liberty. He might be in agreement with the philosophy club's claim: "You would think we don't have free will because of all the laws and rules. But free will is not an absence of being controlled by laws and rules." But Nina's and Morgan's reasons for not believing in negative freedom are different. For Morgan, the constraints that rules put on us do not take away our liberty. They can be a vehicle for freeing ourselves from a world of rampant self-expression and subjectivity in art production. Morgan sees self-expression as indulgence and wonders why anyone would care about it: "I can't explain how it happened. Somehow it did, despite my dubious taste as a kid, when for example, I liked German expressionism. I loved Pollock, but at a time when it was thought, wrongly as we now know, that he was expressing his inner turmoil. Expressionism is tedious because it expresses the self. Why should anyone care? From the beginning, my work was against self-expression, against expressionism."[7] Rules, whether secret or broadcast, allow an artist to construct a work of art rather than compose it, the latter being a personal, subjective, and altogether suspect act. Construction is not simply the building of something. Construction in Morgan's world is the making of something through the issuance and execution of rules as a deprograming technique simultaneously directed toward the audience, artist, and actors.

In *Projection Instructions*, the Projectionist isn't in the film in the traditional sense. The film's real-life projectionist is given instructions that appear on the screen at the same time the narrator speaks them: "Turn sound off. Turn sound on. Turn lamp off. Turn lamp on. Turn volume up. Frame up ..." Each screening of the film is different, depending on who has been tasked with projecting the film. Morgan has explained that the projectionist is being given something like a score and is "free to perform the film as he or she wishes and [Morgan has] nothing to say about it." In another interview, he goes even further, saying, "It is, so to speak, an objective film, one that gives the projectionist the chance to be an interpretive artist."

The audience does not necessarily see it this way. They might understand the unhappy projectionist as being unfairly controlled by the film's specifications. According to Morgan, the audience believes these simple instructions, which really don't require all that much from the projectionist, to be a serious restriction on the projectionist's free will: "I think the audience is in sympathy with the projectionist because he is perceived as being tyrannized by the film's unrelenting demands."[8] At one screening, the projectionist refused to follow the instructions, telling Morgan afterward that she didn't like being told what to do. But Morgan sees the projectionist as possessing a freedom akin to that of the interpretive artist because the instructions can be performed in different ways: "In *Projection Instructions* some instructions are binary but others are variable. The projectionist chooses how loud to make the sound, for example." So, if and when a projectionist totally refuses to obey the film's directives, it is funny that Morgan observes, "Being given the freedom to interpret was not enough." What a graceful response to the renegade projectionist.

I keep picturing nine-year-old Nina as the film's projectionist. At that age Nina would have thought the film was abstract and restrained, if not dry, but I am certain she would have found it funny, especially if she were the projectionist. She would have liked that "the piece of celluloid in the projector" was telling her what to do, and she would've liked being able to perform while hidden from the audience. The film would present all sorts of questions: How had she managed to obtain so much control over the world? What is a projectionist? What does she do? Is there really someone above the audience—in a box, almost floating—who keeps the film world in focus and running smoothly? Who is this person, why must she stay hidden, and who made it that way? This would lead to an even more important question for a child: Are there other situations like this in the world? How often do adults agree to these managed situations, these states of affairs that could be otherwise? I imagine her sparks of laughter in the booth when the words "Throw out of focus." appear on the screen.

1. Morgan Fisher, "Morgan Fisher in Conversation with Melissa Gronlund," in *Morgan Fisher: Conversations*, ed. Jacob Proctor (Aspen, CO: Aspen Art Press, 2014), 52.

2. Timothy O'Connor, "Free Will," *Stanford Encyclopedia of Philosophy*, first published Jan. 7, 2002; substantive revision Aug. 21, 2018. https://plato.stanford.edu/entries/freewill/

3. See Morgan Fisher, *( )* in *Morgan Fisher: Writings*, eds. Sabine Folie and Susanne Titz (Cologne, Germany: Verlag de Buchhandlung Walter König, 2012), pp. 71–75. First published in 2004 as a gallery note for the exhibition "Morgan Fisher. *( )* 'Film Cans and Film Boxes,'" Galerie Buchholz, Cologne, May 14–June 1, 2004.

4. Here I am referring to the films *( )* (2003), *Projectionist Instructions* (1976), *The Director and His Actor Look at Footage Showing Preparations for an Unmade Film (2)* (1968), and *Documentary Footage* (1968).

5. Morgan Fisher, "Morgan Fisher in Conversation with Jean-Philippe Antoine and Christophe Gallois," from *Morgan Fisher: Conversations*, 66, 69.

6. Ibid., 69.

7. Morgan Fisher, "Morgan Fisher in Conversation with William E. Jones," from *Morgan Fisher: Conversations*, 83.

8. Morgan Fisher, "Morgan Fisher in Conversation with Scott MacDonald," from *Morgan Fisher: Conversations*, 99.

Untitled (Tweedledee Tweedledum), 2013
Hydrocal, wood, wallpaper, tobacco, acrylic paint
19 x 60 x 2 in.
(48.3 x 152.4 x 5.1 cm)

following spread

Untitled, 2013
Candle wax, mini blind, resin, epoxy, shoe
20 x 23 x 1 in.
(50.8 x 58.4 x 2.5 cm)

Untitled, 2013
Candle wax, mini blind, resin, epoxy, shoe
20 x 23 x 1 in.
(50.8 x 58.4 x 2.5 cm)

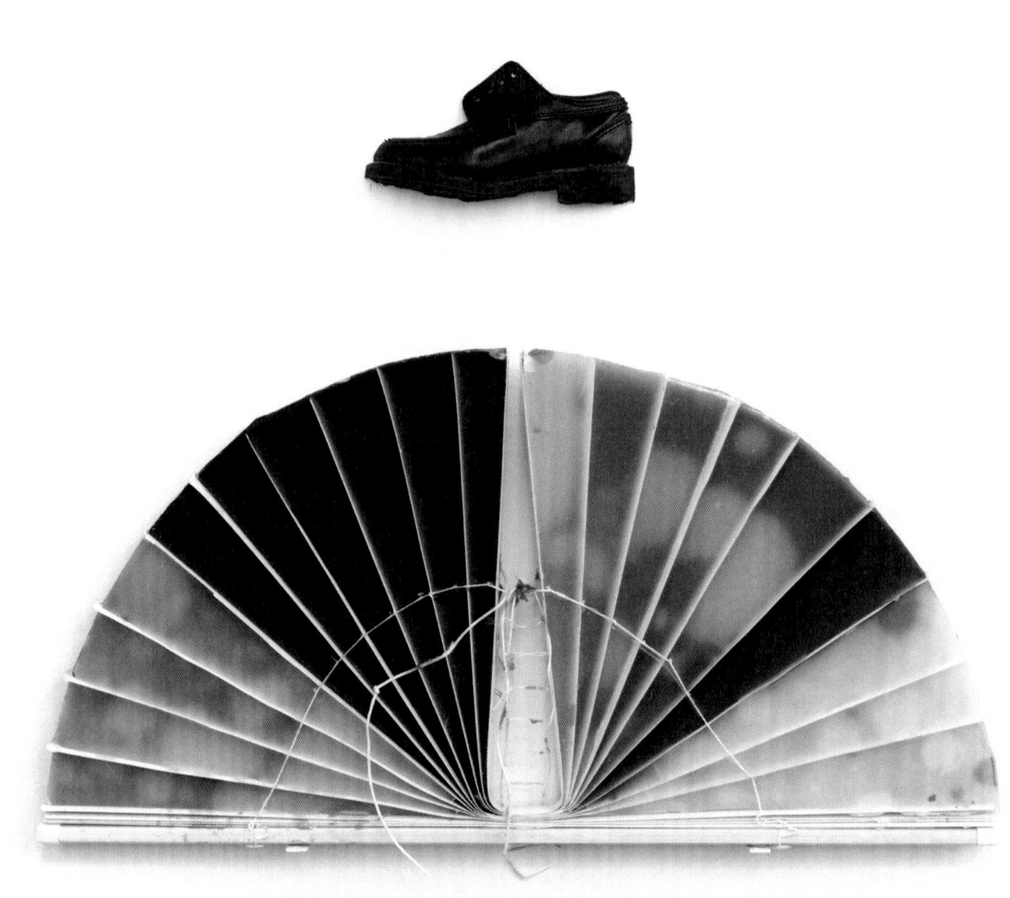

MONSTER AND COOKIE MONSTER WAS BEHIND HIM AND HE GOT SOME COOKIES.

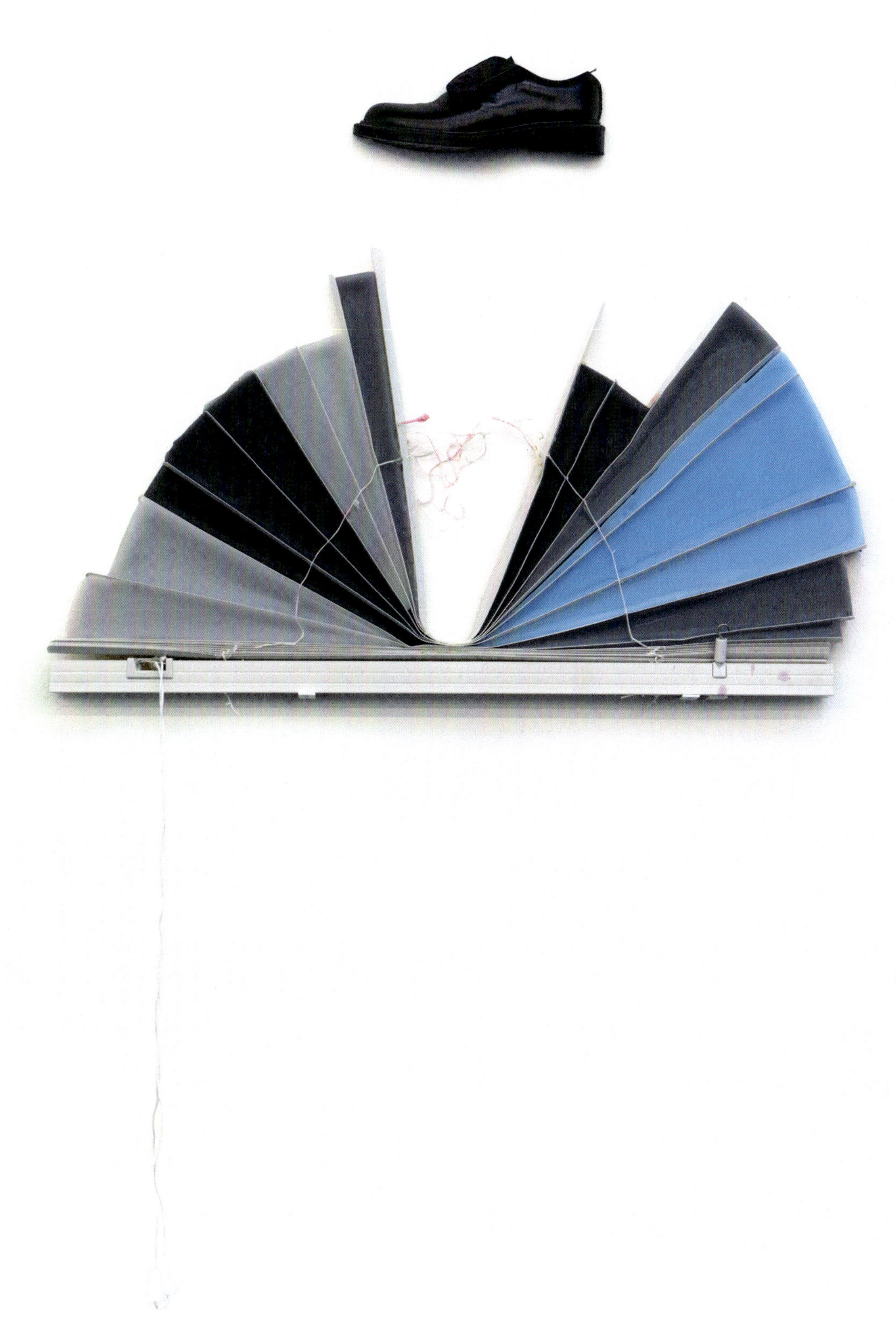

ULLED THEM OUT OF PETER PAN'S OVEN. THEN WENDY WENT TO THE GROCERY

STORE TO BUY SOME PICKLES. WHEN SHE GOT BACK SHE HAD A LITTLE PICK

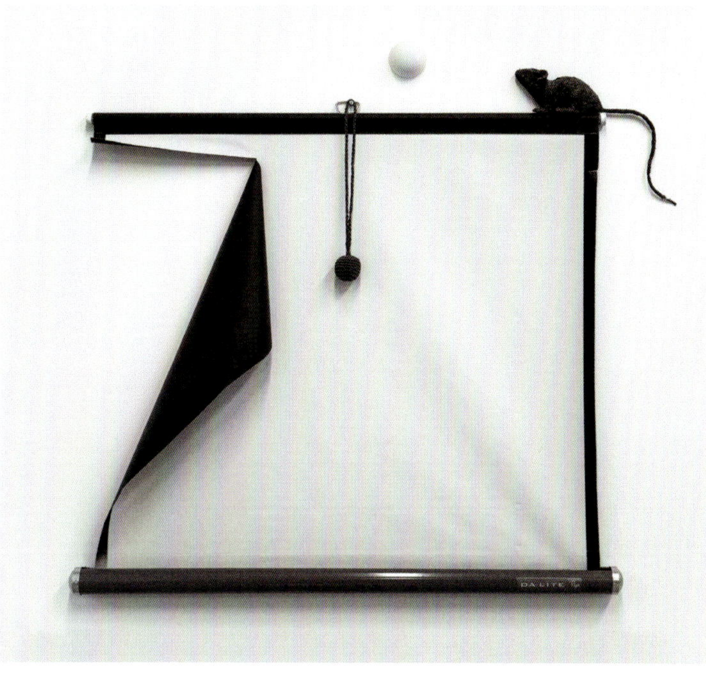

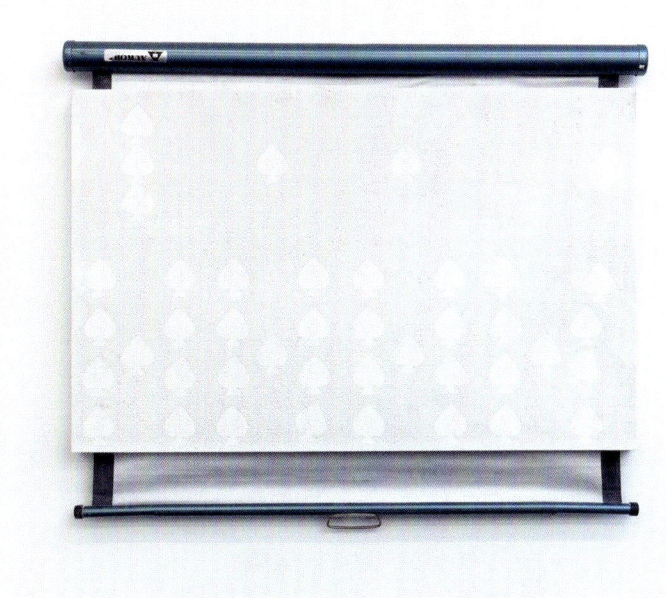

Untitled, 2013
Plaster, wood, metal
34 x 18 x 2 1/4 in. (86.4 x 45.7 x 5.7 cm)

Untitled, 2013
Black and white photograph
33 x 49 in. (83.8 x 124.5 cm)

Untitled, 2013
Plaster, wood, metal
35 x 42 x 2 1/4 in. (88.9 x 106.7 x 5.7 cm)

R THE LITTLE SISTER. NANNY WAS HOLDING THE SISTER ALL NIGHT. SHE

Kyle Dancewicz

Messenger Boys

* * *

Do Lisa Lapinski's sculptures know each other? Is that a dumb question to ask?

Since the late 1990s Lapinski has made sculptures and installations that bring handmade, altered, and reproduced objects together in apparent conversation. Critics who have written on her exhibitions have often imagined that their disparate elements are arranged with some kind of syntax in mind, speaking to each other and the viewer in "an extremely protracted and complicated form of address."[1] But given their stillness, their muteness, their blank stares and expressionless or absent faces, eavesdropping on the conversation between Lapinski's sculptures seems less important than envisioning the structure that determines who can talk to whom, on what terms, and with what vocabulary.

Writing on Haim Steinbach for a catalogue in 2008, Lapinski borrows from Hegel to describe the way that Steinbach's shelves and rows of objects work: "Appearance is not a realm where difference is constant, but one where equals become unequal and unequals become equal (necessarily); and this structure of appearance is the structure of the object that appears."[2] Avoiding a more conventional reading of Steinbach's work as commodity sculpture, or as social history lessons activated by objects on display, Lapinski instead tries to understand what is happening when one object is put next to another, and the two are thought together and thought apart at the same time.

Lapinski's work functions in an expanded field of prepositions, exploding "next to" across space and time. It outlines a realm of appearance filled with sculptures whose forms and titles often reference popular fictional characters, but not the *most* popular fictional characters. She is not concerned with producing an appropriated, off-brand Mickey Mouse, for example, but rather with exercising the floating personas and commercial forms of his lesser-known cousins in a cultural imaginary that is broader, more porous, and less proprietary than Disney's commercial enterprise allows.

Recently, Lapinski's work has invoked the spirit of Little My (1950–), a supporting character from Tove Jansson's (1914–2001) Finnish-Swedish Moomin fairytales, first published as novels in the 1940s. Outside of the United States, Little My and other characters from the Moomin franchise enjoy some degree of ubiquity. Little My, a scowling girl with a crimson hairdo, features on countless products, including a child's chair where her head and torso form the backrest. In Lapinski's *Little My Chair 2* (2011), Little My appears compromised, her stern, ageless face and upper body cut out and replaced with tightly stretched chair caning. Similarly, *Little My Chair #3* (2017) excises Little My's expressive face, using the resulting hole to hang the figure from a modified Shaker peg board on the wall. Throughout Lapinski's work, semi-famous figures like Little My stand in for themselves, but also for the ways in which their identifiable characteristics are chopped up, distributed, and received.

Together, in exhibitions, Little My and other characters meet each other on neutral ground at different phases in their respective processes of dissemination and brand extension. Like Little My, they may enter as reupholstered, almost-found objects, imported into the exhibition from foreign contexts after some heavy, often craft-based altering. They may also be handmade avatars, partial and unrecognizable, as though appearing in a different aspect of their being. In this category, *Tobacco Camel* (2010) is a simplified camel form coated in tobacco shavings. It is a plusher version of Camel's flat cigarette carton logo, but it is not Joe Camel (1987–1997), an attractive, bipedal cartoon camel who appeared as the company's mascot until 1997, when the Federal Trade Commission banished him for appealing too much to minors.[3] Lapinski's sculpture reverts away from the personified, sexualized dromedary, favoring instead an uncanny material affinity between Camel's product and the shaggy, matted hair evoked by the company's name.

Through a related process, *Holly Hobby Lobby Bow #1* (2017), an angular upright ribbon bow form made of wood and a skin of matte black paint, stands in for Holly Hobbie (late 1960s–), a frontier-girl character who appeared in figurines, stationery, and other items that might be found in a greeting card store. In another life Holly Hobbie could have grown up to become an American Girl doll, or even a Disney princess. In Lapinski's sculpture, by unfortunate contrast, Holly's star fades and she emerges in an abstracted, woodworked form, nominally serving as an ambassador for Hobby Lobby, the conservative Christian craft store empire that won the right to deny its employees reproductive health benefits and smuggled 5,500 looted religious artifacts from Iraq. Such is the fate of Holly Hobby, née Hobbie, to collect the scraps of her pioneer attitude and attend to a new, hardened constituency as time moves on.

That Little My, the spirit of Joe Camel, and Holly Hobbie can somehow all exist together in their various deformations, "next to" each other but fragmented and emotionally "beside themselves," so to speak, represents two related registers of appearance functioning in Lapinski's work. Both are marked by desperation. One register senses the processes of dissolution and reconstitution that have resulted, for example, in Little My's debased yet ergonomic form as a little chair.[4] The other tries to string such alienated objects together with tenuous narrative and imagined relations. Together they might behave as a diagram, which, as another artist recently described, is something that "creates a certain dynamic that can be seen as a form. It is not something that follows. It is a machine that is producing something different than itself as part of itself, something that is different each time a repetition occurs."[5] In Lapinski's hands, the diagram is a condition that feels like a crossover special, or an expanded universe, as in the popular branding and content production phenomenon that allows for certain comic book characters to break off into their own side stories. It can also result in the jarring revelation that two separate cinematic worlds are actually the same world, where previously unrelated characters pass seamlessly into and out of each other's lives without much concern for their own histories.

This is not to say that Lapinski is particularly interested in visualizing the commercial machinations of intellectual property or licensing. A higher dimension of her work is concerned with the splintered integrity of characters, objects, and styles as they appear in the present: ubiquitous and severed from their original referents. She engages, for example, with the illustrator Patrick Nagel (1945–1984). In *Th th th th th Snow White* (2010), a series of paintings installed in freestanding shadow boxes framed by a perimeter of concrete breeze blocks, Lapinski reproduces paintings of bikini-clad women realized, probably without direct referent, in the style of

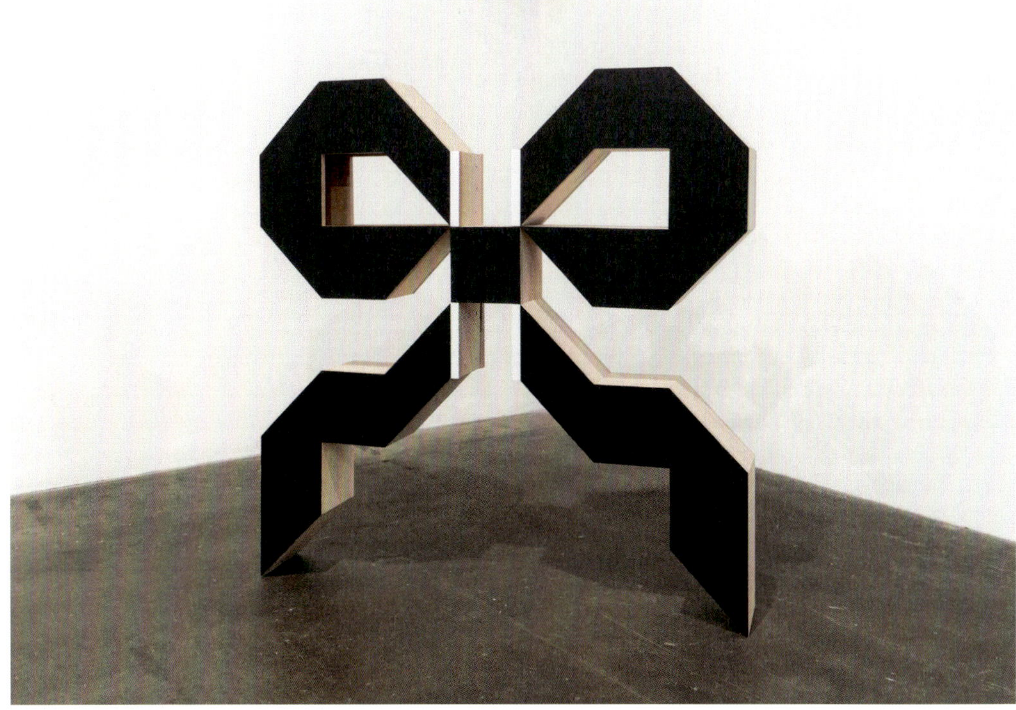

Lisa Lapinski, *Holly Hobby Lobby Bow #1*, 2016. Wood and paint. 49 x 49 x 7 in. (124.5 x 124.5 x 17.8 cm).

HEM ON THE PAVEMENT. (DID THE SISTER GET HURT?) NO, SHE WAS STANDING

Nagel, "the most successful & anonymous American artist of the 1980s."[6] Nagel, like other figures who appear in Lapinski's work, is iconic, but few viewers are likely to make the attribution. Tellingly, Lapinski's paintings aren't copies of Nagel's unnamable works, but instead reproductions of paintings that decorated the windows of a strip mall in Altadena. Nagel's off-iconicity comes back around as ubiquity. History forgets his particular position while his graphic formal tropes, sharply reduced facial features, and bleached-out skins define 1980s popular erotics. Nagel reaches a "higher power of generic style called existence," a diagnosis also worked out in Lapinski's writing on Haim Steinbach, objects, and appearance.[7]

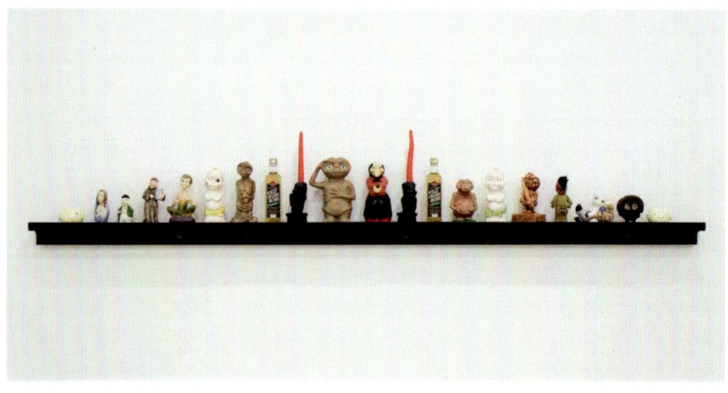

Mike Kelley, *The Allen Ruppersberg, Patrick Painter, Dave Muller, Janese Weingarten, Mike Kelley, Cameron Jamie, Sasha Freedman, Amy Wong, Mary Clare Stevens, Overduin and Kite, Haim Steinbach, Lisa Lapinski Shelf*, 2008. 15 x 95 x 5 in. (38.1 x 241.3 x 12.7 cm).

A sculpture like *Nightstand* (2005) forwards a dynamic of style and ubiquity as well but directs its energies at the textures and aesthetic imperatives of modernism and other standardizing forces. At its core is an assortment of painstakingly handmade Shaker-style sewing chests, all of which serve as pedestals for caned screens, a jewelry display hand, a crystal vase with feathers, and photographs of Art Deco birds by artist Gustave Miklos (1888–1967), another achiever of the "higher power of generic style" that has turned out to be modernist sculpture. *Nightstand* recounts the sweep of early American design into mid-century mass market, entangling legacies of craft practices and industrial aesthetics, all uttered in one breath. The sculpture itself explodes into a mess of parts with its drawers opened and emptied out. The exposed drawers of *Nightstand* perform a constant swing between expression, expressing expression, and expressionlessness in Lapinski's work: it's an exasperated, ecstatic gesture (or gasp) that yields nothing inside, only more on top. Alongside the perverse joy of edging up to Lapinski's work with sympathy or pity for her spiraling subjects, there is a greater and more perverse seduction in doubting that any object, character, image can convey anything about its own "object history," as if it might have nothing to express but an object present, or the mere fact of itself.

There is always a fidgety question to be asked of Lapinski's work. What do all of these people and things have to do with each other? Are Little My, Holly Hobbie, and Snow White (1812–) all on the same page? Maybe a better question to ask is: what kind of familiarity is Lapinski's work about? Generic familiarity like the Miklos birds in *Nightstand*, or the barely legible painting of a skeleton-witch trudging through a swamp perched above them, which looks like a German painting but is actually modeled on a blown-up textile pattern? Or familiar within the idiosyncratic suspension of disbelief that requires Holly Hobbie to appear as a knotted ribbon with an Atariesque silhouette in order for her to communicate with Little My about different expectations for young women in Scandinavia and New England, or whatever else they have in common.

Appearance, Lapinski's work shows, is not pure and direct, nor is it completely structured by external forces of economics, aesthetics, or otherwise. Instead, her work trades in complex, extended interactions of misidentification, misremembering, tracing the intricacies of influence, offshoots, affinities, productive and unproductive associations, false morphological comparisons, dead ends of interpretation, and revised assessments. It picks apart the world to figure out if things are becoming more different or more the same. They definitely know what they've been through, but do Lisa Lapinski's sculptures really know each other? The only work in *Lisa Lapinski: Drunk Hawking* that actually speaks says: "What do you think I am, a messenger boy?"[8]

UP ON THE PAVEMENT. GRAMPY WAS HOLDING BRONS. HE PUT A LITTLE CHAI

1. Giovanni Intra, "Lisa Lapinski: Sculpturicide," *Artext* 76 (Spring 2002), 50–55.

2. Lisa Lapinski, "Raider's Blanket," in *Special Project: Mr. Peanut, Haim Steinbach on Mike Kelley* (Los Angeles: Overduin and Kite, 2008), 17. In an essay on a Steinbach-esque work in a guest bedroom in Mike Kelley's house, Lapinski references part of Hegel's distinction between appearance and essence.

3. Joe Cool typically dresses up in a tuxedo or dresses down in a brown leather jacket and jeans, but he has other outfits, too.

4. For Little My, this is a large-scale, decades-long, international project in licensing. Little My is much better known outside the United States, where there are Moomin adventure parks in Naantali, Finland, and outside of Tokyo, with live costumed characters walking around. The brand's popularity can be attributed to an animated series produced in Japan in 1969, 1972, and, finally, in 1990, when the characters (slipping into the genre and style of anime) took off internationally and it became desirable for them to appear as toys, dishware, and chairs. A company called Små Möbler (Small Furniture) Sweden AB holds the worldwide license for the design of Moomin furniture.

5. Falke Pisano and Lucy Cotter, "Beyond Language: A Dialogue with Falke Pisano," in *Reclaiming Artistic Research*, ed. Lucy Cotter (Berlin: Hatje Cantz Verlag, 2019), 65.

6. Per the subtitle of *The Artist Who Loved Women,* Patrick Nagel's 2016 biography.

7. Lapinski, "Raider's Blanket," 17.

8. *Marker*, 2012. Wood, plaster, tobacco, paper, sound. 28 ½ x 33 x 91 in.

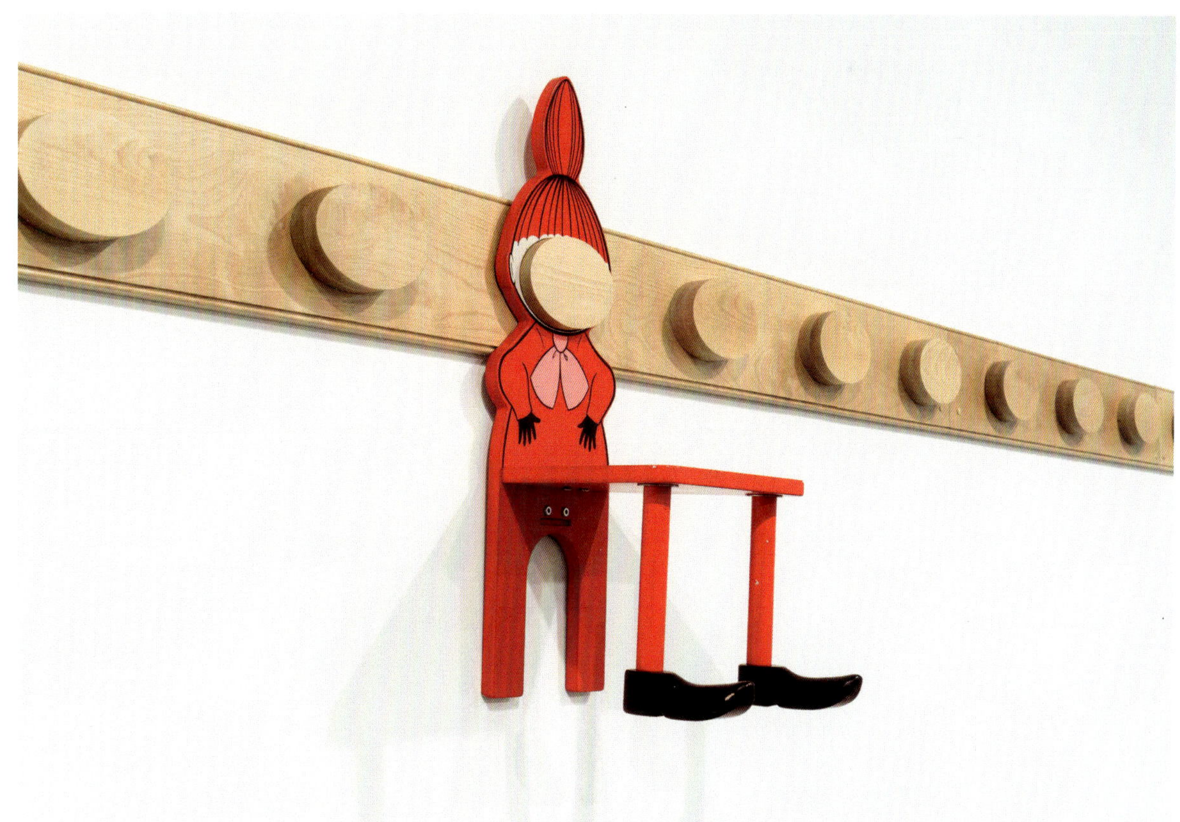

Lisa Lapinski, *Little My Chair #3*, 2017 (detail). Birch, glue, hardware, found chair. Dimensions variable.

N THE PAVEMENT JUST RIGHT FOR BRONS. AND HE PUT BRONS RIGHT ON IT.

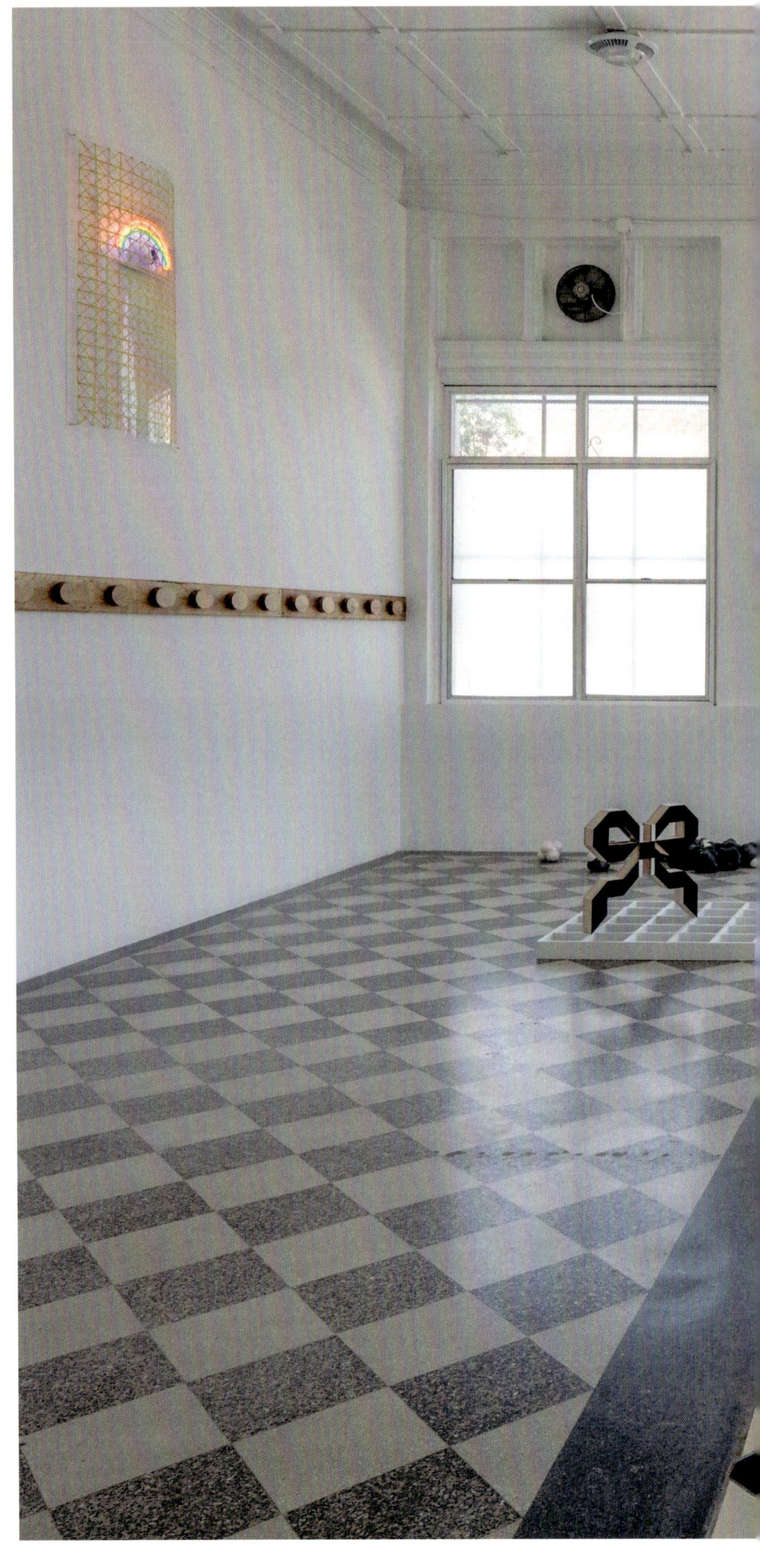

Holly Hobby Lobby
Installation view,
Kristina Kite Gallery,
Los Angeles, September 9–
November 4, 2017

THEN BELLE CAME WITH HER YELLOW DRESS AND BELLE GOT SOME CANDY. SH

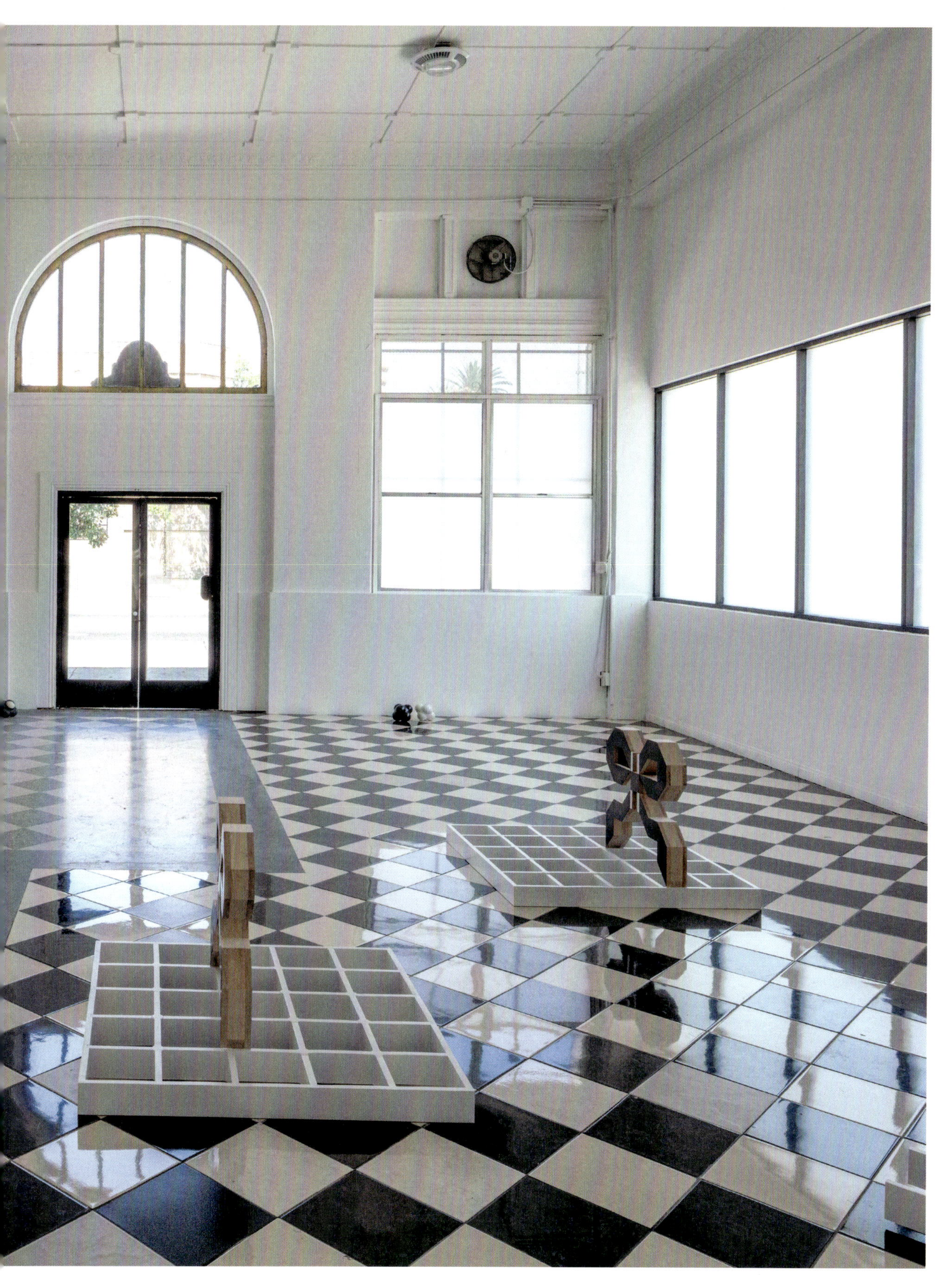

UT OUT THE CANDY ON THE TABLE. BELLE CHEWED A LITTLE BIT OF CANDY.

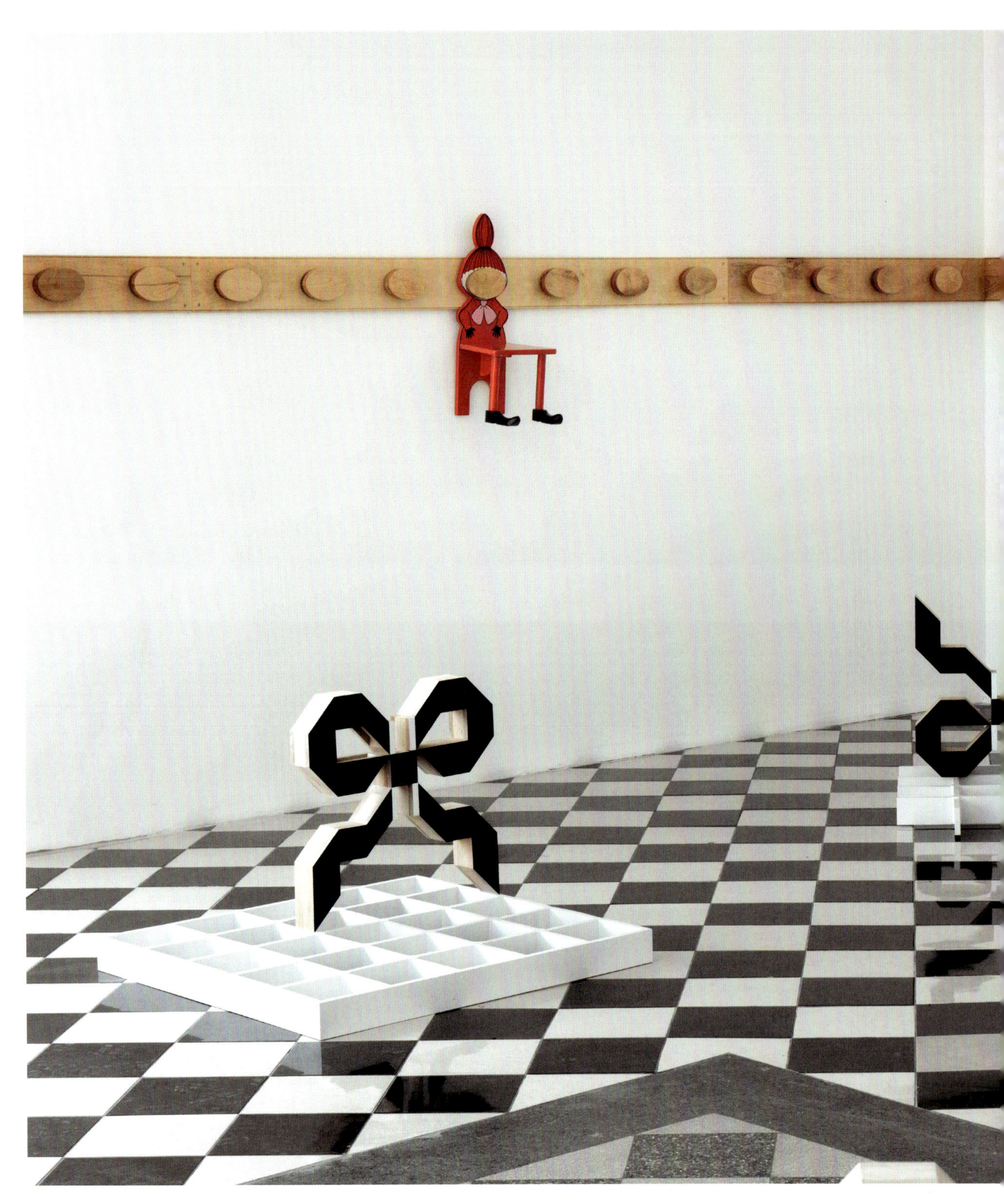

BELLE CALLED OUT WINNIE THE POOH — THAT SCHOOL WAS ALREADY OPEN. BU

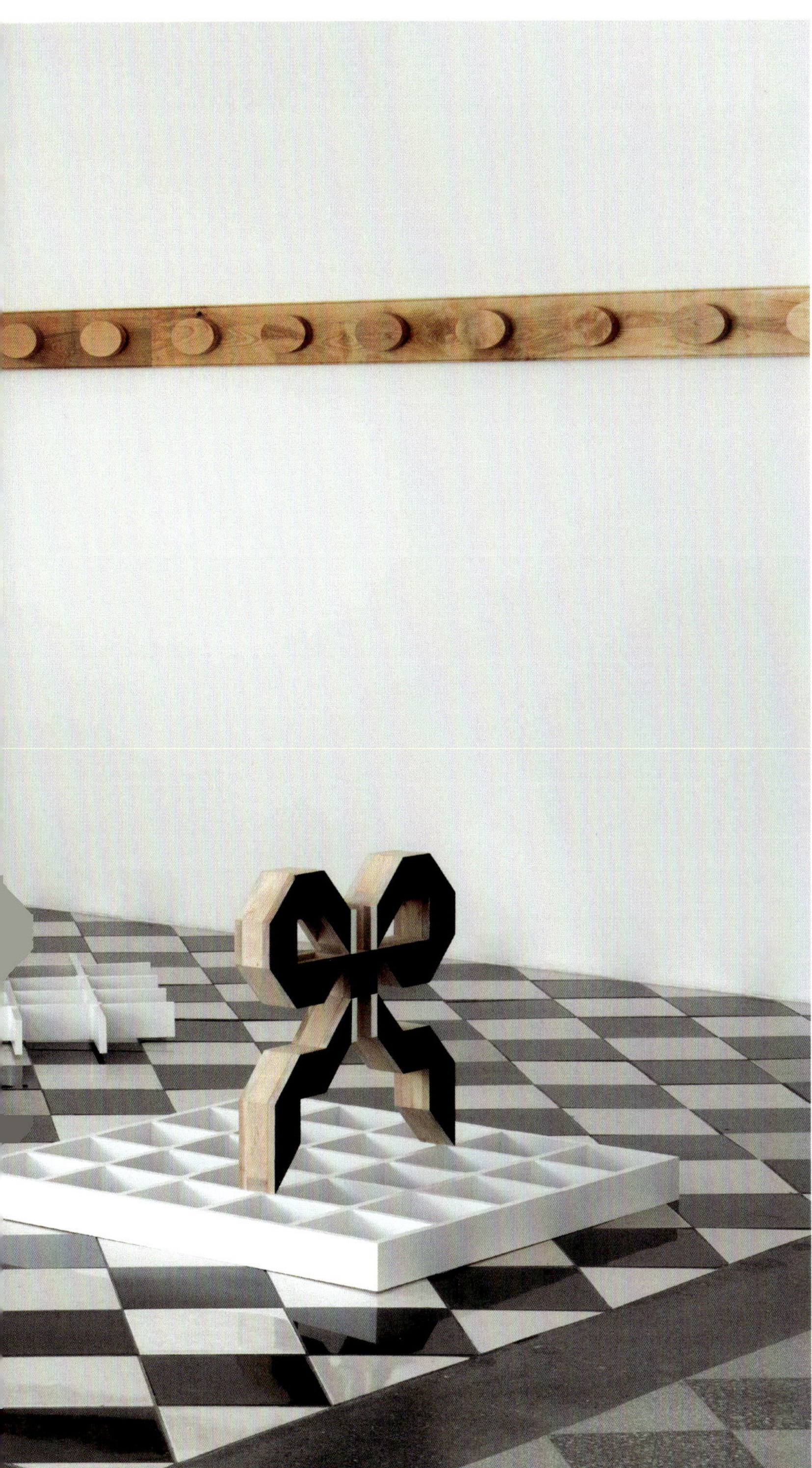

Holly Hobby Lobby
Installation view,
Kristina Kite Gallery,
Los Angeles, September 9–
November 4, 2017

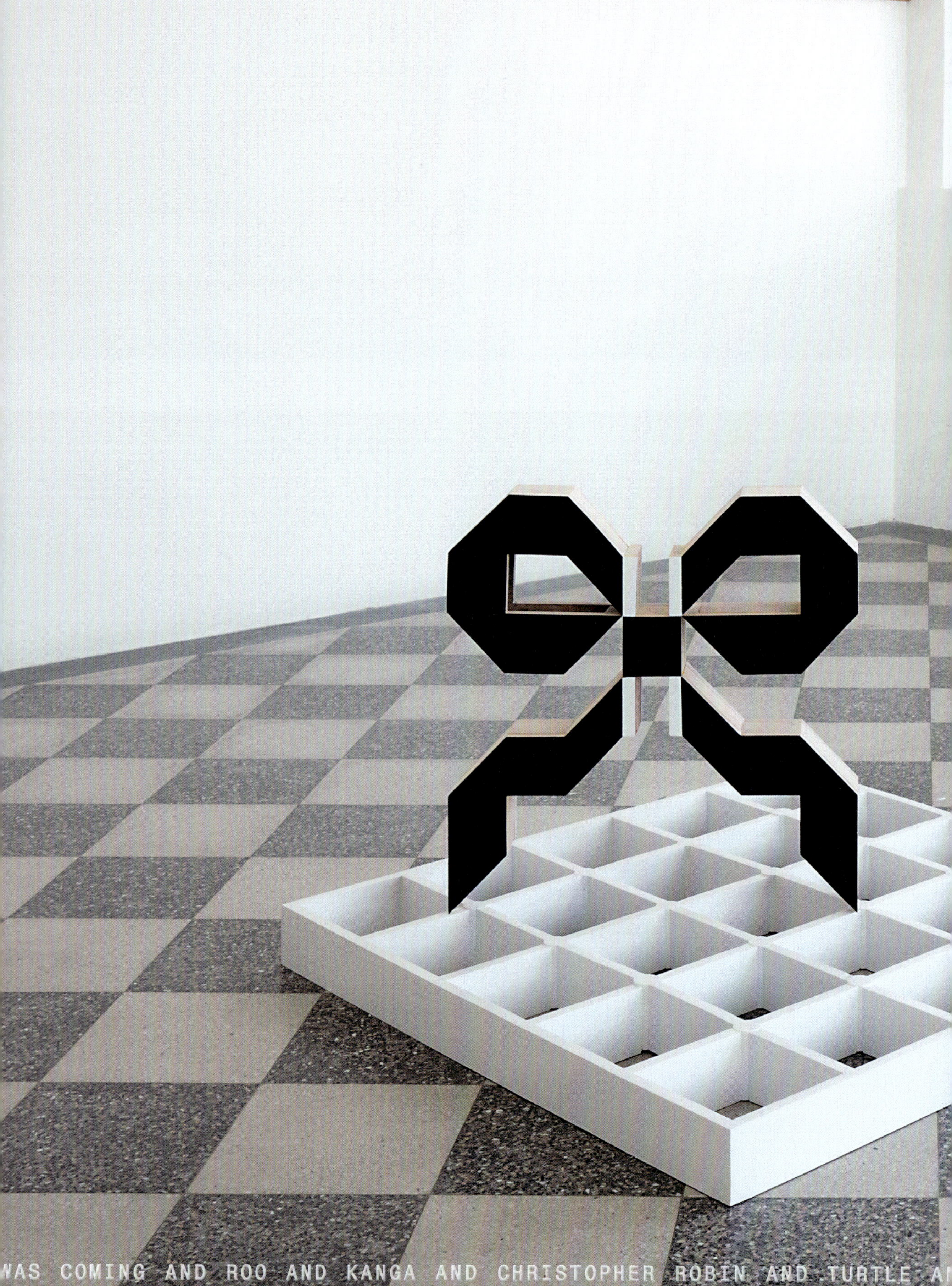

WAS COMING AND ROO AND KANGA AND CHRISTOPHER ROBIN AND TURTLE AN

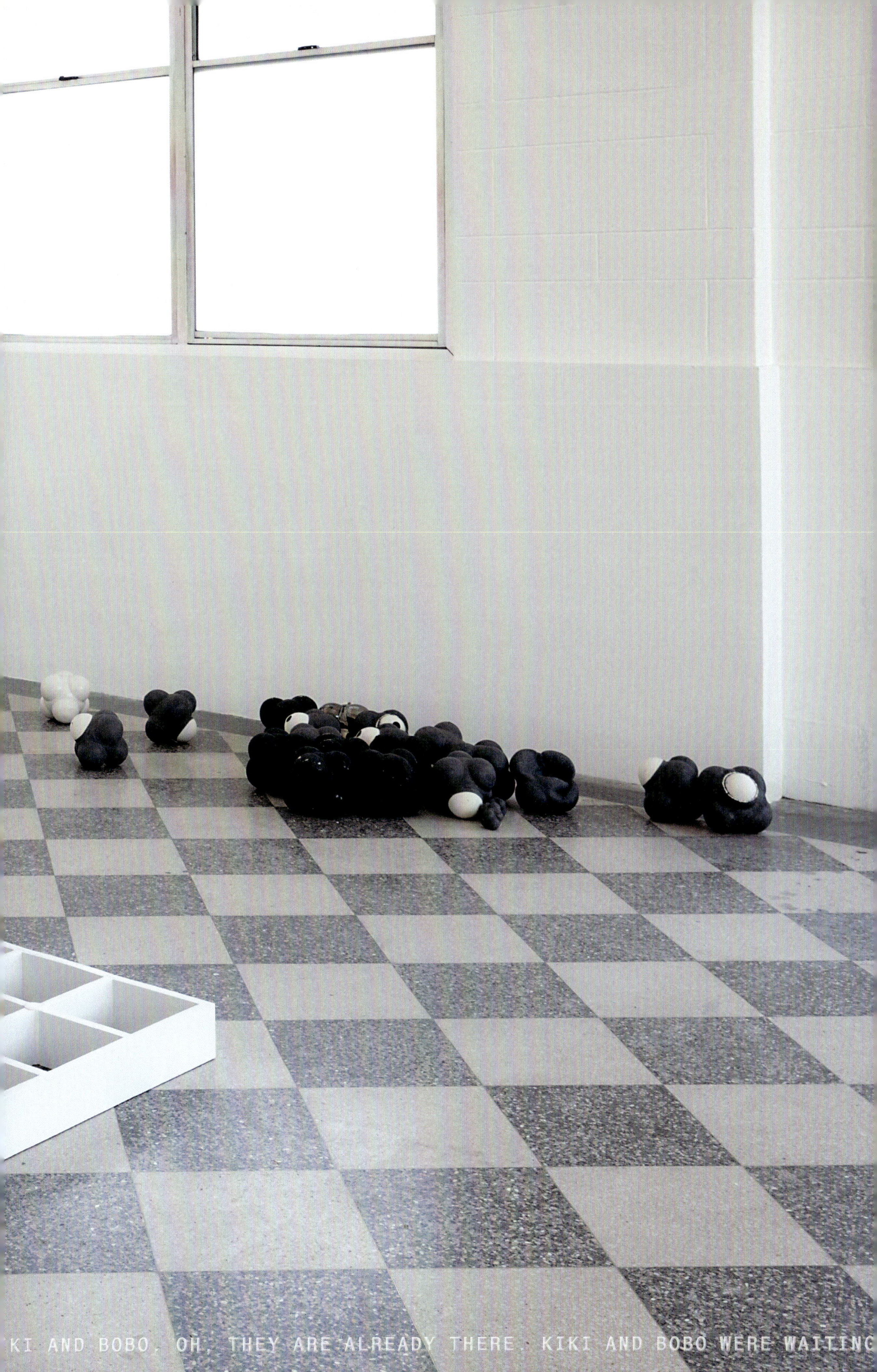

KI AND BOBO. OH, THEY ARE ALREADY THERE. KIKI AND BOBO WERE WAITING

previous spread

Holly Hobby Lobby
Installation view,
Kristina Kite Gallery,
Los Angeles, September 9–
November 4, 2017

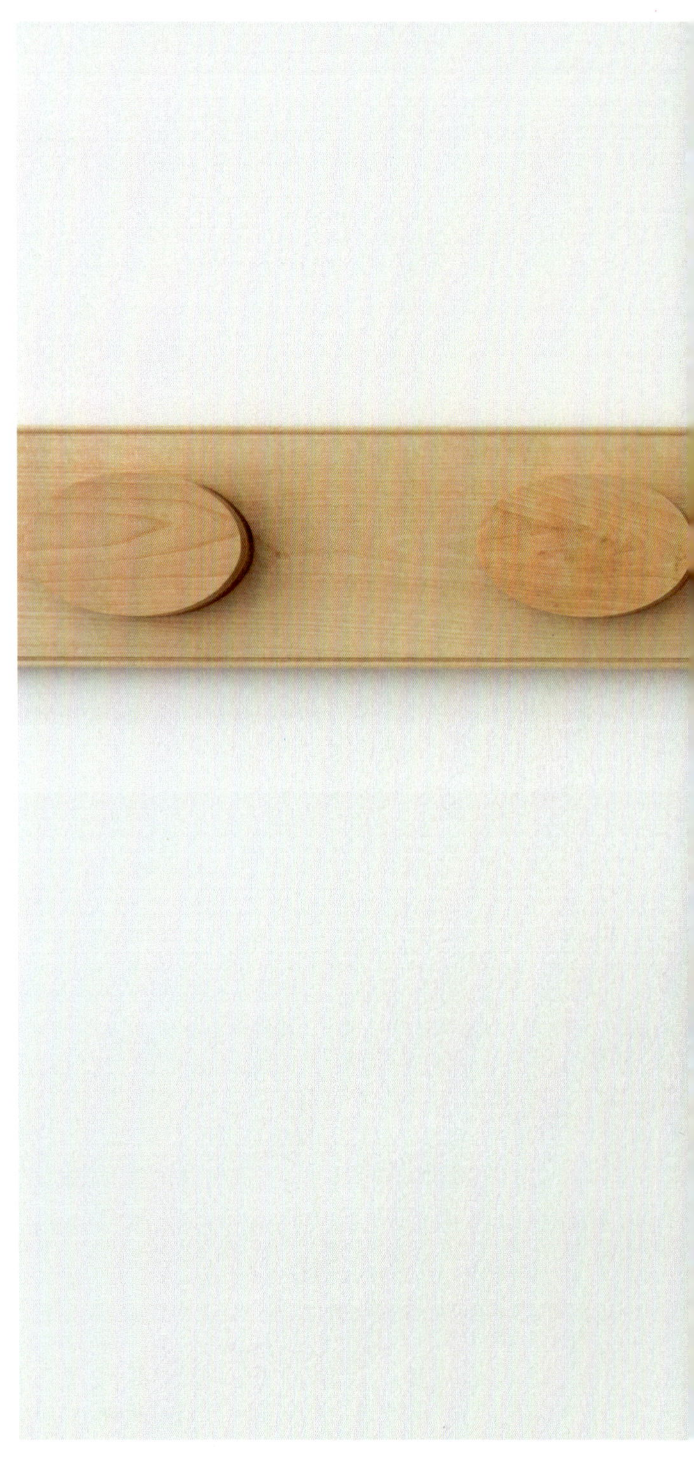

FOR MR. CAMEL. SO THEY LOOKED IN THE SUNNIEST, SUNNIEST PLACE B

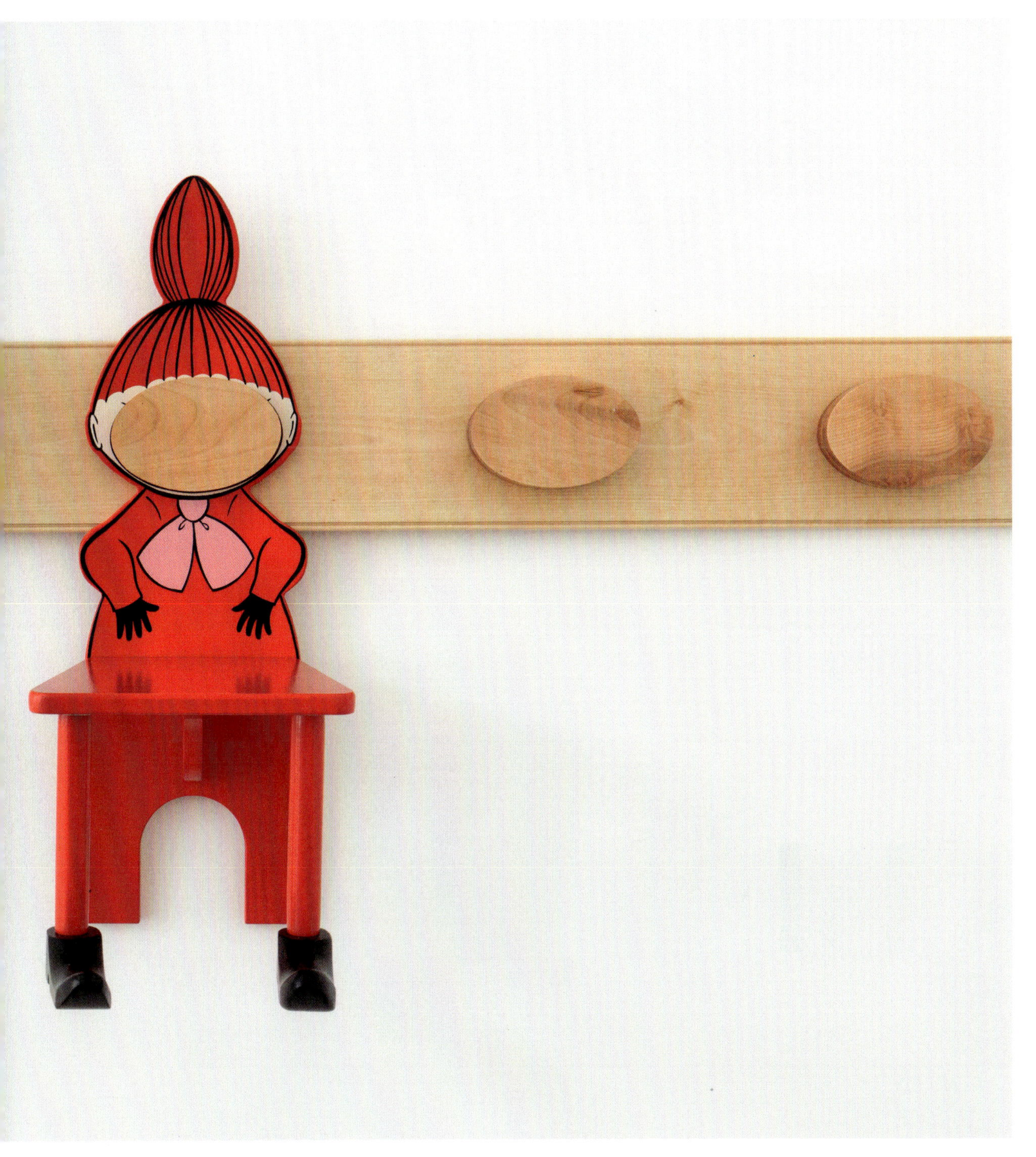

Little My Chair #3, 2017 (detail)
Birch, glue, hardware,
found chair
Dimensions variable

OULDN'T FIND THEM. BUT THEN, "BOO!" HE CAME OUT. THE HORSE SAID,

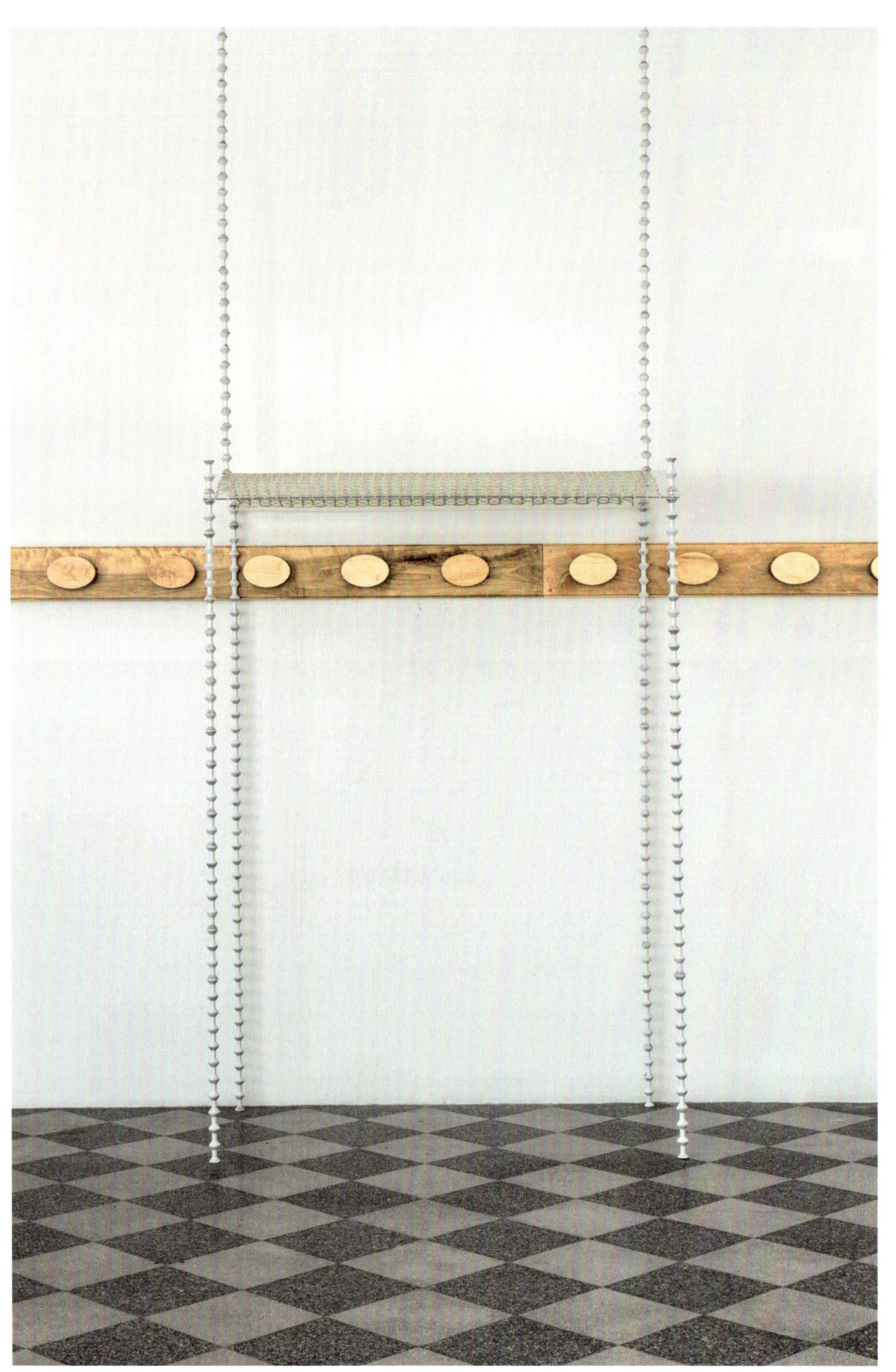

"BOO!" HE CAME OUT. THE TURTLE SAID, "MEOW." THEN FUZZY CAME ALONG AN

Holly Hobby Lobby
Installation view,
Kristina Kite Gallery,
Los Angeles, September 9–
November 4, 2017

INNIE CAME ALONG AND DONALD CAME ALONG AND DAISY DUCK CAME ALONG AND

Sabrina Tarasoff

Guess You Better Unwind It

* * *

Come on, Bambi, get up. Try again. Come on, get up. Get up. Get up. Try again. I'm thumping. That's why they call me Thumper. Thumper! Come on. You can do it. Hop over it. Like this. Hop over it. Like this. You didn't hop far enough. That's it. Now the other one! ...

... and so on, and so forth, Thumper shoves Bambi through his fragile youth, fretting to get somewhere, to move forward, and push through an idea or its actualisation; and this all with a kiddish impatience expressed through pushes, propulsions, props, hops, and thumps. Thumper's pushy excitation aims at moving Bambi from his frail babyishness to more stable states of being, less wobbly, but does so in a series of formal gestures that creates the film's narrative momentum. Their skittish interplay actuates the minute dramas of childhood in its strange temporalities and expectant emotions, in the magical drip-drip-drop of April showers and gauche skids on thin ice, so situating the story in something closely resembling anxiety's affective grammar: paratactic in pace, airborne, thrown. As the duo try to skate across a frozen lake; the script goes: (*Thumper Laughing:*) "*No, no!*" (*Thumper helps Bambi to get up his legs. It's a difficult matter.*) *"Got to watch both ends at the same time!"*

That their wobbly ballet progresses as "a difficult matter," a partial, and inconclusive, and mostly formal arrangement, seemingly, or perhaps *necessarily*, binds it up (or winds it up, like a toy?) with a very Romantic inextricability of fretfulness and ideation. As Thumper laughs at Bambi's entangled limbs, all akimbo, while trying to correctly arrange them: "Guess you better unwind it!" (*It*? What is the "it" referring to? More anon ... maybe.) Like mediums that push motifs ahead, or the kind of anxiety that impels those prone to procrastination, or, ehhh, Adderall, Thumper is literally a *supporting* character: a physical steadying that becomes epistemic in its procedural logic, its gentle push. Dialogue trickles out only in stuttering syllables, a scantness, which, besides the cuteness overload, suggests that meaning in the Bambiverse is found primarily in gestures of anticipation, deferral, and projection. Whether considered for its animated naturalism, or the satisfaction of cartoon subjects going *splat*!, the base structure of Bambi lies in the thrownness of being, the psychic mechanisms that kick in, and the apprehensions that threaten to flatten us into form, ... or, to formalise ones affects as forms ... Or ... (I could say something about Sartre's crackpot theory of skating from *Being* & *Nothingness*, which even he rejected, but ... let's not depress the kids.)

Bambi does not appear in the oeuvre of Lisa Lapinski, even though virtually every other major Disney protagonist *at least* receives a shout-out within a story written by the artist's daughter, Nina, which was used as the press release for an exhibition titled "Th th th th th Snow White," at Taka Ishii Gallery in Kyoto in 2010. "Th th th th th Snow White" culled its name from a phrase stuttered out by the then-almost-three-year-old Nina, who, while hopping up and down on a sofa, exhilarated—moved!—or so I'd imagine given the narrative tone, recited a tale of Carrollesque nonsense inspired by the pages of a Disney franchise picture book featuring the corps d'elite of the Magic Kingdom commingling at a birthday party—Meeko, Wendy, Peter Pan, Tink, Eeyore, Snow White, Donald, Minnie, Belle, ...and in Nina's creative additions, also Grampy [*sic?*], Kiki and Bobo (Muppets?), and ... Mr. Camel? With its eclectic cast of faerie figures, and one cigarette brand icon, Nina's tale advances through a seque-

GOOFY AND ZOE, HUEY, DUEY AND LUEY. THEY CAME WITH...WHAT IS DONALD

nce of paratactic encounters, one figure meeting another, finding friends, hurrying places, being pulled from one thought to another, by bike and foot, dropping things, expecting people, waiting, eating candy, arriving: "Oh, they are already there," she reveals at one point.

Towards the end, "The Rabbit" comes bouncing in, "so happy." And never mind *what* Rabbit, be it Alice's elusive time-keeper or Bambi's overzealous pal: within the illogicality of Nina's feverish birthday fête fan fiction, one Rabbit could stand-in for any other Rabbit. Characters metamorphose into one another, other versions of themselves, or selves that perhaps only ever existed as surfaces to begin with, and so have made themselves open to on-going negotiations, repetitions, and reenactments: "This Time Captain Hook came. Not really Captain Hook. Captain Hook stayed in the cave." (Later, he comes out and peeks back in: "It's a big one.") Nina's narrative strategy hyperbolises Thumper and Bambi's flurried momentum to the point where no other meaning can exist. The plot is lost. It's a carrousel of cartoon defacement that spins out of control, as an overcrowded party might. Nina's story, "a regular story," as she writes, bulldozes over each figure as if to flatten them beyond their usual 2D selves, into something closer resembling a pattern, a frieze, but one that is notably, and oddly, dependent on a spatial grammar—an indecipherable, and so anxiety-provoking, topology of dizzied subjects, coming here and there, hopping up and down, forever.

What of Lisa's own cast of characters? Arthur Rimbaud, Little My, an Analysand, Th th th th th Snow White, someone just referred to as "Sir!", Mr. Camel, who makes a cameo as someone Kiki and Bobo are waiting for in Nina's story, [Clown Type] Face, the so-called Bikini Girls, Mimpy Mimp, Holly Hobby? Could we imagine them, similarly, not as carefully executed characters in scripted conversation, but as blank icons with scant inner lives, whose flimsy contours are subjected to an on-going renegotiation in and/or against time, rubbing away, worn out, and redrawn in the very proximity to one another? Or, in other words, as thrown entities better read through the projective logic of cartoon subjects, whose thoughts are revealed in action, paradoxically appearing through serial desubstantiations? In Nina's story, as in Lisa's works, these characters are crafted in the fret to get somewhere, be it to overcome states of existential recapitulation, psychic automatisms, or obsessive loops, and thereby land in what Kyle Dancewicz called "the expanded field of prepositions, exploding 'next to' ..."

Halt here, mid-sentence, to think about being "next-to:" (closure, completion?) or "next-to": (none): in a context where the grand dénouement is left unresolved, or at least, for now, left looming. Think to, for example, Dorothy, who in the last instance is brought down by exhaustion in the bewitched poppies that precede Emerald City, and so slows down, slips unconscious, into an intoxicated slumber, with her final destination towering nearby. Snow White gets lost in the depths of the Haunted Forest, encountering howling owls, bat caves, and clawing branches in the dark of her imagination, and shrinks to a sob on the cold ground. Alice's tears flood Wonderland, oceanic. Even Goldilocks has to take a nap. The formal slump drops each of our dramatis personae somewhere "next-to" resolution, in the "not-quite-there"—just around, apropos, vis-à-vis, atop, touching, barring, absolutely beside [oneself]. Like so, Lisa's work *functions* in a field of adjacency; its proper operative mode is in the prepositional evasion of a grand finale. Its paradoxical momentum is gained in suspensions, digressions, and states of delay, like abandoned ideas and their ghostly aftermath. Things shoved aside, but still argued for. Ideas freeze-framed in a panic. Disasters averted. Phew.

(Actually, not just yet.)

Think to the sad aftermath of Rimbaud's already-sunken ship, when he'd peaced-out to Ethiopia to trade things, or to Little My's faceless frame, recrafted as a rattan chair; the sculptural Mr. Camel that Lisa created in the absence of cigarettes, and, um, the Chippendale swastikas (yikes) that permeate her sculptures, and things stop feeling safe again. One aversion is always averted by the other, leading to more aversions, in a pattern of resistance and repulsion that probably warrants a prescription (maybe "O'Hara for nerve," as per Elaine Equi), yet ultimately validates its negative momentum by being codified within the spatial free-for-all of art.

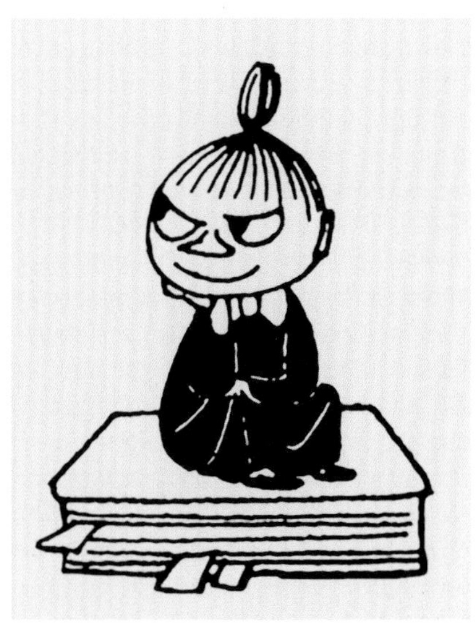

Tove Jansson, *Little My* © Moomin Characters ™

NCLE'S NAME? I THINK IT'S... DONALDS'S UNCLE CAME AND DONALD CAME.

It gets us ... *somewhere*: ahead. Away. Take *[Clown Type] Face* (1999), a piece created during some of Lisa's first days as an art student. Taking cues from action-laden anxiety dreams, moments of dispossession only art school can provide, and that exhaustive thing of dispositioning, which in this case was directly relative to having landed at ArtCenter "later in life," with no preexisting artistic background, Lisa found herself in a small studio with a pile of her father's dead skin that she'd secretly, and neurotically, collected from his floor, and a roll of discount-store wallpaper found somewhere in the Valley. In a moment of Cronenbergian panic, and on Mike Kelley's cue, she'd started to mix the dead skin with paint medium, fretting to figure out how to deal with the remnants of her father's psoriasis as "art."

Thrown into a new fret as the skin-sludge filled her studio with a sweetly corpselike scent, Lisa grabbed the wallpaper and started pasting one piece over another, on and on, for the next six months, until the angsty tapestry hung so heavy against the wall that it started to peel off. Something akin to décollage, or its bathetic apposite. Sealed with a typographic smiley, the kind one might perhaps accompany with a manic white lie, i.e. the classic on-the-verge-of-collapse "I'm fine," *[Clown Type] Face* was created in the intercalation of a somewhat-gross psychic substance placed between form and function—the latter both in the sense of the artist being able to operate in a proper way, *and* present an activity as natural to the circumstance. (At least at surface: a forced smiley when faced with faculty.) The piece assumed anxiety's affective motion and converted it into form, which to paraphrase Sianne Ngai, paradoxically 'relocated, reoriented, or repositioned the "subject thrown"; très Bambi.

Then again, maybe it's not so much Lisa's own thrownness that matters here, or the sad trombone that accompanies [*Clown Type*] *Face*'s sculptural flop, but the shade thrown back into the space at the viewer. After all, much has been made of the interrelations between Lisa's characters, their semantic togetherness, care for one another, or, au contraire, some violence inflicted on each others' misfitted symbolic configurations. Put this into the context of awkwardly nervous impulses, conflicting psychic responses, semantic mishaps, and repetitive face-offs with the aleatory thing of identity, the loss-of-face as a kind of décollage in itself, and it all starts to remind of the kind of high-school shade writ into *Mean Girls*. Alas, I digress: Imagine the Bikini Girls getting into it with Little My, who one day wore rattan instead of getting the memo about a slinky two-piece. Recalling all those times Little My launched into her dominant rhetoric of slippery-slope arguments and self-serving statements, like, "Believe you me, I know. I'm sharp when it comes to things like this," one of the Bikini Girls hisses at My that "everyone knows" today's codes call for a Claudia Schiffer-esque look, not Marcel Breuer-Scandi kiddy chic. When met with Little My's resistance, she snaps, shrieks: "You Can't Sit With Us!" All the other sculptures go silent. Holly Hobby is so embarrassed, she's reduced to a mere bow, in a way that's reminiscent of another Moomin character, Ninny, who in the face of neglect becomes invisible, all but for her bright bow floating mid-air. Mr. Camel is drunk on his own scents, Tom Ford-like. Little My perches herself elsewhere, alone. She thinks to herself, hanging out, "I'm above this:" "Every little creep has a right to be angry."

Highlighted in this passive-aggressive and well-dressed drama of dispositioning are a set of spatial motifs that converge in the production of a particular kind of sculptural subject: outcast, shoved aside, unsecured, and wound-up, certainly, but one whom in such acts of displacement is also individualized. Liberated, for example, by virtue of being reconstituted or differentiated from previous versions of themselves, or, seen another way, moved from one mode of psychic dissemination to another. (Notably, around here I get caught up trying to cram Heidegger mere hours before conclusion, and recall Lisa suggesting to me over the phone, early in this process, to write my text while hopping up and down on my bed, Nina-style. In hopes of shaking the crushing *Dasein*, ... oh god, ... I get up, and up again, and hop over Heidegger, hop hop, as the ... ugh ... "anxiety throws *Dasein* back upon that which it is anxious about—its authentic potentiality for being-in-the ..."—I exhaust myself—"... world.")

Still, this projective logic, however exhausting, holds, as the anxiety embedded into Lisa's works functions to blur a distinction between the being-*here* or *there* of her iconographic cast, their semantic rapid cycling, and revise whatever symbolic mandates have been attached to them prior. Which is to stay, Lisa throws her subjects under the bus, leaving them defaced, flattened, repeated or compressed in (or by?) space, so as to forfeit their meaning in the public, everyday world for a shiny, new, and sometimes mostly decorative symbolic realm. These characters are simply, if not somewhat cruelly, pushed out of their contexts, over the edge of recognition, and into a semantic [free fall]: fun! Like Disney princesses that tumble out of their respective forever after's into an anachronistic birthday party, more than likely a bit boozed-up, the artist gives license (through her practice? Or characters that function as mouthpieces for some unspeakable angst?) to unwind from the real.

Typically, I would try to tie this together in a neat Holly Hobby bow by suggesting that I *know* what the "it" unwound is in both the choreographed disarray of Bambi's limbs and Lisa's arrangements, but, I suspect the fallibilities of Thumper's kiddish articulation get us closer to the truth than any neat resolve. When Thumper sighs that they'd better unwind "it," instead of Bambi's legs, which would correctly be referred to as "them," or "the legs," we fall into a realm of identification. To unwind "it," is to unwind that thing, that person, me, you, someone previously mentioned. *That one*: over there: the subject to a preposition. Whatever ”it” is in Lisa’s works, is always in motion. Or, at least “it” has found a way to function, through, or despite the fret—or maybe I mean fête?

HE CAVE AND SAW WHAT THE CROCODILES DID. THEY WERE HAVING A PICNIC

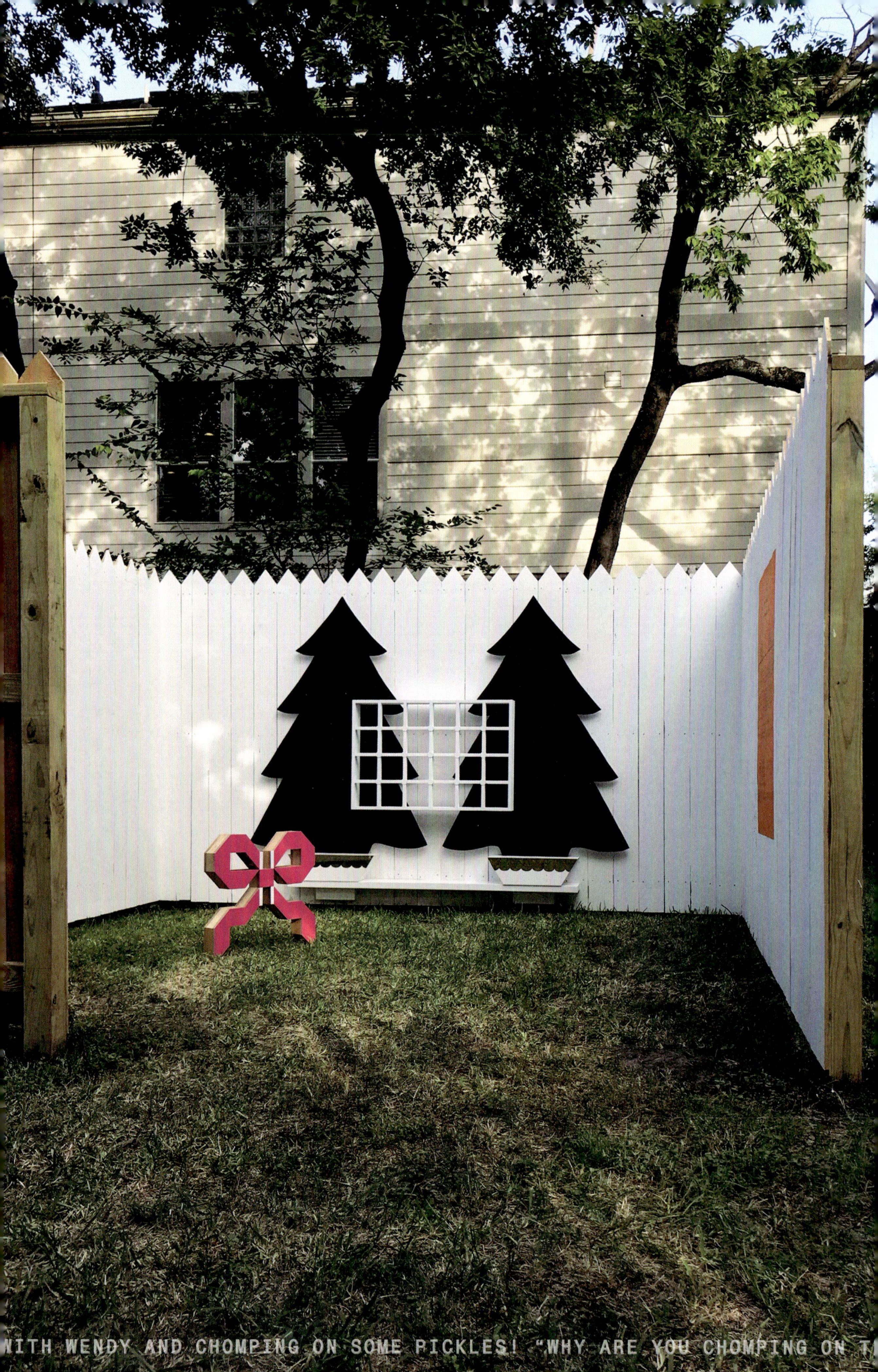

WITH WENDY AND CHOMPING ON SOME PICKLES! “WHY ARE YOU CHOMPING ON T

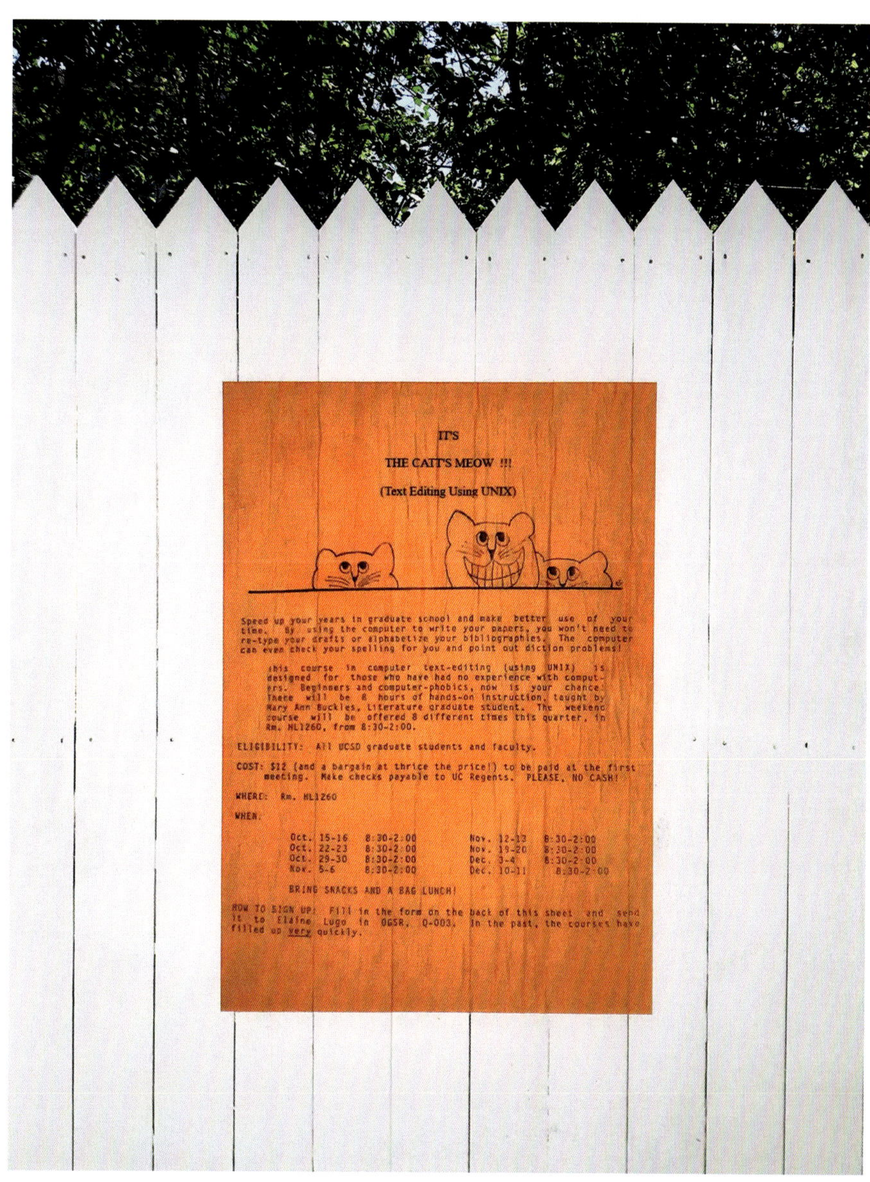

Snoopy Mitosis
Installation view, Sylvia's Sculpture Garden at F Gallery, Houston, October 20, 2019–January 31, 2020

Snoopy Mitosis
Installation view, Sylvia's Sculpture Garden at F Gallery, Houston, October 20, 2019–January 31, 2020

ISTER'S PICKLES?" WE'RE SHARING THE PICKLES WITH WENDY'S SISTER. SO

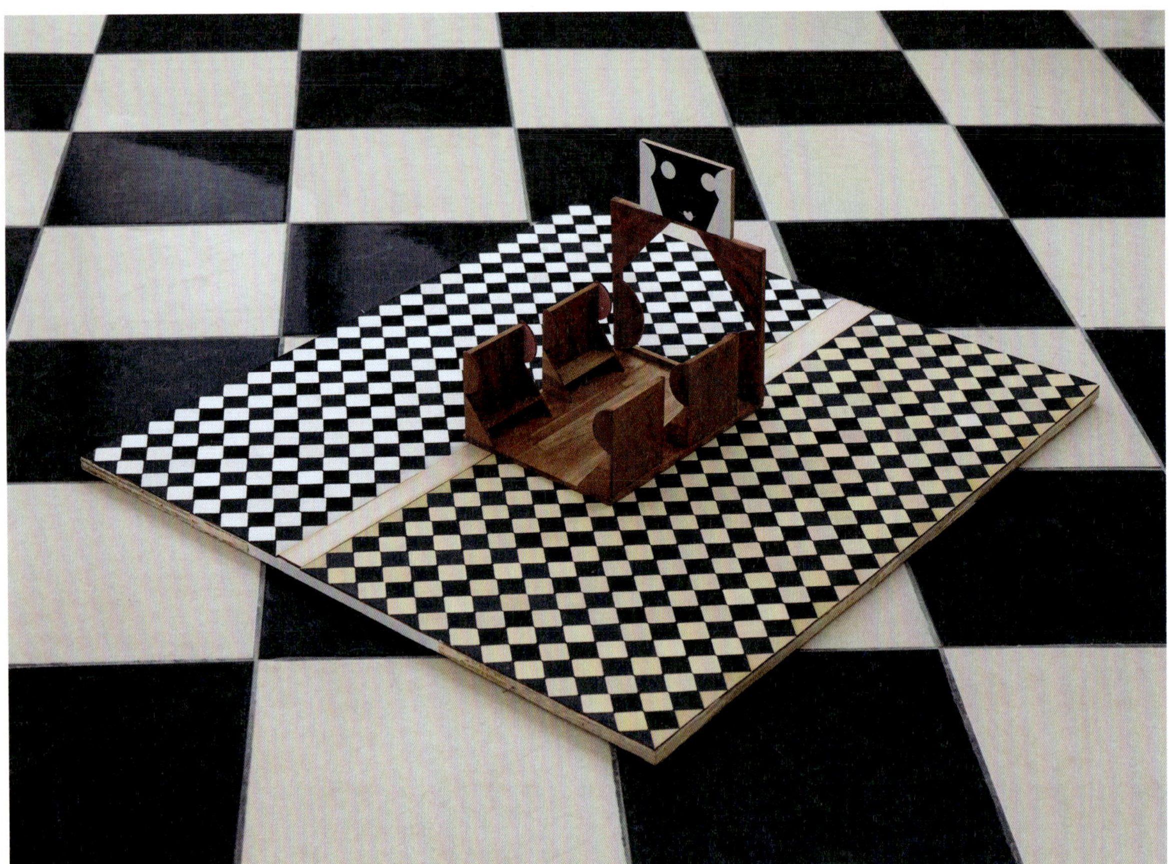

Black Cat Portal, 2021 (detail)
Wood and acrylic paint
2 parts: 31 1/2 x 28 x 10 1/2 in.
(80 x 71.1 x 26.7 cm);
24 x 8 3/4 in. (61 x 22.2 cm)

Black Cat Portal, 2021 (detail)
Wood and acrylic paint
2 parts: 31 1/2 x 28 x 10 1/2 in.
(80 x 71.1 x 26.7 cm);
24 x 8 3/4 in. (61 x 22.2 cm)

CAPTAIN HOOK LEFT. HE PEEKED INSIDE THE CAVE. IT'S A BIG ONE. IT

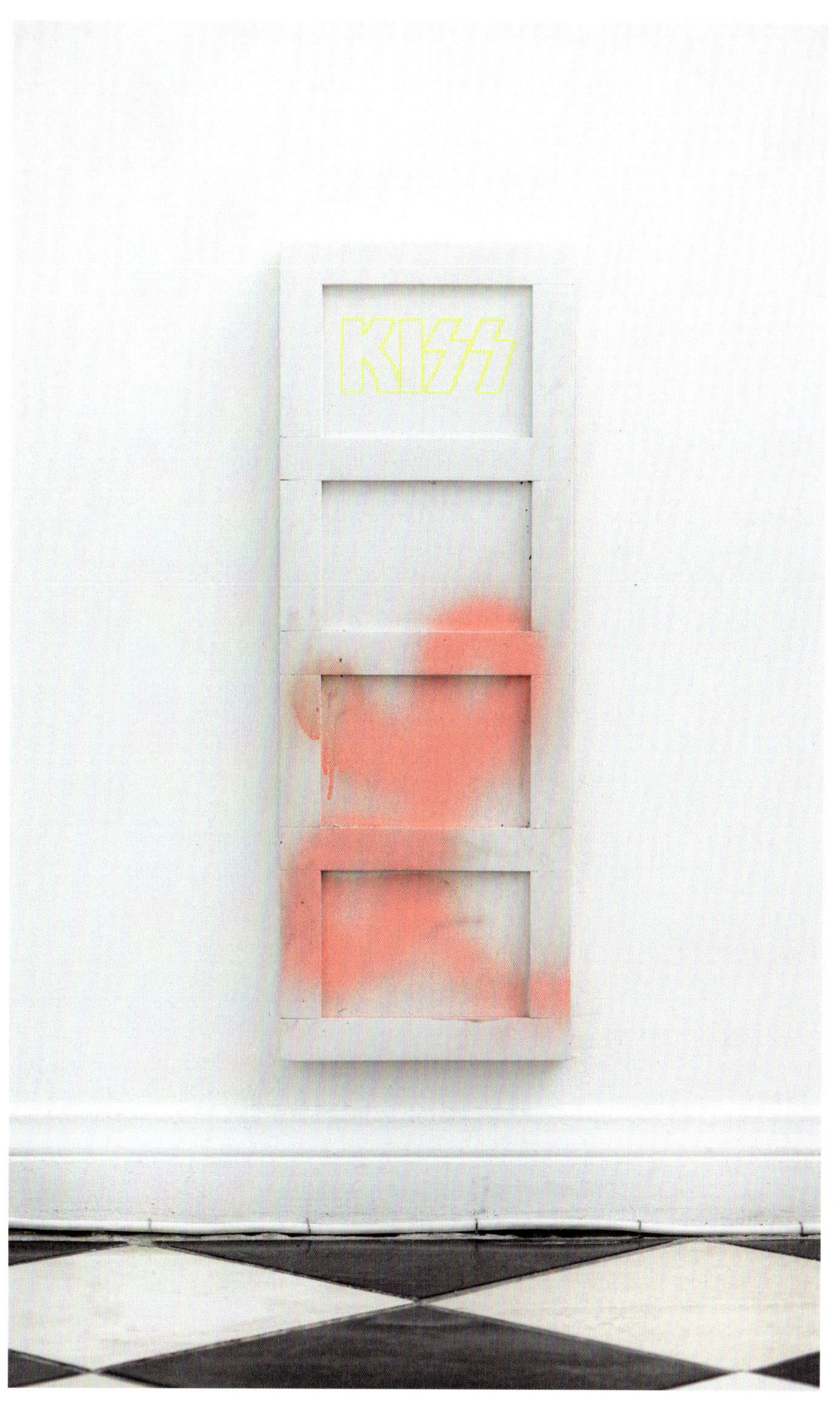

ELLOW. IT’S NOT BROWN. CAPTAIN HOOK SAW WHAT ALL THE CROCODILES DID.

Lisa Lapinski: Drunk Hawking
Visual Arts Center, University of Texas at Austin, January 24–March 6, 2020

1
Gus
1997–98
Screen print on paper
28 x 22 in. (71.1 x 55.9 cm) framed

2
Miss Swiss
1997–98
Screen print on paper
28 x 22 in. (71.1 x 55.9 cm) framed

3
Glub, Glub
1997–98
Screen print on paper
28 x 22 in. (71.1 x 55.9 cm) framed

4
[Clown Type] face
1999
Wallpaper, glue, Xerox, mold, hearts of palm can, paint
Dimensions variable
Approx. 36 in. (91.4 cm) square
Collection of Eileen Cohen

5
Rod Cross
2003
Screen print on paper, custom frame
71 x 57 in. (180.3 x 144.8 cm)
Collection of Mike Kelley Foundation for the Arts, Los Angeles

6
Successful Schizophrenia
2004
Screen print on paper
9 panels, 18 x 24 in. (45.7 x 61 cm) each

7
Nightstand
2005
Walnut hardwood, polyurethane, acrylic paint, panel and canvas, photographs, caning, glass, feather
Dimensions variable

8
I Clown (Version A)
2008
Photograph
16 x 24 in. (40.6 x 61 cm)

9
I Clown (Version B)
2008
Photograph
16 x 24 in. (40.6 x 61 cm)

10
Stands for Mosques
2008
Plywood, Bondo, paint
Four triangular blocks: 17 1/2 x 35 x 25 1/2 in. (44.5 x 88.9 x 64.8 cm) each
Two triangular blocks: 17 1/2 x 35 x 24 in. (44.5 x 88.9 x 61 cm) each

THEY HAD ONE OUT OF THE CAVE. CAPTAIN HOOK SAID, "WHERE IS ALL T

11
Untitled
2010
Wallpaper, glue, ink, paint
Series of 8
Rainbow: 22 x 7 in. (55.9 x 17.8 cm)
Pink Heart: 20 x 26 in. (50.8 x 66 cm)
Gold Flower: 20 x 26 in. (50.8 x 66 cm)
Pink and Blue: 21 x 27 in. (53.3 x 68.6 cm)

12
Th th th th th Snow White (Magenta)
2010
Slip cast ceramic, wood, paint on plywood, hardware
78 x 56 x 6 in. (198.1 x 142.2 x 15.2 cm)

13
Th th th th th Snow White (Blue)
2010
Slip cast ceramic, wood, paint on plywood, hardware
78 x 56 x 6 in. (198.1 x 142.2 x 15.2 cm)

14
Th th th th th Snow White (Green)
2010
Slip cast ceramic, wood, paint on plywood, hardware
78 x 56 x 6 in. (198.1 x 142.2 x 15.2 cm)

15
Tobacco Camel
2010
Foam and Tobacco
41 x 52 x 11 in. (104.1 x 132.1 x 27.9 cm)
Collection of Peter Remes

16
Disk #2
2010
Epoxy, shoe, metal, colorant, paint
44 x 58 x 2 1/4 in. (111.8 x 147.3 x 5.7 cm)

17
Little My Chair 2
2011
Found chair and cane
15 x 11 x 30 in. (38.1 x 27.9 x 76.2 cm)
Collection of a lady

18
Untitled
2011
Wallpaper, glue, wood, tobacco
Series of 2: 29 x 20 x 1 in. each
(73.7 x 50.8 x 2.5 cm)

19
Marker
2012
Wood, plaster, tobacco, paper, sound
28 1/2 x 33 x 91 in. (72.4 x 83.8 x 231.1 cm)

20
Untitled (Trieste)
2013
Plexiglass, papier-mâché, tobacco, wood, paint
84 x 66 x 20 in. (213.4 x 167.6 x 50.8 cm)

21
Untitled (steel blue projection screen/spades)
2014
Projection screen, plaster
42 x 36 x 2 1/2 in. (106.7 x 91.4 x 6.4 cm)

22
Untitled (1/2 green projection screen/clovers)
2014
Projection screen, plaster
18 x 34 x 2 1/2 in. (45.7 x 86.4 x 6.4 cm)

23
Captain Hook at Eton (single palm)
2014
Black and white photograph
41 x 27 3/4 x 1 3/4 in. (104.1 x 70.5 x 4.4 cm) framed

24
Captain Hook at Eton (projection screen with rat)
2014
Black and white photograph
49 x 33 x 1 3/4 in. (124.5 x 83.8 x 4.4 cm) framed

25
Untitled
2015
Hoe, wax, resin, blinds, wax colorant
23 x 11 x 60 in. (58.4 x 27.9 x 152.4 cm)

26
Little My Chair #3
2017
Wood, glue, found chair
Dimensions variable
19 Panels: 7 1/4 x 29–96 x 3/4 each
(18.4 x 73.7–243.8 x 1.9 cm)

27
Holly Hobby Lobby Bow #1
2017
Wood and paint
49 x 49 x 7 in. (124.5 x 124.5 x 17.8 cm)

28
Untitled
2017
Plexiglas, cane, paint, neon
34 x 59 x 4 in. (86.4 x 149.9 x 10.2 cm)

29
Untitled
2019
Hoe, wax, resin, blinds, wax colorant
23 x 12 x 60 in. (58.4 x 30.5 x 152.4 cm)

Unless otherwise noted, all works courtesy of the artist and Kristina Kite Gallery, Los Angeles.

GRAHAM BADER is Associate Professor and Chair of Art History at Rice University. The author of *Hall of Mirrors: Roy Lichtenstein and the Face of Painting in the 1960s* (MIT Press, 2010), *Poisoned Abstraction: Kurt Schwitters between Revolution and Exile* (Yale University Press, 2021), and editor of *October Files: Roy Lichtenstein* (MIT Press, 2009), he has published widely on topics across modern and contemporary art.

KYLE DANCEWICZ is Deputy Director at Sculpture Center, New York. He has recently organized solo exhibitions and projects with Lydia Ourahmane, ektor garcia, Matt Keegan, and Jesse Wine. Other projects include the New York iteration of *Liz Larner: Don't put it back like it was*, co-organized with the Walker Art Center, Minneapolis. Dancewicz holds a BA in art history from Harvard University and is completing an MA at Hunter College. Prior to working at Sculpture Center, he managed Mad. Sq. Art, the public art program of Madison Square Park Conservancy, New York. Independently, he has worked with the lumber room in Portland, Oregon, and has contributed writing to various exhibition catalogues.

BRUCE HAINLEY is the author of *Under the Sign of [sic]: Sturtevant's Volte-Face*, among other books. He edited Gary Indiana's *Vile Days: The Village Voice Art Columns 1985–1988* and co-wrote with John Waters *Art—A Sex Book*.

VIOLA SCHMITT is based in Vienna and is a professor of linguistics at the Humboldt-University Berlin, specializing in the formal semantics of natural languages.

MACKENZIE STEVENS is the Director of the Visual Arts Center at the University of Texas at Austin, where she has organized exhibitions with Carmen Argote, Nikita Gale, Juan Pablo González, Madeline Hollander, Luiz Roque, and Kenneth Tam among others. She organized *Drunk Hawking*, a mid-career survey with Lisa Lapinski in 2020. Stevens previously worked at the Hammer Museum in Los Angeles, where she organized exhibitions, performances, and public programs and contributed to the first North American retrospective of Jimmie Durham. She was also part of the curatorial team for *Made in L.A. 2016: a, the, though, only* and *Made in L.A. 2018*.

SABRINA TARASOFF is an independent writer, artist, and critic based in Paris. She earned her BFA at the school previously known as Parsons Paris while also acting as codirector of the independent exhibition space Shanaynay. She is a contributing editor at *Mousse Magazine* and writes regularly for *Artforum*, *Flash Art*, and *X-TRA Contemporary Art Quarterly*. Her writing focuses on the mysterious movement between popular culture, poetry, and art, with a particularly keen eye on the nebulous "poet gang" that formed around the Wednesday Night Poetry series at Beyond Baroque Literary Art Center from 1976 to 1986. Her installation *Beyond Baroque* for *Made in L.A. 2020* ruminated on this foundational literary art center. She also runs the Summer Room, an annual residency at Treignac Projet in Treignac, France.

Lisa Lapinski: Miss Swiss
is published by

Inventory Press
2305 Hyperion Ave
Los Angeles, CA 90027
inventorypress.com

and

Visual Arts Center
University of Texas at Austin
2300 Trinity St
Austin, TX 78712
utvac.org

Cover Image
Lisa Lapinski, *Mimpy Mimp #9*, 2011 (detail).
Wood, ceramic, Plexiglas, hardware, and found box
55 1/2 x 44 1/4 x 6 1/4 in. (141 x 112.5 x 16.3 cm)

"Is free will a question?" originally appeared in *Morgan Fisher/Passing Time*, published by REDCAT, 2019.

Editor
MacKenzie Stevens

Copyeditor
Eugenia Bell

Design
Apogee Graphics

Printed and bound in Belgium by die Keure printing

ISBN: 978-1-941753-47-7
LCCN: 2023904001

Distributed by
ARTBOOK | D.A.P.
75 Broad St, Suite 630
New York, NY 10004
artbook.com

Many thanks to Will Fowler, Nina Fowler, Bruce Hainley, Kristina Kite, MacKenzie Stevens, Graham Bader, Kyle Dancewicz, Sabrina Tarasoff, Viola Schmitt, Laura Owens, Asha Schechter, Connie Chang, Mary Thompson, Nerissa Cooney, Adam Michaels, Shannon Harvey, Eugenia Bell, Kaila Tierra Schedeen, Marc Silva, John Sparagana, Kathleen Canning, Caroline Thomas, Bennett Simpson, Anna Helm, Patrick Jackson, Rebecca Matalon, Adam Marnie, Natasha Bowdoin, Josh Bernstein, Tom Watson, Fredrik Nilsen, Anna Fritz, Mitchell Syrop, Hirsch Perlman, Milena Williams, Rachel Boyle, Misako, Jeffrey Rosen, John Rasmussen, Megan McCready, Morgan Fisher, Janice Evans, and Betty Lapinski.

—Lisa Lapinski

Published on the occasion of the exhibition *Drunk Hawking*, organized by the Visual Arts Center at the University of Texas at Austin.

Credits
pp. 10–19, 24–25 Courtesy of Richard Telles Fine Art, Los Angeles; p. 21 Courtesy of Haim Steinbach; p. 26 © Mike Kelley Foundation for the Arts. All Rights Reserved / VAGA at ARS, New York; pp. 28, 34–36, 62–66, 68–69 Courtesy of Johann König Gallery, Berlin, Germany; p. 30 Courtesy of the Strong National Museum of Play; p. 32 Digital image © Whitney Museum of American Art / Licensed by Scala / Art Resource, New York; pp. 38–39 Courtesy of Casey Kaplan, New York; p. 40–43, 57; Courtesy of The Museum of Contemporary Art, Los Angeles; pp. 31, 46–49, 51 Courtesy of Taka Ishii Gallery, Kyoto, Japan; pp. 53, 101–110, 118–119 Courtesy of Kristina Kite Gallery, Los Angeles; p. 54 Courtesy of John Risley, Jr.; p. 54 Digital Image © The Museum of Modern Art/ Licensed by SCALA / Art Resource, New York; p. 60 Courtesy of the Museum of Modern and Contemporary Art of Trento and Rovereto; p. 70–71 Courtesy of Marianne Boesky Gallery, New York; p. 100 © Mike Kelley Foundation for the Arts. All Rights Reserved / VAGA at ARS, New York; p. 113 Digital Image © Tove Jansson, Rights and Brands, Stockholm; pp. 116–17 Courtesy Sylvia's Garden at F Gallery, Houston.

Photography
pp. 6–7: MacKenzie Stevens; p. 8: Sandy Carson; pp. 12–19, 24–27, 29: Fredrik Nilsen; p. 21 David Lubarsky; pp. 40–43, 53, 57, 101–10, 118–19: Brian Forrest; pp. 31, 46–49, 51: Yasushi Ichikawa; pp. 116–17: Adam Marnie.

Collections
pp. 12–13, 56: Collection of Eileen Cohen; pp. 18–19: Museum of Contemporary Art (MOCA), Los Angeles; p. 24: Collection of Anne Goldstein; p. 26: Mike Kelley Foundation; p. 27: Collection of Kourosh Larizadeh and Luis Pardo; p. 28: Collection of Peter Remes; p. 29: Gift of Laurence Rickels, Museum of Contemporary Art (MOCA), Los Angeles; p. 30: Strong National Museum of Play; p. 32: Whitney Museum of American Art; p. 54: Museum of Modern Art, New York; p. 60: Museum of Modern and Contemporary Art of Trento and Rovereto; p. 66: Collection of a lady.

THERE. THEN RABBIT CAME BOUNCING UP. HE WAS SO HAPPY. HE CAME BOUNCI

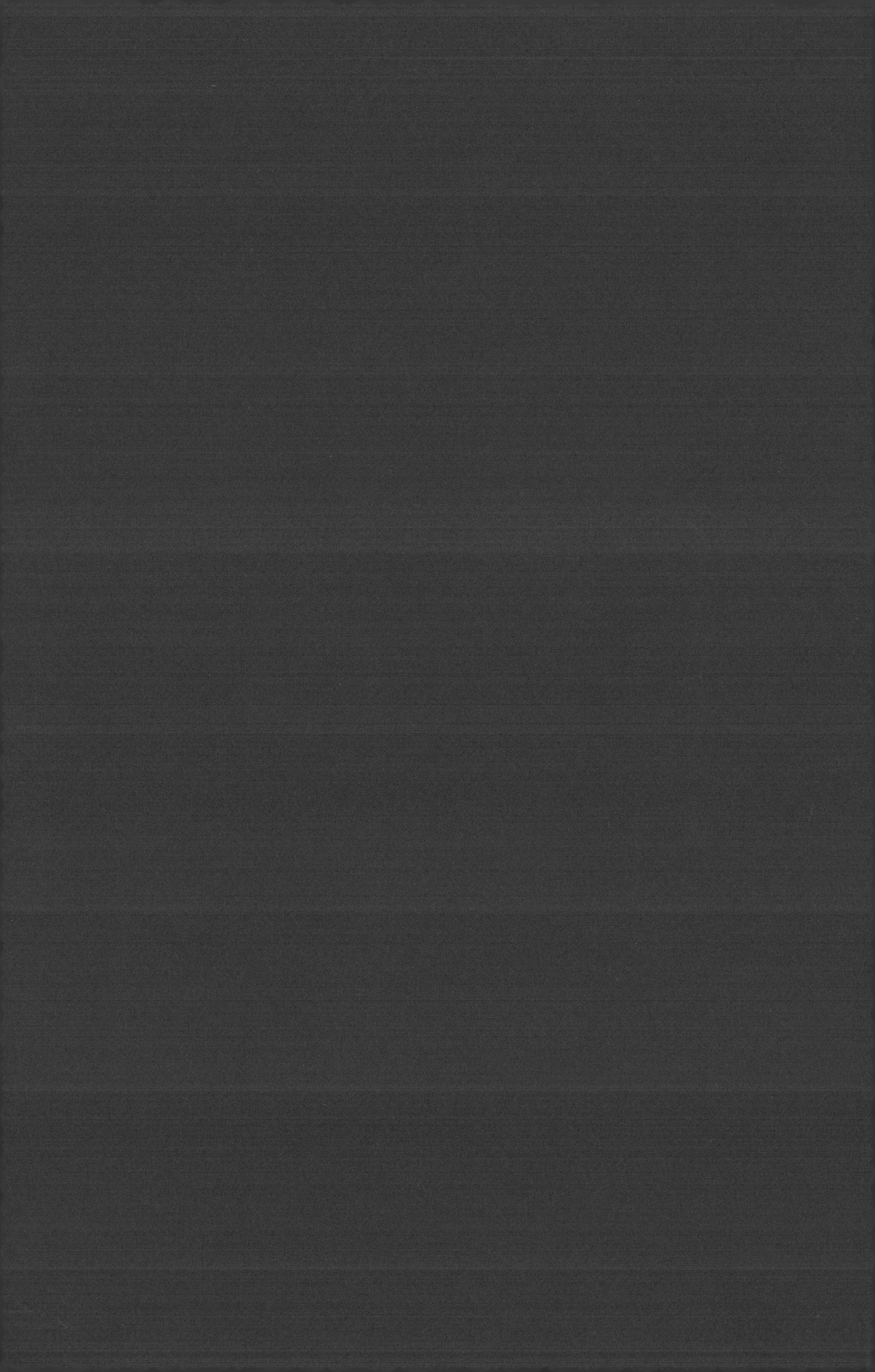